READING LATIN POETRY

READING
LATIN
POETRY

ROGER A. HORNSBY

UNIVERSITY OF OKLAHOMA PRESS
NORMAN

LIBRARY OF CONGRESS CATALOG CARD NUMBER: 67–10322

Copyright 1967 by the University of Oklahoma Press, Publishing Division of the University. Composed and printed at Norman, Oklahoma, U.S.A., by the University of Oklahoma Press. First edition.

TO L.J.H. AND J.L.G.H.

C 1

PREFACE

W<small>RITTEN FROM A CONVICTION</small> that not the least of Rome's achievements was its poetry, this book attempts to show the enduring value of that achievement and its relevance for us today. The history of Rome does not lack for modern apologists, but its literature has too often been made to subserve the cause of history in a way irrelevant to itself and pernicious ultimately to history. Imaginative literature concerns the thoughts, feelings, and attitudes of men, and so offers an access to history more valuable than the mere illustration of a particular historical phenomenon. It is the literary critic, rather perhaps than the historian, who can discover this particular access. But literary criticism itself has suffered from a surfeit of historical scholarship. It has tended, at least in England and America, to concentrate on history and its problems, to the great detriment of the literature itself whose remarkable merit has, for the most part, been all but obscured.

Recently, however, a critical approach to literature comparable to what has long been found among European scholars has begun to appear in scattered articles. Nevertheless, no book as yet has been published which seeks to awaken in the student of Roman literature a critical awareness and to inculcate in him some notions on how to proceed towards a critical analysis and evaluation of a literary text. This book aims at such goals.

The premise of the book is that a poem is an organic whole in which all parts function naturally together. Nevertheless, to perceive the organic nature of poetry it is necessary to analyze the role of the various parts of the poem, such as language, meter, imagery, and ideas, as well as its organization; hence the division of the book into chapters dealing with these different aspects. Each succeeding chapter builds on the previous ones. The subject of metrics, usually relegated to appendices, has been introduced early in the book since it is regarded as a vital, indeed a primordial, aspect of poetry. The chapter on metrics also corrects, it is hoped, the undue emphasis usually given to stanzaic forms, by stressing other aspects of metrics which are too often neglected or ignored. Too frequently students emerge from poetry courses knowing only the nomenclature and not the relevance of stanzas.

Within each chapter the progression has also been from the simple to the more complex. Comments and essays on individual poems, as well as the more general introductory remarks, illustrate the main points of each chapter. Like the chapters themselves, the commentaries on the poems become progressively more detailed, but none is meant to be an exhaustive analysis of the particular poem. Furthermore, only a certain number of the poems are commented on; but following each poem there are, in addition to notes explaining grammatical, syntactical, and other points, a number of questions designed to lead the student into the heart of the poem. In some cases, these questions are very searching and, if fully and carefully answered, should reveal the essential meaning and significance of the text. In other cases, the questions are rather general; the reason is to encourage the student to work out some of the poems for himself; leaving to the student the pleasure of discovery is, after all, sound pedagogy.

The notes and questions assume that the reader has easy access to a good lexicon with copious citations so that ambiguities and shades of meaning may be observed. A vocabulary has been deliberately omitted from the book, in the conviction that not only must it be inadequate but also that such aids lull the student into a false sense of security.

Although instructors are free, of course, to do what they will with the book, it is suggested that the poem dealt with be read, translated, scanned (after Chapter I), and puzzling grammar points be cleared up; then that the questions be answered. There is more than enough material here for a term or, should that happy event be possible, for a year's course.

The texts of the poems are all taken from the standard Oxford or Teubner editions. Where crucial changes in the readings have been made, these have been indicated in either the notes or the questions.

My indebtedness to the critical work of previous writers on individual Latin poets is obvious as well as great. No less considerable is the debt I owe to the pervasive contemporary criticism of English poetry, especially that of Yvor Winters and F. R. Leavis. But my deepest obligation, apparent everywhere in this volume, is to Cleanth Brooks and Robert Penn Warren's *Understanding Poetry*.

This book owes its origin and arrangement to my classes in Latin poetry. But, in addition, it is my pleasure to thank for their generous comments on the manuscript Professor Oscar E. Nybakken of the University of Iowa, Professor Myra Uhlfelder of Bryn Mawr College, Professor Margaret Forbes of the University of Minnesota, and Professor James A. Hitt of the University of Texas. Especially do I owe a deep debt of gratitude to the late Professor Norma Young of the University of Iowa, whose patient and detailed reading of the entire manuscript of this book eliminated more blemishes than even she realized. For the typing of the final manuscript I am indebted to Mrs. Donna Sandrock and Mrs. Constance Merker. But chiefly I wish to thank for her endless patience and keen critical judgment my wife.

For a grant-in-aid toward publication of this book I am grateful to the University of Iowa.

Roger A. Hornsby

January 2, 1967
Iowa City, Iowa

CONTENTS

READING LATIN POETRY

THE DRAMATIC NATURE
OF POETRY

I

A POEM IS A STATEMENT in words about a human experience; not all statements in words about human experience, however, constitute a poem. Scientists as well as historians, philosophers, and novelists describe experiences that involve human beings; indeed, our daily conversations largely revolve around statements of this sort, yet none of us would assert that we were then uttering poetry. Frontinus' work on war, Livy's *Ab Urbe Condita*, Petronius' *Satyricon*, and Cicero's *Correspondence* all involve statements about the experiences of human beings, but none of them, we admit, is a poem. Nevertheless, poetry, along with gossip, fiction writing, history, philosophy, and science, has a common source in the impulse that men have to communicate their reactions to life. The manner and the quality of that communication are what distinguish poetry from other forms of discourse.

Purely scientific communication contains no judgment of value, but merely of fact, and it is wholly devoid of emotion. Scientific writing of the sort we find in the works of Frontinus or Cato contains rational statements with but slight attempt to judge and to communicate the feeling which the understanding of the experience ought to evoke. Frontinus in his treatise on the morality of war is not trying to communicate a feeling or even a judgment on the art of war; yet war is a topic capable of engaging emotions and necessitating a moral judgment. Poetry is like scientific writing in that it involves rational statements about human experiences, but it differs in that it judges the experience and communicates an appropriate feeling.

History, novels, and letters of the intimate sort found in Cicero's *Correspondence* seek to make rational statements and to form judgments. Furthermore, they frequently communicate some degree of feeling appropriate to the understanding of the experience. In his *Gallic Wars* Caesar gives very little indication of his own feelings on the pacification of Gaul. On the other hand, Livy (in the description of Cannae) attempts to interpret the experience and to communicate the horror of it. Petronius judges Trimalchio in the *Satyricon* at the same time as he elicits an emotional response from the reader. The reader of Cicero's letters shares in the orator's panic at his exile. But prose writing of the sort illustrated by these examples is only partially concerned with rendering as full a statement as possible about a particular human situation. Livy, Petronius, and possibly even Cicero, attempted to render more fully the experiences they wrote about than did Caesar. But none of them intended as full an understanding nor as deep a communication of the feeling appropriate to that understanding as a poet might have. The history, the novel, the letter might be located on a scale of which the poles are scientific prose and poetry. The history, the novel, the letter veer now toward one end, now toward the other. The poem differs in that it employs language more precisely and embraces meaning more subtly than do other forms of communication.

A poem, then, to refine the earlier definition, is a rational statement about a human experience which judges the experience and communicates the feeling which the understanding should elicit. Poetry finds its deepest source in the human impulse to communicate thoughts, feelings, and attitudes, matters which concern all of us most of the time and which engage our most passionate attention. The desire to speak of what so intensely concerns us comes from our even more passionate desire to understand ourselves and our world, to make sense of our experiences and our feelings, to create order out of chaos. The greatest poetry precisely does this; it gives us insight into ourselves and the world.

Poetry, then, is not separate from ordinary life, but deals explicitly with the very concerns of human beings. Poetry employs as its basic tool the language of ordinary people. The vocabulary of modern poetry does not differ from that of the street, nor did it in ancient Rome. Critics and scholars frequently comment on a supposed distinction in vocabulary between Latin poetry and prose, but this seeming difference is perhaps no more real than it is in English, and had more of the writings of the ancient world come down to us, it might have been revealed as negligible or nonexistent. But, although poetry employs ordinary language, it employs it in a heightened, intensified way. How it is heightened and intensified is in part the subject of this book.

But first, two things need to be said about what poetry is not. It is not a finely decorated surface beneath which a thought, fine or otherwise, lurks; it is not a "pill of truth" which is sugar-coated to render it palatable. An idea by itself does not make a poem, even if the idea is a good one. Ideas necessarily form part of poetry, and they affect the vocabulary, the rhythm, the figurative language of a poem, and are in turn affected by them. All these elements interact and modify one another, so that the poem is different from the bald idea. This point will be demonstrated repeatedly in the book.

A poem, furthermore, is not an expression of pure emotion. Those who so define poetry would be compelled to admit, for example, that a poem describing the taste of an apple or the scent of a rose is the same as the actual experience. Or a poem about the death of a brother would arouse in the reader the response of grief that an actual death might prompt. Manifestly, this is not the case, for a vast difference exists between the description and the actuality. No one, simply by reading, satisfies his sense of taste or smell, nor has so intense a feeling of grief as an actual bereavement causes. Poetry involves emotion, but a poet interprets the original experience; he does not "purely express it." More will be said about this matter later in the book.

These two common and fallacious notions about poetry arise from a failure to understand that a poem is an organic whole. Meter, figurative language, ideas are not mechanically combined, but are

{5}

in an intimate and fundamental relationship. This interrelationship of the elements of a poem is what is important. In a good poem no single element can be moved or shifted without profoundly changing the poem and making it into something different. The relationship of the elements in individual poems is the chief concern of this book. Although when we talk about poetry, we should be wary of using analogies since they so often mislead; nevertheless, one might be risked if we say that a poem is analogous to a tree with its organic life, but not to the concrete blocks of a building which are mechanically related to one another.

Bearing these provisos in mind, let us turn to one of the most important and obvious aspects of poetry, its dramatic organization. Every poem implies a speaker of the poem, either the poet or someone else who tells of an event, a situation, an idea. At the same time there is the response of that person to this event, situation, or idea; thoughts and feelings, if nothing else, have been set in motion. In this way every poem contains an action; it is a little drama. This aspect of poetry can be illustrated in the following poem:

Publius Vergilius Maro (70–19 B.C.)

Eclogue I

Meliboeus   *Tityrus*

M. Tityre, tu patulae recubans sub tegmine fagi
    siluestrem tenui musam meditaris auena:
    nos patriae finis et dulcia linquimus arua.
    nos patriam fugimus: tu, Tityre, lentus in umbra
5   formosam resonare doces Amaryllida siluas.
T. O Meliboee, deus nobis haec otia fecit.
    namque erit ille mihi semper deus, illius aram
    saepe tener nostris ab ouilibus imbuet agnus.
    ille meas errare boues, ut cernis, et ipsum
10   ludere quae uellem calamo permisit agresti.
M. Non equidem inuideo, miror magis; undique totis
    usque adeo turbatur agris. en, ipse capellas

protinus aeger ago; hanc etiam uix, Tityre, duco.
hic inter densas corylos modo namque gemellos,
15 spem gregis, a, silice in nuda conixa reliquit.
saepe malum hoc nobis, si mens non laeua fuisset,
de caelo tactas memini praedicere quercus.
sed tamen iste deus qui sit, da, Tityre, nobis.
T. Urbem quam dicunt Romam, Meliboee, putaui
20 stultus ego huic nostrae similem, quo saepe solemus
pastores ouium teneros depellere fetus.
sic canibus catulos similis, sic matribus haedos
noram, sic paruis componere magna solebam.
uerum haec tantum alias inter caput extulit urbes
25 quantum lenta solent inter uiburna cupressi.
M. Et quae tanta fuit Romam tibi causa uidendi?
T. Libertas, quae sera tamen respexit inertem,
candidior postquam tondenti barba cadebat,
respexit tamen et longo post tempore uenit,
30 postquam nos Amaryllis habet, Galatea reliquit.
namque, fatebor enim, dum me Galatea tenebat,
nec spes libertatis erat nec cura peculi.
quamuis multa meis exiret uictima saeptis,
pinguis et ingratae premeretur caseus urbi,
35 non umquam grauis aere domum mihi dextra redibat.
M. Mirabar quid maesta deos, Amarylli, uocares,
cui pendere sua patereris in arbore poma;
Tityrus hinc aberat. ipsae te, Tityre, pinus,
ipsi te fontes, ipsa haec arbusta uocabant.
40 T. Quid facerem? neque seruitio me exire licebat
nec tam praesentis alibi cognoscere diuos.
hic illum uidi iuvenem, Meliboee, quotannis
bis senos cui nostra dies altaria fumant.
hic mihi responsum primus dedit ille petenti:
45 "pascite ut ante boues, pueri; summittite tauros."
M. Fortunate senex, ergo tua rura manebunt.
et tibi magna satis, quamuis lapis omnia nudus
limosoque palus obducat pascua iunco:

{7}

non insueta grauis temptabunt pabula fetas,
50   nec mala uicini pecoris contagia laedent.
fortunate senex, hic inter flumina nota
et fontis sacros frigus captabis opacum.
hinc tibi quae semper uicino ab limite saepes
Hyblaeis apibus florem depasta salicti
55   saepe leui somnum suadebit inire susurro:
hinc alta sub rupe canet frondator ad auras;
nec tamen interea raucae, tua cura, palumbes,
nec gemere aëria cessabit turtur ab ulmo.

T. Ante leues ergo pascentur in aethere cerui,
60   et freta destituent nudos in litore piscis,
ante pererratis amborum finibus exsul
aut Ararim Parthus bibet aut Germania Tigrim,
quam nostro illius labatur pectore uultus.

M. At nos hinc alii sitientis ibimus Afros,
65   pars Scythiam et rapidum cretae ueniemus Oaxen
et penitus toto diuisos orbe Britannos.
en umquam patrios longo post tempore finis
pauperis et tuguri congestum caespite culmen,
post aliquot, mea regna, uidens mirabor aristas?
70   impius haec tam culta noualia miles habebit,
barbarus has segetes: en quo discordia ciuis
produxit miseros: his nos conseuimus agros!
insere nunc, Meliboee, piros, pone ordine uitis.
ite meae, quondam felix pecus, ite capellae.
75   non ego uos posthac viridi proiectus in antro
dumosa pendere procul de rupe uidebo;
carmina nulla canam; non me pascente, capellae,
florentem cytisum et salices carpetis amaras.

T. Hic tamen hanc mecum poteras requiescere noctem
80   fronde super uiridi: sunt nobis mitia poma,
castaneae molles et pressi copia lactis,
et iam summa procul uillarum culmina fumant,
maioresque cadunt altis de montibus umbrae.

Notes

Meter: Dactylic Hexameter.

5. *formosam Amaryllida*—cognate accusative. *Amaryllida* is a Greek accusative.

9. *errare, ludere*—objective infinitives with *permisit*; a grecism.

10. *uellem*—may be a subjunctive by attraction, for *ludere* would ordinarily be a subjunctive; more likely this is an imitation of the Greek generalizing clause which would use the subjunctive or optative. It may also have the connotations of a wish possible of realization which in Greek requires the optative; hence the use here of an imperfect subjunctive.

15. *silice in nuda*—i.e., so that they died.

16. the apodosis is to be understood.

18. *qui*—for *quis.*
    da—for *dic.*

28. *tondenti*—understand *mihi*; dative of reference.

35. *aere*—ablative of means.
    mihi—dative of reference.

36. *Amarylli*—ultima is short; a Greek vocative.

37. *sua*—i.e., each kind on its own tree.

38. *aberāt*—ultima is long; an archaism.

40. *facerem*—deliberative subjunctive.

44. *responsum*—used of the "reply" of an oracle.

49. *grauis*—and so sickly.

53-55. *tibi*—indirect object with *suadebit.*
    apibus—dative of agent with *depasta.*
    florem—Greek accusative or accusative of respect with *depasta.*
    depasta—the past passive participle with middle force.
    inire—complementary infinitive after *suadebit.*
    somnum—object of *inire.*
    susurro—instrumental ablative.

65. *cretae*—the passage is vexed, but *cretae*, not *Cretae*, seems preferable.

66. *orbe*—ablative of separation.

69. *post*—adverbial.

79. *poteras*—although unusual, it may be, as many suggest, a polite invitation. There is also a probability that the form imitates Greek, which uses an imperfect indicative for a wish in the present that something might be other than it now is.

From reading the epic we are aware of how dramatic that poem can be. Book II of the *Aeneid*, for example, vividly recounts the fall of Troy but does so by means of Aeneas' telling the story to Dido. If we forget that fact, we are in danger of missing some of the great complexity of the drama being enacted between Dido and Aeneas. In Vergil's *Eclogue* a similar situation occurs, but one which is much less complex. The poem is a dialogue between two characters who in their conversation perform a little drama.

The action of the drama—the plot, one might say—is whether Meliboeus will succeed in finding some succor for his present misery. The poem begins with a dialogue contrasting the respective states of Meliboeus and Tityrus. We are aware that some sort of upheaval in the social world is occurring, one which ruins some and ignores others. That the dislocation has cruelly and capriciously touched Meliboeus he makes clear in vv. 11–17. He not unnaturally wants to find out how Tityrus has managed to escape. He asks what god is it that gave such aid (v. 18).

But Tityrus answers him strangely; for he now speaks not of a god but of the City of Rome. Indeed he describes Rome in so strange a way that one is inclined to wonder with Meliboeus what Tityrus had to do with Rome. Tityrus proceeds to an even stranger account of why he went to Rome; he was without funds so long as he and Galatea were lovers, but then he met Amaryllis who was not apparently so extravagant and who helped him save his money so that he could go to Rome to buy his liberty. In the series of speeches between the two men up to v. 35, the action has proceeded on the basis of questions and answers. The character of the two men has been suggested by the way the one asks and the other answers. Meliboeus reveals himself as a realist capable of accepting a situation and of trying to find some way of helping himself. He comments to the point on the effect of what it means to be dispossessed (vv. 3–4, 11–14); at the same time he reveals his essentially pragmatic character when he remarks that he never trusted to "signs" (vv. 16–17). Finally, his questions are all straightforward and intelligent.

Tityrus on the other hand appears evasive and slightly muddled because, as the poem progresses, he becomes entangled in his own evasions. In answering Meliboeus' first question, he evades the issue with his reference to a god who has granted him his happy home and life. When he finds that Meliboeus is not to be put off, he concocts a tale about going to Rome. Meliboeus obviously views Tityrus' remarks on seeing Rome with a jaundiced eye (v. 26). Simple country folk do not ordinarily go to Rome. But Tityrus proceeds to compound his difficulties by his account of buying his liberty. Surely it was not necessary to go to Rome for such a purpose. Rather than say outright that he does not want to tell Meliboeus how he came to be so well off, he blunders into a series of evasions whose consequences he has not thought out.

But Meliboeus, a rational and practical man, recognizes Tityrus' evasions, and plays along with them in his address to Amaryllis (vv. 36–39). Tityrus continues to bumble on with his suspicious story of a god's giving him his freedom. The answer of the oracle is surely one of the strangest to a request for liberty. It cannot be taken seriously as more than an impromptu response of Tityrus to an immediate difficulty of his own making. Meliboeus so takes it. Although Meliboeus speaks ironically of what Tityrus possesses, he does so with considerable imagination and subtlety, especially in vv. 53–58. Tityrus, not completely unaware that Meliboeus might be treating his story with something less than solemnity, proceeds to a series of exaggerated protestations which involve impossible conditions in his attempt to bolster his case. His response is not unlike that of a disregarded child who stamps his foot to affirm his story.

Meliboeus picks up the tactless remarks of Tityrus and applies them to his own plight. Meliboeus implies in his speech that as far as he is concerned all the conditions of Tityrus' protestations have been met, for he is about to go as an exile to the ends of the earth.

Meliboeus makes his statements fully aware now that Tityrus is not going to answer his original question. But he has another purpose in mind, for his speech does make an appeal to Tityrus, that of want to plenty. It is precisely the kind of appeal, as the sequel shows, that Tityrus can understand. Tityrus, touched by the speech and by Meliboeus' plight, invites him to spend the night. Meliboeus has gained his objective.

The action of the poem unfolds entirely through dialogue. We can easily see the dramatic quality of this poem. Furthermore, since the action of a drama necessarily involves characters, they too are revealed in the poem through the dialogue. The kind of man each is, each declares from his own mouth. The response of both men to the social upheaval afflicting their country is sharply delineated: Meliboeus, the practical man, who accepts the world as it is and tries to make his way in it; Tityrus, the slightly irresponsible man, who ignores the social scene and lives well in spite of it.

Through his organization of the drama Vergil permits us to observe that this is the way the world is. Although the background suggests the possibility of a tragic handling of the material, tragedy does not overwhelm the poem. In fact, as we read and perceive the relationships between the two men, we realize that this poem concerns life as it actually exists: the good and intelligent do not always go down to utter ruin or rise to great triumph; they make do in the world where the feckless are often successful. Acceptance of the necessary compromises with the world such as Meliboeus makes is often a sign of intelligent, realistic, day-to-day living.

QUESTIONS

1. The comments and essays on various poems in this book are not meant as exhaustive ones. If a poem can be exhausted in a prose commentary, it probably is not a good one. We should be able to return again and again to a work of art to perceive more and more about it. For example, examine verses 46–58 and 64–78. How does the organization of those passages encourage the interpretation suggested in the essay? How are the passages alike? How do they differ?

2. Why should Meliboeus address Tityrus as "fortunate senex"?

3. How do Meliboeus' first verses (1–5) help prepare the way for the drama of the poem?

4. Can the epithet "free" be applied to both Tityrus and Meliboeus? Is there any distinction to be observed when it refers to either? What does the poem suggest or hint about the idea of freedom?

⟨§⟩

Gaius Valerius Catullus (c.84–54 B.C.)

XLV

Acmen Septimius suos amores
tenens in gremio, "mea" inquit, "Acme,
ni te perdite amo atque amare porro
omnes sum assidue paratus annos,
5   quantum qui pote plurimum perire,
solus in Libya Indiaque tosta
caesio ueniam obuius leoni."
hoc ut dixit, Amor sinistra ut ante,
dextra sternuit approbationem.
10   at Acme leuiter caput reflectens
et dulcis pueri ebrios ocellos
illo purpureo ore suauiata,
"sic," inquit, "mea uita, Septimille,
huic uni domino usque seruiamus,
15   ut multo mihi maior acriorque
ignis mollibus ardet in medullis."
hoc ut dixit, Amor sinistra ut ante,
dextra sternuit approbationem.
nunc ab auspicio bono profecti
20   mutuis animis amant amantur.
unam Septimius misellus Acmen
mauult quam Syrias Britanniasque:
uno in Septimio fidelis Acme
facit delicias libidinesque.
25   quis ullos homines beatiores
uidit, quis Venerem auspicatiorem?

NOTES

Meter: Phalaecean or Hendecasyllabic

1. *amores*—usually used by Catullus for an intimate relationship, not always that of friendship.

3. *porro*—"in time to come."

5. *pote*—for *potest.*

10. *caput reflectens*—i.e., bending backwards in order to turn her face upward towards Septimius.

20. *amant amantur*—no connective; such an arrangement is called then asyndeton.

Like Vergil's first *Eclogue*, this poem presents a little drama within the poem. Catullus, however, does not rely exclusively on dialogue to tell the story of this poem. The scene is described not by the lovers but by the poet who also addresses his audience or readers. The "drama" within the poem revolves around Acme's and Septimius' protestations of undying love, but it is complicated by descriptions from the poet—Amor's sneeze of approbation—and comments on the felicity of the lovers (vv. 19–26). We, the readers, see the action of the lovers and recognize that the vows of deathless love will last no longer than the passion which inspired them. Our enjoyment of the poem stems not only from the scene of a boy and girl kissing, but also from our detached amusement at their affair.

Although the poet does not tell us what to think about Septimius and Acme, he nevertheless leads us to certain conclusions by the way he presents the scene. Poetry, like drama, does not tell us what is going on, but rather shows us. The lovers are embracing with passion (vv. 1–2, 10–12). Such an embrace is pleasurable, we can readily infer. Further, the declarations of the lovers are received with favor, for Amor sneezes his approval. However, there is something ambiguous about Amor's approval, not in what he does, but in how he is described doing it. The ambiguity arises from the phrase *Amor sinistra ut ante/ dextra sternuit approbationem* (vv. 8–9, 17–18). *Sinistra* and *dextra* suggest that there is something two-sided about the approval, i.e., what Acme and Septimius say is fine for the moment, but not to be taken too seriously. The ambiguity is further heightened by the exaggerated language the poet uses in lines 19–26, in which he speaks of this affair as though it were a solemn undertaking, like going off to war (observe references to good auspices, to Syria and Britain). But in the last line by means of *Venerem* he conveys the notion that this is, after all, a rather lighthearted love affair.

By such means has the poet presented his scene and allowed us to infer his comments. The readers become the witty spectators of this amusing little drama.

QUESTIONS

1. Carefully examine vv. 10–12. What do the words *ebrios ocellos*, *purpureo*, and *suauiata* mean? How do they help further the "action" of the poem?

2. What do *delicias libidinesque* (v. 24) mean? How do they aid the poem?

3. In the light of discussion on this poem what do you make of the fact that *dixit* (vv. 8, 17), *sternuit* (9, 18), and *uidit* (26) are the only past tenses in the poem? What does that fact suggest about the tenses of the other verbs in the poem? Does such an arrangement of verb tenses emphasize in any way the dramatic quality of the poem?

4. What does *beatiores* (v. 25) mean? What is the purpose in using this word?

❧

Quintus Horatius Flaccus (65–8 B.C.)
Ode III. 9
Donec gratus eram tibi
nec quisquam potior bracchia candidae
ceruici iuuenis dabat,
Persarum uigui rege beatior.
5   "donec non alia magis

arsisti neque erat Lydia post Chloen,
 multi Lydia nominis
Romana uigui clarior Ilia."
 me nunc Thraessa Chloe regit,
10 dulcis docta modos et citharae sciens,
 pro qua non metuam mori,
si parcent animae fata superstiti.
 "me torret face mutua
Thurini Calais filius Ornyti,
15 pro quo bis patiar mori,
si parcent puero fata superstiti."
 quid si prisca redit Venus
diductosque iugo cogit aeneo,
 si flaua excutitur Chloe
20 reiectaeque patet ianua Lydiae?
 "quamquam sidere pulchrior
ille est, tu leuior cortice et improbo
 iracundior Hadria,
tecum uiuere amem, tecum obeam libens."

Notes

Meter: Second Asclepiadean.

 2. *quisquam*—used adjectivally with *iuuenis*.

 3. *ceruici*—in prose the word is regularly plural. Horace sometimes uses the singular for the plural in order to represent a group, a class, or a pair.

 dabat—for *circumdabat*.

 4. *Persarum rege*—proverbial for wealth and, thus, happiness.

 5. *alia*—ablative of cause.

 6. *post*—after in rank.

 7. *multi nominis*—genitive of quality.

 10. *modos*—the accusative frequently in poetry appears after *doctus*, as an accusative of respect.

 sciens—regularly in Augustan and later poetry takes the genitive on the analogy of *peritus*.

12. *animae*—refers to Chloe.

superstiti—a proleptic adjective, the intention of which is to anticipate objections and so to weaken their force. Here the word means "and allow her to live."

14. *Thurini*—of Thurii, a southern Italian city on the site of Sybaris; extremely wealthy.

15. *mori*—the infinitive is poetic after *patior*, as is *uiuere* in line 24.

QUESTIONS

1. What is the dramatic situation of the poem? How do we know it? How effective is dialogue for such a use? What are its limitations? Its assets?

2. What purpose do the adjectives attached to the names of Chloe and Calais have? Are they effectively employed?

3. Compare this poem with Catullus XLV.

This poem uses a dramatic situation similar to that of Catullus' poem, XLV. But unlike that one, and like Vergil's first *Eclogue*, the drama of the poem is told exclusively through the dialogue. The action of the poem concerns two friends, once lovers but now separated, who finally return to one another. But these lovers are much more wary with one another than the ones treated with amused detachment by Catullus. Observe the simple declarations about the past and present each makes (vv. 1–15). Even when the man proposes a renewal of their old affair, it is done with some hesitancy, as though he wanted to be certain of the girl before beginning anew with Lydia. Lydia, herself, responds in the same way, for she too has her prudent moments. Observe the use of *obeam* in v. 24, where the ambiguity is deliberate: "I will go to meet you," i.e., the door is open (in answer to v. 20) and "I will die with you." The couple is more sophisticated than Catullus' pair. The poet lets them reveal themselves without commentary. Through their dialogue the guarded quality of their feelings becomes clear at the same time that they commit themselves to a new and risky relationship.

The dramatic nature of poetry has been stressed in the first three poems in this book. But that is not their only merit; the questions to the poems should make this clear.

⋅⋅⋅

Marcus Valerius Martialis (c.40–104 A.D.)
Epigram I. 13

Casta suo gladium cum traderet Arria Paeto,
    quem de uisceribus strinxerat ipsa suis,
"Si qua fides, uulnus quod feci non dolet," inquit,
    "sed tu quod facies, hoc mihi, Paete, dolet."

NOTES

Meter: Elegiac Couplet.

1. *Paeto*—Caecina Paetus who aided Camillus Scribonianus in a revolt against the emperor Claudius. Arrested, he was taken to Rome and condemned to death. His wife, Arria, advised him to commit suicide and thereby set an example for others rather than incur disgrace by execution.

4. *facies*—a prediction; more effective than the imperative or the subjunctive of exhortation.

QUESTIONS

1. Examine carefully the dramatic qualities of this poem, then write a brief essay on the drama of the poem.

⋅⋅⋅

Gaius Valerius Catullus (c.84–54 B.C.)
X

Varus me meus ad suos amores
uisum duxerat e foro otiosum,
scortillum, ut mihi tum repente uisum est,
non sane illepidum neque inuenustum.
5 huc ut uenimus, incidere nobis
sermones uarii, in quibus, quid esset

iam Bithynia, quo modo se haberet,
et quonam mihi profuisset aere.
respondi id quod erat, nihil neque ipsis
10   nec praetoribus esse nec cohorti,
cur quisquam caput unctius referret,
praesertim quibus esset irrumator
praetor non faceret pili cohortem.
"at certe tamen," inquiunt, "quod illic
15   natum dicitur esse, comparasti
ad lecticam homines." ego, ut puellae
unum me facerem beatiorem,
"non," inquam, "mihi tam fuit maligne,
ut, prouincia quod mala incidisset,
20   non possem octo homines parare rectos."
at mi nullus erat neque hic neque illic,
fractum qui ueteris pedem grabati
in collo sibi collocare posset.
hic illa, ut decuit cinaediorem,
25   "quaeso," inquit, "mihi, mi Catulle, paulum
istos commoda: nam uolo ad Sarapim
deferri." "mane," inquii puellae,
"istud quod modo dixeram, me habere,
fugit me ratio: meus sodalis—
30   Cinna est Gaius—is sibi parauit.
uerum, utrum illius an mei, quid ad me?
utor tam bene quam mihi pararim.
sed tu insulsa male et molesta uiuis,
per quam non licet esse neglegentem."

Notes

Meter: Phalaecean or Hendecasyllabic.

1. *Varus*—a friend of Catullus, but who he is is unclear.
3. *scortillum*—this diminutive occurs only here.
   repente—"at first sight."
7. *Bithynia*—bequeathed by Nicomedes III to Rome in 74 B.C.

when it was organized as a province. Western Pontus was added to it in 65 B.C. when Pompey overthrew Mithridates. Governed by propraetors until 27 B.C., it then became a senatorial province. It did not have much importance during the Republic when compared with Asia, and it possessed the merest of Greek culture.

11. *cur* . . .—indirect question dependent on *nihil*. The point lies in the expensiveness of oil which only the rich could use.

18. *mihi*—dative of reference.

22. *grabati*—a Macedonian word for bedstead with the implication of poverty.

26. *commodă*—the short ultima is colloquial usage.

Sarapim—an Egyptian deity whose influence reached Rome during the time of Sulla. Invalids especially flocked to Sarapis.

27. *mane*—note the hiatus (see glossary) and the shortening of the final vowel.

28. *istud*—a grecism; an accusative of specification; *me habere* is in apposition.

29. *fugit me ratio*—colloquialism.

30. *Cinna Gaius*—i.e., C. Helvius Cinna.

31. Understand *attinet*.

QUESTIONS

1. What does the description of the scene, vv. 1–5, contribute to the dramatic unraveling of the poem?

2. In vv. 6–8, what is the significance of the order of the questions? Is there any order to the classes mentioned in vv. 9ff.?

3. From v. 28 to the end what is deliberately omitted? Why? What effect does such an omission create?

4. Certain words and phrases such as the diminutive *scortillum*, *illepidum*, *inuenustum*, *sermones*, and certain other constructions such as direct quotation in various passages are indicative of urban colloquial speech. With the aid of Harper's *Latin Dictionary* and the notes above, find other examples in the poem. Indicate what purpose such colloquialisms serve.

5. Although a slight poem, it nevertheless manages to present a scene involving three persons. Carefully examine how the charac-

ter of each person is conveyed. What evaluation can we make of each? What information permits us to make such judgments?

&§∾

Quintus Horatius Flaccus (65–8 B.C.)

Ode. I.37

Nunc est bibendum, nunc pede libero
pulsanda tellus, nunc Saliaribus
   ornare puluinar deorum
     tempus erat dapibus, sodales.
5 antehac nefas depromere Caecubum
cellis auitis, dum Capitolio
   regina dementis ruinas
     funus et imperio parabat
contaminato cum grege turpium
10 morbo uirorum, quidlibet impotens
   sperare fortunaque dulci
     ebria. sed minuit furorem
uix una sospes nauis ab ignibus,
mentemque lymphatam Mareotico
15   redegit in ueros timores
     Caesar ab Italia uolantem
remis adurgens, accipiter uelut
mollis columbas aut leporem citus
   uenator in campis niualis
20   Haemoniae, daret ut catenis
fatale monstrum; quae generosius
perire quaerens nec muliebriter
   expauit ensem nec latentis
     classe cita reparauit oras;
25 ausa et iacentem uisere regiam
uultu sereno, fortis et asperas
   tractare serpentis, ut atrum
     corpore combiberet uenenum,
deliberata morte ferocior,

30   saeuis Liburnis scilicet inuidens
     privata deduci superbo
     non humilis mulier triumpho.

Notes

Meter: Alcaic Stanza.

2. *Saliaribus . . . dapibus*—proverbial for their sumptuousness. The Salii were an ancient priesthood in Rome.

3. *puluinar*—singular for plural.

5. *antehac*—dissyllable.
   nefas—diaeresis (see glossary) follows this word.

10. *uirorum*—ironical, for the men were eunuchs.
   sperare—depends on *impotens* and is explanatory; a grecism.

13. Reference is to battle of Actium; fire broke out among Antony's ships and destroyed them. Cleopatra escaped with sixty vessels.

14. No pause in this line.

16. *Italia*—the first *i* is lengthened.

22. *perire*—depends on *quaerens*; an infinitive of purpose.

27. *tractare*—depends on *fortis.*
   serpentes—according to the traditional account, she met her death from the bite of an asp concealed in her bosom.

30. *Liburnis*—indirect object of *inuidens; deduci* is direct object.

31. *priuata*—predicate position.

Although she is not named, the lady in question is Cleopatra, and the event which lies outside the poem but to which reference is made is the defeat and death of Antony and Cleopatra at the hands of Octavian. Poets often use historical data of this sort and assume that it is commonly known. In reading Latin or Greek poetry we frequently need historical notes which would have been unnecessary for an ancient audience. But the importance of references to historical events is not in their mention, but in how the poet uses them. Do they, we need constantly to ask ourselves, give us insight? Do they aid the poem's purpose?

This poem, furthermore, opens with a line reminiscent of a

poem of the Greek poet Alcaeus which dealt with the overthrow of a tyrant of his state. Such reminiscence is common too in poetry. But again we must constantly ask ourselves what purpose is served by such an allusion. Does it help our understanding of the poem? Or is it simply decorative, that is, not functional? Look up the fragment of Alcaeus' poem, compare the two, and then decide.

QUESTIONS

1. In this ode, commonly called the "Cleopatra Ode," carefully examine what historical scenes and events are referred to and what relevance they have to the poem.

2. Examine and comment on all the verbs of this poem. What is the time sequence of the poem? What is the dramatic scene of the poem? When, supposedly, does the scene occur?

3. Explain whether you think the comparison in lines 17–21 is reasonable or justified.

4. Is the attitude towards Cleopatra in this poem consistent, or does it change? Account for your answer.

5. Write an essay on the dramatic aspect of the poem.

RES METRICA

2

CONCENTRATION of detail and intensity of expression distinguish poetry from prose. Although both poetry and prose may communicate through form, poetry does so with greater precision and subtlety so that the connection between the concentration of detail and intensity of expression looms larger than in prose. The close organization of a poem, especially in Latin poetry, is most obvious in the use of rhythmical language. Rhythm is frequently regarded as the chief distinction between poetry and prose. But, prose, as almost any passage of Cicero's orations or philosophical essays demonstrates, also embodies rhythm. The use of rhythmical language as a criterion of difference is false, for it is one of degree, not of kind. Rhythm is one among the many elements of a poem. Its value lies in its power "to modulate and define emotion, so that a finer adjustment of emotion to thought may be possible."[1] Rhythm, then, is one of the means of organizing a poem.

In Latin poetry, rhythm is based primarily on a pattern of long and short syllables. The unit of rhythm is the *foot*. The arrangement of feet in verses is the *meter*; e.g., the hexameter which is a succession of five feet, either dactyls or spondees, plus one spondee or a dactyl with one short syllable missing. In lyric poetry several such meters are arranged into stanzaic forms, which have acquired certain names, such as the Alcaic, the Sapphic, the Elegiac. We shall go more fully into these matters later.

Metrics in Latin require more attention than in English be-

[1] Yvor Winters, *On Modern Poets* (Meridian Books, New York, 1959), 145.

cause of our unfamiliarity with the metrical units and stanzaic forms. Moreover, Latin is a foreign tongue in which we only rarely feel "at home." Because of our familiarity with English, metrics in English poetry do not create such a seemingly enormous block to our grasp of the poem. Latin metrics are not so difficult that we cannot, with some practice, come to an awareness of their effect. In understanding metrics, as in all other skills, ease comes with familiarity.

Classical Latin poetry, being based primarily on a pattern of long and short syllables, is called quantitative verse. Latin also has a stress accent, i.e., the accented sound is uttered more loudly than the unaccented, which to some degree affects the rhythm, but for classical poetry (all the poems in this book, for example), stress is of somewhat minor importance.

"Long and short syllables" refers roughly to the length of time it takes to utter the sound of the syllable. Classical writers felt that a long syllable took twice as long to utter as a short one. But in order to know the quantity of a syllable, i.e., the length of time required, one has first to know what the syllable consists of, and where it begins and ends. Hence syllabic division is the first step in mastering Latin prosody. Every syllable in Latin contains either a vowel or a diphthong, and a Latin word has as many syllables as it has vowels and diphthongs. The syllable may consist solely of a vowel or diphthong, or may have consonants on either side or on both sides of it, e.g., *a-gres-tis, de-us.*

I. Within a word a syllable ends (A) with its vowel or diphthong if another vowel or diphthong immediately follows, or (B) if the succeeding consonants or consonant can normally begin a word in classical Latin, e.g., *de-a, me-o, re-gi-na*; *pu-bli-cum, a-qua, a-cri.*

II. Within the word a syllable ends with a consonant or consonants only when the consonants do not normally occur at the beginning of a word in classical Latin. No word begins with such combinations as *rb, mb, lp, ll, rr, tt, gn, mn, ps, ntr,* or *nct,* or *ct.*

Therefore, within a word the division occurs between those letters, e.g., *ar-bo-re, am-bo, cul-pa, nol-le, fer-re, mit-to*; *ig-nis, om-ni, ip-se*; *an-tro*; *sanc-to*. Words like *gnomon, Mnemosyne, psittacus*, and *Ctesiphon* are Greek in origin, and such words as *gnarus* are archaic. They are not classical words. *X* and *z* are double consonants, for they represent, respectively, *cs* and *ds*. Such words as *saxo, exeo, gaza* are divided: *sac-so*; *ec-se-o*; *gad-sa*.

Three exceptions occur to I (B). The first concerns *s* within the word. Although *s* and one or more consonants may begin a classical Latin word, the same group may not begin a syllable within a word. The *s* goes with the preceding syllable:

sci-o but *fus-ca*
spe-ro but *as-pe-ra*
stre-nu-us but *cas-tra*

The second exception involves words compounded with a preposition ending in a mute (g, d, b, c, [k], t, p,) followed by a liquid (l or r). In such words the division occurs immediately after the prepositional element, e.g., *ab-ri-pi-o, ob-ru-o, sub-li-mi*.

The third exception concerns any word where a liquid follows a mute. Here poets allowed themselves freedom of choice, for the mute and the liquid could either go together or be divided, e.g., *pa-tris* or *pat-ris*; *a-gris* or *ag-ris*. The division in this case depends on the exigencies of the metrical pattern.

One may infer that because of these exceptions one should divide *monstro* as *mons-tro* not *mon-stro*, but *constitisse* as *con-sti-tis-se* not *cons-ti-tis-se* and *inscia* as *in-sci-a* not *ins-ci-a*, and similarly with words such as *abs-ci-do, abs-te-mi-a*. But all such syllabification is inferential.

Greek words were generally treated as Latin ones, but occasionally one finds exceptions wherein a word is divided as though it were Greek, e.g., *At-las* and *A-tlas* both occur.

Liaison

One further point needs to be observed before we move to a consideration of the quantity of syllables, and that is liaison. In the pronunciation of Latin words in both poetry and prose, liaison occurs in the following ways between the final syllable of one word and the initial syllable of the next word:

I. If a word ends with a consonant other than *m* and is followed by a word beginning with a vowel or diphthong, alone or preceded only by *h*, the final consonant is detached from the first word and joined to the initial syllable of the next, e.g.,

hoc ut dic-sit A-mor si-nis-tra ut an-te (Cat. XLV.8.)

nunc a-b aus-spi-ci-o bo-no pro-fec-ti (Cat. XLV.19.)

mu-tu-i-s a-ni-mi-s a-man-t a-man-tur (Cat. XLV.20.)

II. If a word ends in a vowel or diphthong (with or without *m*) and comes before a word beginning with a vowel or diphthong, either alone or preceded only by *h*, the final vowel of the first word is elided. Hence this form of liaison is called elision, a squeezing out. The two syllables are reduced to one whose character is mainly that of the second vowel or diphthong, although a trace of the first vowel or diphthong is felt to be there, e.g.,

il-lǽ est, tu le-ui-or cor-ti-cǽ e-t im-pro-bo
(Hor. *O.* III.9.22)

te-cum ui-ue-rǽ a-mem, te-cǘ(m) ob-e-am li-bens
(Hor. *O.* III.9.24)

sae-pe ma-lǘ(ḿ) (h)oc no-bis, si mens non lae-va fuis-set
(Vergil *Ecl.* I.16)

Initial *h* in classical Latin was either not pronounced or very faintly pronounced. Every *h* should be bracketed in scanning. Final *m*, when followed by an initial vowel or diphthong, apparently imparted only a nasal quality to the preceding vowel. When followed by a consonant, final *m* is, of course, pronounced, e.g., *tecum uiuere.* Occasionally we find two words which do not elide although all the conditions for elision are present. This failure of elision is called *hiatus*, e.g., *deferri. "mane," inquii puellae* (Cat. X.27). No elision occurs between the *e* of *mane* and the *i* of *inquii* although it seems possible. The poet wants a pause after *mane*, to emphasize the word by separating it from *inquii.*

III. When a word ending in a vowel or a vowel plus *m* precedes *es* or *est* (from *esse*), prodelision occurs, for the *e* of *es* or *est* is elided. Thus:

femina est or *bonum est* becomes

feminá͡ 'st or *bonū͡(m) 'st.*

When a colloquial effect is especially desired, prodelisions frequently occur with *-us es* or *est*:

iratus es becomes *iratū͡ 's*

audiendus est becomes *audiendū͡ 'st.*

Such are the possibilities of liaison in classical Latin poetry. They are all frequent and must be carefully observed. No liaison, however, occurs when one word ends in a consonant and the next begins with a consonant other than *h* or when one word ends with a vowel and the next begins with a consonant. (Liaison between verses will be taken up later.)

Test your ability in syllabification by dividing into syllables all the words of one of the poems in the first section of this book and indicating all the forms of liaison which occur.

Quantity of Syllables

Before we can assign the quantity of a Latin syllable, we should determine whether it is open or closed. An open syllable ends in a vowel or diphthong, e.g., *a-qua*, *ma-la*. A closed syllable ends in a consonant or consonants, e.g., *cer-tum*, *con-dit*.

An open syllable has the quantity of its vowel or diphthong. It is, therefore, long if it has a long vowel or diphthong and short if it has a short vowel: *ă-quā* (abl.), *bŏ-nă*, *mă-lă*, *ă-nĭ-mō*, *cāe-lō*, *āe-quă*.

All closed syllables are long, regardless of the quantity of the vowel. The syllables *ēst* and *ĕst* are both long, for both are closed, although the *e* is long in one word and short in the other. The words *īnfelix* and *ĭndoctus* both have long first syllables, although only the *i* of the prefix of *īnfelix* is long. Since syllables, not vowels, are the units of classical verse, the quantity of the syllable is what must be determined.

Some apparent exceptions exist to what has been said about open and closed syllables. *Hĭc* (masculine nominative singular) and *hŏc* (neuter nominative singular) both have short vowels. *Hoc* was originally *hŏd-ce* with a short *o*. This first changed to *hoc-ce* and then to *hŏc* with short *o*. But in classical Latin, despite the spelling, the pronunciation, especially before words beginning with a vowel or *h* plus a vowel, was *hocc*. Hence in syllabifying it is necessary to restore the second *c*, e.g.,

(h)oc-c opu-s (h)ic la-bo-r est   (Vergil, *Aen.* VI.129)

The syllable, *hoc*, is long, for it is closed.

Hic began as *hŏ-ce*, which became *hĕ-ce*, then *hĕc*, and finally *hĭc*. The second *c*, as in *hoc(c)*, is technically not legitimate to the word so that a scansion such as the following occurs:

(h)īc uĭ-r (h)ĭ-c ēst . . .   (Vergil, *Aen.* VI.791)

But, because of the close association with *hoc(c)*, *hic* acquired an extra *c* so that we usually find:

(h)īc-c ă-lĭ-ē-nŭs ŏ-uīs cūs-tōs . . .   (Vergil, *Ecl.* III.5)

Be careful to distinguish this *hĭc* from *hīc*, the adverb, whose vowel is always long and whose *c* is single.

In words such as *aio, eius, maior, peior, Gaius, Maia,* and *Troia,* the first vowel is short, though the syllable is long. What has happened is that the consonantal *i* was doubled in pronunciation and was even sometimes spelled *ai-io, ei-ius, mai-ior, pei-ior,* etc. Hence, although the vowel is short, the syllable, because it is closed, is long. This same phenomenon occurs with the compounds and derivatives of *iacere: eicere, obicere, subicere, obex,* etc. The *i* must be doubled in scansion:

ob-ii-ci-t il-le   (Vergil, *Aen.* VI.421)

The *o* of *ob* is short, but the syllable is long.

Return now to the passage previously divided into syllables

and in which liaisons were indicated, and mark the quantity of every syllable.

Meters

Theoretically, we have all the information we need to work out the metrical arrangement of any verse of poetry. In a sense this is correct, for if the words are properly pronounced and the quantities of the syllables given clearly, the metrics of every verse become apparent, or will become so with practice. However, some additional information is useful, especially for the beginner.

The meter most frequently encountered by students in Latin poetry is the hexameter, and that will do well as a beginning for these comments on metrics. The ideal hexameter is a line consisting of six dactyls:

$$-\cup\cup|-\cup\cup|-\cup\cup|-\cup\cup|-\cup\cup|-\cup\cup$$

Each dactyl or spondee is called a foot. In any foot the poet may substitute a spondee for the dactyl. The verse could then appear:

$$--|--|--|--|--|--$$

In the usual hexameter, however, the last foot is not a true dactyl but either a dactyl with one short syllable missing or a spondee. Further, the fifth foot almost always is a dactyl. When a spondee does occur in that position, the verse is called spondaic, no matter what kind of foot appears in the first four feet. What usually happens in hexameters is indicated by the following passage from Statius' *Siluae*:

Cri-mi-ne quo me-ru-i, iu-ue-nis pla-ci-dis-si-me di uum,

quo-ue er-ro-re mi-ser, do-ni-s ut so-lu-s e-ge-rem,

Som-ne, tu-is? ta-ce-t om-ne pe-cus uo-lu-cres-que fe-rae-que

et si-mu-lant fes-sos cur-ua-ta ca-cu-mi-na som-nos,

nec tru-ci-bus flu-ui-i-s i-dem so-nu-s; oc-ci-di-t (h)or-ror

ae-quo-ri-s, et ter-ris ma-ri-a ad-cli-na-ta qui-es-cunt.

(*Siluae* V.4.1–6)

The first verse clearly indicates the metrical pattern, beginning with the normal dactylic hexameter verse. The other verses vary that pattern.

Some other observations, which will hold true for other types of meter as well, need to be made. In reading poetry the necessity of pausing, either at the end of the verse or within it, becomes apparent. The pauses in poetry are determined by the sense of the passage; that is, by what an intelligent reading of the passage requires. In a long verse, such as the hexameter, a pause occurs usually somewhere in the line as well as frequently at the end. Pauses within the verse are of two kinds: diaeresis and caesura. In the passage quoted above, the metrical pattern of dactyls and spondees does not usually agree with the syllabification of the words themselves. That is, there is an overlap in the pattern so that one word ends in the middle of a foot and the next one begins a foot as in v. 3. But occasionally a word and a foot end together as in *crimine* (v. 1), *donis ut* (v. 2), *cacumina* (v. 4), *occidit* (v. 5), *aequoris, terris mari (a)* (v. 6). The coincidence of the ending of word and foot is called diaeresis. A string of diaereses gives a jerky effect to the verse, and so a succession of them was avoided except for special effects. When the sense also requires us to stop, the diaeresis then, as in v. 6, becomes a distinct pause; it is as though everything had stopped. As in v. 5: *idem sonus*; *occidit*, such a diaeresis is indicated by ‖ , and is known as diaeresis-pause.

Diaeresis was generally avoided in the middle of the verse which is the weakest point. But the other pause, caesura, was frequently used here. Caesura occurs when a word ends before the metrical foot is complete. The effect is that of suspense. The ear, having been conditioned to a regular pattern of long and short syllables, hears that pattern. When it is not completed or when it is interrupted, a slight sense of anticipation is created which carries through the pause and the ending of the foot. Caesura has the tendency to bind the foot together unlike diaeresis which tends to separate the verse. To determine the caesura of the line, just as the diaeresis-pause, we have to pay attention to the sense of the passage. For example, one would not pause after *donis* or *ut* in v. 2, or after *idem* in v. 5, or even after *crimine* in v. 1, but those lines contain a caesura. Frequently the caesura occurs where there is a mark of punctuation as appears after *miser* in v. 2 or *tuis* in v. 3. Caesura, indicated by ‖ , is of two kinds in the hexameter. When it falls after the first long syllable, it is called masculine ($-‖\smile\smile$); after the first short, it is called feminine ($-\smile‖\smile$). It usually occurs in the third foot, although sometimes in the second or the fourth, and sometimes in both. A line with a diaeresis-pause does not usually contain a caesura.

A pause frequently occurs at the end of a verse, especially when a mark of punctuation occurs there or when the final syllable is not a long one, as in v. 3. A verse with a pause at the end is called end-stopped and is indicated by | . When no pause falls at the end, the verse is called a run-on line, as v. 5.

In every foot of a hexameter the first syllable, which is a long one, has naturally greater emphasis than the rest of the foot. This emphasis is called the ictus, or beat of the foot. Sometimes this beat coincides with the normal accent of the word, but just as often it does not. Although it is possible to compose a verse where both stresses coincide, the cost in the hexameter is the excessive use of diaeresis. Therefore conflict arises. Sometimes the conflict is deliberately sought as Vergil frequently did in the *Aeneid*. But in general a compromise was agreed on so that, in the hexameter, coincidence of ictus and accent occurs in the last two feet and usually at the beginning of the verse.

The six lines of *Siluae* V.4 are syllabified and scanned with diaeresis-pause (II), caesura (‖), end-stop (|), ictus (″), and accent (′) indicated.

Cri-mi-ne'quo me-ru-i,'iu-ue-nis pla-ci-dis-si-me'di-uum,|

quo-ue er-ro-re mi-ser,‖do-ni-s ut'so-lu-s e-ge-rem,|

Som-ne, tu-is?‖ta-ce-t om-ne pe-cus'uo-lu-cres-que fe-rae-que|

et si-mu-lant fes-sos'cur-ua-ta ca-cu-mi-na'som-nos,|

nec tru-ci-bus flu-ui-i-si-dem so-nu-s; oc-ci-di-t (h)or-ror

ae-quo-ri-s, et ter-ris'ma-ri-x ad-cli-na-ta qui-es-cunt.'

After you have examined the metrics of a passage, observe what effect, if any, there is in the placing of diaeresis or caesura. In v. 1, for example, the *crimen* is set off by the diaeresis for the sake of emphasis, and the caesura of the line, though normal, emphasizes the invocation. The caesurae of v. 3 are effective. The first one occurs in the second foot where the question is emphatic, but the effect of the caesura hastens us on in a manner that a diaeresis-pause would not. The caesura in the fourth foot is slight, for there is only a slight separation intended between the beasts and the birds. The pause at the end of the verse avoids the collision of *que* and *et*. The diaeresis of v. 4 emphasizes the word *cacumina* and aids the suggestion of the peaks. *Curuata cacumina* metrically reinforces the image of the phrase. The long-delayed pause of v. 5, which is a diaeresis-pause, and the run-on line and the diaeresis of the first foot of v. 6, markedly underscore the three words, *occidit*, *horror*, *aequoris*, and their concepts, as well as prepare for the quiet close of the rest of the verse.

Certain other metrical phenomena, which it will be well to illustrate, exist in the passage. Assonance, or the repetition of the same sound or a closely similar one within or at the end of the word, occurs in the repetition of the *m*, the *o*, and the *s* sounds in vv. 1–3. The sound coupled with the sense of the passage furthers the suggestions of the question, emphasizes the softness of sleep, and the sense of puzzlement. Alliteration, another device at the disposal of the poet, is the repetition of the same sound at the beginning of a word, as in *curuata cacumina*. Alliteration there helps to reinforce the idea of those words. Rhyme, the repetition of the same sound at the end of the words, appears in *fessos . . . somnos* in v. 4. In Latin poetry of the classical period, rhyme was generally avoided except for special effects such as here where the rhyme emphasized by the caesura binds the two words together.

Such then are the metrical considerations which help shape the idea of this poem's first six verses. In discussing them we have been careful not to say that such and such creates this or that effect. The reason for the avoidance is that metrics and metrical matters cannot be divorced from the words involved. The *s* and *m* sounds of *iuuenis placidissime diuum* do not of themselves, even when combined with the long vowels, create the illusion of "softness." The same sounds in another context might help to suggest something else: fear or hatred. Words are the important elements; they carry the meaning, and their sounds when skillfully used may reinforce that meaning.

Here is the entire poem. Carefully mark the scansion and pauses in vv. 7–19, and observe the use of alliteration, assonance, and rhyme. The starred verses are especially noteworthy.

Publius Papinius Statius (c.40 or 45–96 A.D.)

Siluae V.4

Crimine quo merui, iuuenis placidissime diuum,
quoue errore miser, donis ut solus egerem,
Somne, tuis? tacet omne pecus uolucresque feraeque
* et simulant fessos curuata cacumina somnos,
5 * nec trucibus fluuiis idem sonus; occidit horror
aequoris, et terris maria adclinata quiescunt.
* septima iam rediens Phoebe mihi respicit aegras
stare genas; totidem Oetaeae Paphiaeque reuisunt
lampades et totiens nostros Tithonia questus
10 praeterit et gelido spargit miserata flagello.
* unde ego sufficiam? non si mihi lumina mille
quae sacer alterna tantum statione tenebat
* Argus et haud umquam uigilabat corpore toto.
* at nunc heu! si aliquis longa sub nocte puellae
15 bracchia nexa tenens ultro te, Somne, repellit,
inde ueni nec te totas infundere pennas
luminibus compello meis (hoc turba precetur
* laetior): extremo me tange cacumine uirgae,
sufficit, aut leuiter suspenso poplite transi.

NOTES

8. *Oetaeae Paphiaeque*—i.e., the morning and evening stars. *Oetaeae* is a reference to the mountain range between Thessaly and

{34}

Aetolia where Hercules ascended the funeral pyre; *Paphiaeque* is a reference to the planet of Paphian Venus.

9. *Tithonia*—i.e., the dawn, Aurora, uses a whip to chase the stars from the heaven; from it fall the dewdrops upon the poet. Tithonus was the husband of Aurora.

12. *sacer*—because sent by Juno.

QUESTIONS

1. What purpose does the invocation serve?
2. How are concrete details employed in the poem?

Incertus Auctor

Heia, uiri, nostrum reboans echo sonet heia!
arbiter effusi late maris ore sereno
placatum strauit pelagus posuitque procellam,
edomitique uago sederunt pondere fluctus.
5 Heia, uiri, nostrum reboans echo sonet heia!
annisu parili tremat ictibus acta carina.
nunc dabit arridens pelago concordia caeli
uentorum motu praegnanti currere uelo.
Heia, uiri, nostrum reboans echo sonet heia!
10 aequora prora secet delphinis aemula saltu
atque gemat largum, promat seseque lacertis,
pone trahens canum deducat et orbita sulcum.
Heia, uiri, nostrum reboans echo sonet heia!
persultet Phorci chorus aequora: nos tamen heia.
15 conuulsum remis spumet mare: nos tamen heia.
uocibus adsiduis litus resonet "tamen heia."

NOTES

Meter: Dactylic Hexameter.
2. *arbiter*—i.e., Neptune.
10. *aemula*—as a noun it usually takes a genitive.
11. *largum*—an internal accusative.
    lacertis—ablative of means.

14. *Phorcus*—a sea god.

QUESTIONS

1. Show what part meter plays in this poem. How does it help to organize the thought and content of the poem? A further exercise: Return to the first poem of this book, Vergil's *Eclogue* I. Choose a passage of some length and comment on its metrical qualities.

Elegiac Couplet

Closely connected with the hexameter is the elegiac couplet which consists of two verses, the first a hexameter of the sort just discussed. The second is called a "pentameter," but it is the same as a hexameter except that the third and sixth feet omit the last half of the dactyl, i.e., two short syllables or one long one. In the second verse the first two feet may have substitutions of spondees, but the fourth and fifth feet show no such substitutions. The line has no regular caesura, but a diaeresis-pause occurs in the third foot:

Ō-dĭ ĕ-t ă-mo. ‖ Quā-rē ĭd fă-cĭ-am for-tas-sĕ rĕ-qui-ris
Nēs-cĭ-ŏ, sed fĭ-ĕ-rĭ sen-tĭ-ŏ e-t ex-crŭ-cĭ-or.

(Catullus LXXXV)

Nīl nĭ-mĭ-um- stŭ-dĕ-o, ‖ Cae-sar tĭ-bĭ uel-lĕ plă-ce-rĕ
nēc scĭ-rĕ ut-rūm sis-āl-bŭ-ṣ a-n a-tĕr (h)ŏ-mo.

(Catullus XCIII)

In v. 2 of Catullus LXXXV the regular pentameter appears. In v. 2 of Catullus XCIII the variant appears. Though these poems may appear unusual in that they are only two verses each, they do indicate one general tendency of the elegiac couplet, that of self-containment. The couplet generally attempts to express a complete thought within itself. But such is only a goal and does not necessarily have to be met. Observe, however, the diaeresis-pause in both pentameters of both couplets. Since each poem is fundamentally a dactylic one, the dactylic rhythm is thus reasserted at the end of the couplet. Older grammarians gave the name pentameter to the second verse by scanning it as five feet in the following manner:

$$- \overline{\smile\smile} | - \overline{\smile\smile} | - \ \ - | \smile\smile - | \smile\smile - |$$

In this method the fourth and fifth feet would be anapests ($\smile\smile-$). If the verse were so scanned, the definite pause of the diaeresis would be ignored; hence the reluctance today to scan the second verse of the couplet in this fashion. The couplet in effect turns on the diaeresis, as can be observed in the two poems by Catullus. *Fieri* in the first one forms a kind of suspense after the *nescio, sed.* We listen for the next word somewhat impatiently. The *sis* in the second poem affords an even better illustration. Because of the *utrum*, we know that alternatives are to be presented to us. The *sis* reminds us that those alternatives are to characterize the man; hence our eagerness to know what is to be predicated of the *sis*.

Diaeresis and diaeresis-pause, instead of being avoided as they generally are in hexameters, are deliberately sought in the second verse of the elegiac couplet. Other verse forms also deliberately use diaeresis and diaeresis-pause. This fact well illustrates the danger of making absolute rules. Poems require various means for their success; what may work in one poem may prove disastrous in another.

QUESTIONS

1. At various points in these two poems elision occurs. Does the elision seem merely mechanical, or does it serve some other function whereby the poem is tightly bound together?

2. Carefully analyze the accent and ictus of both poems. How are accent and ictus used? Is the use skillful or not? Does it reveal any particular or noteworthy phenomena about the poem?

Iambic Meters

So far we have been discussing verse forms which are primarily dactylic or spondaic. The other major system of versification is based on the iamb ($\smile-$). The iamb is not counted in quite the same way as the dactyl or spondee, each of which is a foot. Two iambs make a unit, technically a dipody ($\smile-\smile-|$). (Each half is called a foot.) An iambic verse may consist of two or more such dipodies.

One of the commonest is the iambic trimeter, which is used in the following poem, where each verse contains three dipodies or six iambs:

Phă-sēl-lŭ-s̱ il̄-lĕ,‖quem ŭi-dē-tĭ-s, (h̄)os-pĭ-tes,|
ā-ĭt fŭ-ĭs-sē‖na-ŭi-ŭm|ce-lēr-rĭ-mŭs,|

(Catullus IV.1–2)

The whole poem is iambic trimeter and will be discussed in detail in a later section of the book. For the moment simply observe the pattern, and notice that rarely does a dipody end with the end of a word. Caesura usually occurs in the second dipody. Note also that the first syllable of *ait* is long. The diaeresis of v. 2 calls attention to itself. A pause occurs there, which in this instance, though slight, makes the last dipody of the verse, consisting of a single word, important. Our attention is forced on the word. In addition the case of the word is odd for Latin; it is nominative when we would expect accusative. What the poet does is force our attention on the use of the nominative, which indicates, among other things, that the boat is making a claim for itself. The personification is thus emphasized by the meter as well as by the construction.

When the iambic trimeter alternates with the iambic dimeter, ◡–◡–|◡–◡–| , the couplet is called the iambic strophe.

A variant of the pure iambic trimeter is the verse form known as the choliambic, the lame iambic, which has the following scheme:

◡̆ ⸗ ◡ ◡̆ ⸗ | ◡̆ ‖ ⸗ ◡ ⸗ | ◡ ⸗ ⸗ ◡̆ ‖

Mĭ-sēr Că-tūl-le,‖dē-sĭ-na-s̱ ĭ-nep-tĭ-rē
ēt quōd ŭĭ - des̄ˡˡpĕ-rĭs-sĕ per-dĭ-tum dū-cas

(Catullus VIII.1–2)

In this brief sample from a poem which appears later in the book, observe that v. 1 sets the pattern. Caesura occurs in the third foot as in the iambic trimeter, and in the sixth foot the pattern of iambs is reversed by the use of a trochee (–◡). The reversal in this case suggests the ineptness which the verse speaks of. In v. 2, which has some variations, note the long syllable of the first foot, the diaeresis at the end of the first dipody, the use of a spondee in the final foot rather than a trochee, and the alliteration of *perisse perditum*. All these devices emphasize and encourage the emotional acceptance of the thought of the verse. They clearly modulate and define the emotion expressed by the verse.

Trochaic verse is the reverse of iambic. The "pure" form of it is the trochaic tetrameter catalectic, consisting of four dipodies, the last of which lacks a syllable (catalectic, cut off):

$$-\,\cup\,-\,\underset{\smile}{}\,|\,-\,\cup\,-\,\underset{\smile}{}\,|\,-\,\cup\,-\,\underset{\smile}{}\,|\,-\,\cup\,\underset{\smile}{}$$

Ām-nǐ-s̄ ǐ-ba-ṭ ǐn-tě-r̄ ar-ǔa ual-lě fu-sus fri-gǐ-da

(Tiberianus, *Amnis ibat*, 1)

The meter rarely appears in Latin poetry. This example is taken from a poem which will be discussed in Chapter III, and which shows some metrical peculiarities. A more common trochaic verse is the Phalaecean or hendecasyllabic, popularized in Latin poetry by Catullus. It is a trochaic verse of five trochees, but in the second foot a dactyl is substituted for a trochee. Moreover, the first trochee may have either syllable long or short. The last trochee may have a final syllable which is either long or short. The pattern is:

$$\underset{\smile}{}\,\underset{\smile}{}\,|\,{\overset{\prime\prime}{}}\,\cup\,\cup\,|\,-\,\cup\,|\,-\,\cup\,|\,-\,\underset{\smile}{}$$

Syllabify and scan the following poem:

> *Gaius Valerius Catullus* (c.84–54 B.C.)
> ### XXVII
> Minister uetuli puer Falerni
> inger mi calices amariores,
> ut lex Postumiae iubet magistrae
> ebrioso acino ebriosioris.
> 5   at uos quo lubet hinc abite, lymphae,
> uini pernicies, et ad seueros
> migrate: hic merus est Thyonianus.

NOTES
Meter: Phalaecean or Hendecasyllabic

1. *Falerni*—regarded as one of the fine wines.

2. *inger*—the only instance of the shortened imperative form.

3. *lex magistrae*—ruler of the feast, chosen by lot, decreed the proportion of water to wine and the proposal and drinking of toasts. The whole notion derives from the Greek symposium, but note that here a woman is in command.

6. *uini pernicies*—i.e., water ruins wine.

seueros—i.e., sober.

7. *Thyonianus*—Bacchus was called Thyoneus because his mother was Theban Semele, or Thyone.

The Phalaecean comes close to a prose rhythm, but it permits a wide variety of effects, from one of formality to that of this poem. Here the effect of the poem does not rest exclusively on the meter. The elision in v. 4 suggests the slurred speech of the man who has drunk too much, the idea with which the verse is concerned. The last verse has an effect similar to that of v. 4, as does the particular form of the imperative in v. 2. All these details reinforce the thought of the poem—the joy of drinking.

QUESTIONS

1. Comment on the use of the comparative in v. 4. Is it appropriate and suggestive?

2. How are adjectives generally used in this poem?

3. Comment on use of assonance and alliteration in the poem.

4. Write an essay on the dramatic situation of the poem and the part the meter plays in the poem.

Stanzaic Forms

So far we have dealt primarily with poems in which the verses repeat the same metrical pattern. However, some indication has been made of stanzaic forms such as the elegiac couplet and the iambic strophe, both of which are composed of two lines. Latin poetry also shows complex stanzas which involve both dactylic and iambic measures, either separately or in combination. The most common and best known are the Alcaic and Sapphic strophes. These two forms derive from Greek poetry. Catullus used the

Sapphic strophe, but Horace firmly incorporated that form along with the Alcaic into Latin poetry.

The verse pattern of the Alcaic is:

$$\underset{}{\smile} \mid \perp \smile \mid \perp \ -\text{II} \perp \smile \smile \mid \perp \smile \mid \smile \qquad \text{(Greater Alcaic)}$$

$$\underset{}{\smile} \mid \perp \smile \mid \perp \ -\text{II} \perp \smile \smile \mid \perp \smile \mid \smile \qquad \text{(Greater Alcaic)}$$

$$\underset{}{\smile} \mid \perp \smile \mid \perp \ - \mid \perp \smile \mid \perp \ \smile \qquad \text{(Trochaic dimeter)}$$

$$\perp \smile \smile \mid \perp \smile \smile \mid \perp \smile \mid \perp \ \smile \qquad \text{(Lesser Alcaic)}$$

The syllable which opens the first three verses is called an anacrusis, which means a "prelude" before the measure proper. It does not count as a foot. The last foot of the first two verses is catalectic, for the second syllable is missing. Diaeresis-pause regularly occurs in the first two verses, although on occasion it is avoided. The verse form is a mixture of trochaic and dactylic feet. The names in brackets are the technical names of the various lines.

The following poem has been syllabified and scanned as an illustration of the Alcaic stanza:

Quintus Horatius Flaccus (65–8 B.C.)
Ode I.26

Mu-si-ş a-mi-cus tris-ti-ti-a(m) et me-tus

tra-dam pro-ter-ui-ş in ma-re Cre-ti-cum

    por-ta-re uen-tis, quis su-b Arc-to

    rex ge-li-dae me-tu-a-tu-r o-rae,

5 quid Ti-ri-da-ten ter-re-a-t, u-ni-ce

se-cu-ru-s! O quae fon-ti-bu-ş in-te-gris

    gau-des a-pri-cos nec-te flo-res

    nec-te me-o La-mi-ae co-ro-nam

Pi-ple-i dul-cis! Nil si-ne te me-i

10 pro-sunt (h)o-no-res: (h)unc fi-di-bus no-uis

    (h)unc Les-bi-o sac-ra-re plec-tro

    te-que tu-as-que de-cet so-ro-res.

NOTES

Meter: Alcaic Stanza.

3. *portare*—an infinitive of purpose; a grecism.

quis rex—probably alludes to Dacian King Cotiso, who in 30 B.C. threatened the northern frontier of Roman territory.

sub arcto—"under the Bear," i.e., in the North.

metuatur and *terreat*—both clauses are grammatical objects of *securus.*

metuatur—regard it as impersonal, or understand *a nobis.*

5. *Tiridāten*—In 31 B.C. Tiridātes moved against the usurper Phraates who had murdered his father and brother for the Parthian throne. Tiridātes, unsuccessful, fled to Augustus in 30 B.C. for aid.

9. *Piplei*—Greek vocative singular; a dweller at Piplea, a fountain in Pieria.

te—i.e., *Musa (Piplei).*

10. The verse refers to Aeolic lyric poetry, which Horace prides himself on having introduced into Latin.

The poem discusses how the power of the Muses, of art, can immortalize a man and remove him from the usual cares of the world. It is fairly simple and straightforward in theme. But the metrical pattern when closely observed or attentively listened to indicates some subtlety. Each of the first two verses of the stanzas contains the diaeresis-pause after the second foot, after which the meter changes from trochees to dactyls. But note that dactyls are in one sense trochees with an extra short syllable, a sort of lengthened trochee. Adjusted to the trochees of the start of the line, the ear easily accommodates the dactyl after the diaeresis-pause, especially since the next measure is trochaic. Only v. 10 lacks a diaeresis in the third foot. Although the elision in v. 1 and the liaison in v. 5 underemphasize the diaeresis, it nonetheless is present.

Diaeresis-pause occurs in vv. 3 and 7 at the end of the second foot, but not in v. 11, which has a masculine caesura at the same point. Finally, vv. 4 and 8 have a masculine caesura in the second foot but not v. 12 which has a feminine caesura.

The third stanza then shows three differences from the established pattern of the poem in its three final verses: the omission of diaeresis in the third foot of v. 10, and at the end of the second foot in v. 11, and the feminine caesura in v. 12. The subtle changes in the pauses, especially the use of caesura in unexpected ways, reinforces the thought of the stanza and helps to convey the attitude being expressed, that of the intimate relationship between the poet and the Muses. The notion is further emphasized by the use of repetition, assonance, alliteration, and rhyme in the last three verses.

QUESTIONS

1. Examine the poem for instances of rhyme and alliteration other than in the last three lines. Do they play any part in the organization of the poem?

2. Carefully explain the meaning and use of *sacrare* in v. 11.

3. Explain the number of *metus* in v. 1. Why is that word used?

4. Explain the use of *Lesbio* in v. 11.

Sapphic Stanza

The other stanza form made famous by Horace is the Sapphic. It too was a Greek form supposedly invented and employed by Sappho of Lesbos. The pattern is:

$$\underline{\smile}\,\smile/\underline{\smile}\,-\,/\,\underline{\smile}\,//\,\smile\,\smile/\,\underline{\smile}\,\smile/\underline{\smile}\,\bar{\smile} \qquad \text{(Lesser Sapphic)}$$

$$\underline{\smile}\,\smile/\underline{\smile}\,-\,/\,\underline{\smile}\,//\,\smile\,\smile/\,\underline{\smile}\,\smile/\underline{\smile}\,\bar{\smile} \qquad \text{(Lesser Sapphic)}$$

$$\underline{\smile}\,\smile/\underline{\smile}\,-\,/\,\underline{\smile}\,//\,\smile\,\smile/\,\underline{\smile}\,\smile/\underline{\smile}\,\bar{\smile} \qquad \text{(Lesser Sapphic)}$$

$$\underline{\smile}\,\smile\,\smile/\underline{\smile}\,\bar{\smile} \qquad \text{(Adonic)}$$

Like the Alcaic, this stanza is basically a trochaic verse with a dactyl in the third foot which regularly contains a caesura, usually masculine but sometimes feminine.

Horace's *Ode* I.30 well illustrates the Sapphic stanza.

Ō Vĕ-nus, rē-gī-nă ‖ Cnĭ-dī Pă-phī-quĕ
spēr-ñe-dī-lēc-tam ‖ Cȳ-prŏn et ŭŏ-can-tis
tū-rĕ te mūl-tō ‖ Glȳ-cĕ-rae dĕ-cō-ram
trāns-fĕ-r ĭ-n ae-dem.

5 Fer-uĭ-dus tē-cum‖pŭ-e-r̄ et sŏ-lū-tis
Gra-tĭ-ae zo-nis‖pro-pĕ-rent-que Nym-phae
et pă-rum co-mis‖sĭ-nĕ te Iŭ-uen-tas
Mer-cŭ-rĭ-ŭs-quĕ.

Notes

1. Cnidi Paphique—Cnidos, a Doric city of Caria; Paphos on the western coast of Cyprus—both where Venus was worshiped.
2. Cypron—a Greek accusative.

In the first verse the caesura is a feminine one emphasizing the word *regina*, which characterizes the royal power of Venus. The pause at the end of the verse and the diaeresis in v. 2 of the first foot emphasize the imperative. Also in v. 2 the position of *et* draws attention to itself and suggests that the succeeding clause is important. The same word is likewise emphasized in vv. 5–7, where the cohesion of the attendants of Venus is indicated. *Et* is normally not of such emphatic importance. But here it underlines the notions expressed in the poem. In the first two instances (vv. 2 and 5), observe that diaeresis occurs although its effect is partially lessened by the liaisons. The last *et* (v. 7) has an even stronger effect than those of vv. 2 and 5, for it appears at the beginning of the verse. Liaison is skillfully used in v. 4 to emphasize the purpose of the command. The use of the imperatives *sperne* and *transfer* and the emphasis on *et* are reinforced at the end of the first stanza by the liaisons of the last verse. Through the use of a single word a similar effect is achieved in v. 8. The emphasis of the ideas conveyed by the use of the name of the god is reinforced by its solitary position.

As an exercise on the importance of metrics examine the following poem. The verse pattern is:

⏒ ⏒ | – ⏑ ⏑ | – ⏑ | ⏒	(Second Glyconic catalectic)
⏒ ⏒ | – ⏑ ⏑ | – ⏑ | ⏒	(Second Glyconic catalectic)
⏒ ⏒ | – ⏑ ⏑ | – ⏑ | ⏒	(Second Glyconic catalectic)
⏒ ⏒ | – ⏑ ⏑ | – –	(Second Pherecratic acatalectic)

The starred verses are hypermetric; that is, the verse has an extra syllable. The final syllable of the verse ends in a vowel plus *m* and is elided with the initial vowel or *h* plus vowel of the first syllable of the next verse. Hypermetric verses are common enough in Latin poetry. Try to state as clearly as possible what effect the hypermetric verses have in this poem.

Gaius Valerius Catullus (c.84–54 B.C.)

XXXIV

Dianae sumus in fide
puellae et pueri integri;
Dianam pueri integri
    puellaeque canamus.
5   o Latonia, maximi
magna progenies Iouis,
quam mater prope Deliam
    deposiuit oliuam,
montium domina ut fores
10   siluarumque uirentium
  *saltuumque reconditorum
    amniumque sonantum;
tu Lucina dolentibus
Iuno dicat puerperis,
15   tu potens Triuia et notho es
    dicta lumine Luna.
tu cursu, dea, menstruo
metiens iter annuum,
rustica agricolae bonis
20   tecta frugibus exples.
sis quocumque tibi placet
  *sancta nomine, Romulique,
antique ut solita es, bona
    sospites ope gentem.

Notes

A festival hymn to Diana written to be sung by a chorus of

boys and girls, perhaps responsively. The poem may have been inspired by the festival of Diana at her temple on the Aventine during the full moon of August.

2. *integri*—modifies both nouns.

8. *deposiuit*—an archaic form.

14. *Iuno*—regarded as the deity who brought back the moon-light after its monthly eclipse. In certain aspects often identified with Diana.

Questions

1. Write an analysis of the metrical qualities of this poem, and indicate what part they play in the poem.

2. Why is the form of *deposiuit* appropriate? Are there other such usages in the poem?

Other Verse Forms

The remaining verse forms which appear in this book will be given in outline. They are combinations of feet and lines already discussed. The names are attached only for convenience and need not be memorized. If a student follows the rules for scansion indicated in this chapter, he should have no serious difficulty in analyzing the metrics of any poem, no matter how unfamiliar he may be with the particular verse form. Nevertheless, the verse form of every poem is given in the notes on each poem.

First Asclepiadean

$$-\ -\ |\ -\ \cup\ \cup\ |\ -\ \|\ -\ \cup\ \cup\ |\ -\ \cup\ |\ \overset{\smile}{-}$$

Second Asclepiadean

$$-\ \overset{\smile}{-}\ |\ -\ \cup\ \cup\ |\ -\ \cup\ |\ -\quad \text{(Glyconic)}$$
$$-\ -\ |\ -\ \cup\ \cup\ |\ -\ \|\ -\ \cup\ \cup\ |\ -\ \cup\ \overset{\smile}{-}$$

Exercise

Examine the metrics of Horace's *Ode* III.9. Do they reinforce what has already been said about that poem?

Third Asclepiadean

```
— — | — ◡ ◡ | — ‖ — ◡ ◡ | — ◡ | ⌣̆
— — | — ◡ ◡ | — ‖ — ◡ ◡ | — ◡ | ⌣̆
— — | — ◡ ◡ | — ‖ — ◡ ◡ | — ◡ | ⌣̆
— ⌣̆ | — ◡ ◡ | — ◡ | —      (Glyconic)
```

Fourth Asclepiadean

```
— — | — ◡ ◡ | — ‖ — ◡ ◡ | — ◡ | ⌣̆
— — | — ◡ ◡ | — ‖ — ◡ ◡ | — ◡ | ⌣̆
      — — | — ◡ ◡ | — ⌣̆     (Pherecratic)
      — ⌣̆ | — ◡ ◡ | — ◡ | ⌣̆  (Glyconic)
```

First Archilochian

```
— ◡ ◡ | — ◡ ◡ | — ‖ ◡ ◡ | — ◡ ◡ | — ◡ ◡ | — ⌣̆  (Hexameter)
      — ◡ ◡ | — ◡ ◡ | —           (Dactylic Trimeter
                                    catalectic)
```

Fourth Archilochian

```
— ◡̃◡̃ | — ◡̃◡̃ | — ‖ ◡̃◡̃ | — ◡ ◡ | — ◡ | — ◡ | — ◡  (Greater
                                                Archilochian)
◡ — ◡ — | ◡ ‖ — ◡ — | ◡ — ◡        (Iambic Trimeter catalectic)
```

Second Pythiambic

```
— ◡ ◡ | — ◡ ◡ | — ‖ ◡ ◡ | — ◡ ◡ | — ◡ ◡ | — ⌣̆  (Hexameter)
      ◡ — ◡ — | ◡ ‖ — ◡ — | ◡ — ◡ —      (Iambic Trimeter)
```

Sapphic Major

```
      — ◡ ◡ | — ◡ — ◡̄           (Aristophanic)
— ◡ | — — | — ‖ ◡ ◡ | — | — ◡ ◡ | — ◡ — ◡̄  (Greater Sapphic)
```

Ionic a maiore

```
— — ◡ ◡ | — — ◡ ◡ | — ◡ — ◡ | — —
```

A final word remains to be said about metrical matters. It is obvious from the foregoing that one needs to know how to pronounce Latin correctly, to know the quantities of vowels, and to pay attention to syllabification. Such information is imperative for the reading of Latin poetry. If one is unfamiliar with the quantities of the vowels in particular words, he should look them up in a dictionary and become familiar with them. The names of particular verses or stanzas are not of great importance. They may serve as short cuts, but in the long run a mechanical reliance on them is harmful. Careful attention to syllables, observation of quantity, and a sensible reading of the passage are far more useful than memorizing stanzaic forms.

This chapter has discussed metrics in some detail. In the ensuing poems in this book one should apply the lessons of this chapter, for skill in reading and analyzing Latin poetry comes only from experience. Therefore it would be well for the student to scan and analyze every poem he reads, noting the variations of forms which the poem employs, and accounting as fully as possible for those variations. Although some of the comments and questions on succeeding poems are about metrics, especially when some new phenomenon is met, metrical analysis will be generally assumed. Such work should be done as part of the class preparation. If it has been well done, the evidence will appear in the reading in Latin during class time. For, as is probably obvious by now, all the preliminaries of scanning and analyzing subserve the understanding of the poem and can be expressed in the oral reading of Latin poetry. Paying attention to quantity of syllable and the various pauses, as well as the other effects of the line or stanza, including, of course, the sense of the passage, increases the awareness we acquire in reading and listening to poetry.

DESCRIPTIVE POEMS
3

Poems describe not only actions but also scenes, or objects, or persons. But descriptive poems cannot avoid being dramatic, no matter how much the poet tries to remove his personality from the poem and to present a poem of "pure" description. In choosing to comment on one detail or a small group of details from the myriad of objects which exist in the world, the poet dramatizes that detail. The poet's choice invests the object with importance and forces the reader to ponder why this particular object and not some other was chosen. The poem, if it is successful, illuminates that very point by indicating what human values and concerns prompted the poet's choice, and thus will give the reader a new way of perceiving reality. That kind of insight is the great claim poetry has on our attention. Poems of description as well as poems where the narrative dominates are concerned with this "human event," which is the central fact of poetry.

⌘

Tiberianus (Fourth Century A.D.)

Amnis ibat

Amnis ibat inter arua ualle fusus frigida,
luce ridens calculorum, flore pictus herbido.
caerulas superne laurus et uirecta myrtea
leniter motabat aura blandiente sibilo.
5   subter autem molle gramen flore adulto creuerat:

*tum croco solum rubebat et lucebat liliis
et nemus fragrabat omne uiolarum sub spiritu.
inter ista dona ueris gemmeasque gratias
omnium regina odorum uel colorum Lucifer
10   aureo flore eminebat, cura Cypridis, rosa.
roscidum nemus rigebat inter uda gramina:
fonte crebro murmurabant hinc et inde riuuli,
*antra muscus et uirentes intus hederae uicerant,
*quae fluenta labibunda guttis ibant lucidis.
15   has per umbras omnis ales plus canora quam putes
cantibus uernis strepebat et susurris dulcibus;
hic loquentis murmur amnis concinebat frondibus,
quas melos uocalis aurae musa Zephyri mouerat.
sic euntem per uirecta pulcra odora et musica
20   ales amnis aura lucus flos et umbra iuuerat.

NOTES

Meter: Trochaic Tetrameter Catalectic. The starred lines show
    metrical peculiarities.

2. *calculus*—diminutive of *calx*; used in voting and in reckoning.

9. *Lucifer*—in Greek, Phosphoros; in Latin, when the morning
star is referred to, it is called Lucifer; when the evening star,
Hesperos.

10. *Cypridis*—i.e., Aphrodite, the Roman Venus.

This poem well illustrates certain aspects of descriptive poetry
which repay observation. Poetry is distinct from life, although all
poetry has its foundation in life as it is observed by human beings.
No poem reproduces the actuality of the scene or event. Here we
do not see the actual river and its banks and nearby grove. Al-
though much is described, many of the details of which a visitor to
the scene would be conscious are omitted. Presumably he would
know where he is, but the reader of the poem is not even informed
what river this is. Also a visitor would feel the sting of flies and the
earth under his feet and he would be conscious, in short, of his
physical surroundings. There are poems which attempt to suggest

these physical impressions, but all that is excluded here. Our attention is specifically directed to certain details in order that a definite mood may be created and a particular attitude adopted. The mood is one of peacefulness which is suggested by the flat verb of the opening line. The river does not rush or tumble. Were we to substitute *ruit* or *ruebat* (metrical considerations aside) for *ibat*, the effect would be quite different. The mood is sustained and emphasized by the use of *leniter* and *blandiente* in the description of the flowers.

Furthermore, the poem appeals not to the actuality but to the remembrance of sensations. Four senses are suggested in the poem. But observe that our physical senses are not actually involved; as we read the poem we do not smell the flowers, feel the breeze, touch the ground, hear the murmuring of the leaves of the trees. We are invited or charmed by the poem into summoning a remembrance of these sensual experiences. The very fact that we do not have these actual sensations is played upon in the poem by the tenses of the verbs, which are all either imperfect or pluperfect. The poet deliberately exploits this means of reminding us of the past in the description of the past.

What then is the purpose of such a summoning of past time? As has been said, the mood established by the presentation of the details of the poem is one of peacefulness. In our daily life we are hardly at peace. The physical distractions of the world are too much with us. What the poem attempts then is to prompt a remembrance of a more peaceful time and place, removed from the bustle of the present and the confinement of locale. The very anonymity of the river helps foster the mood of tranquillity.

This poem happens to have been written by an author who was a *praefectus praetorio* in Gaul in A.D. 335. That he was a late Roman poet is indicated in the poem itself by the use of long syllables where the meter calls for short syllables. *Lucebat* and *guttis* in lines 6 and 14 appear in positions where the syllable ought to be short. This change in quantity seems to indicate that Latin verse was changing from a measure based on the quantity of the syllable to one based on stress. The latter form had always existed in classical Latin poetry, but in the late empire it finally came to dominate, helping to pave the way for the rise of the vernacular tongues.

But what is of paramount interest in this poem is that it presents a mood not so often found in Latin poetry. Other poems in this book will suggest similar moods, but rarely with such a deliberate, almost nostalgic feeling for another place.

QUESTIONS

1. Carefully examine the organization of the poem to show the gradation of sensual suggestions.

2. Explain the construction of *euntem* in line 19. To whom does the word refer? What effect does it have occurring so late in the poem? Why?

3. What part does meter play in this poem?

◄§§►

Petronius Arbiter (d. 66 A.D.)
O Litus vita

O litus uita mihi dulcius, o mare! felix
    cui licet ad terras ire subinde meas!
o formosa dies! hoc quondam rure solebam
    Naidas alterna sollicitare manu.
5 hic fontis lacus est, illic sinus egerit algas:
    haec statio est tacitis fida cupidinibus.
peruixi; neque enim fortuna malignior unquam
    eripiet nobis quod prior hora dedit.

NOTES

Meter: Elegiac Couplet.

  1. *felix*—in predicate position with an *est* understood.

QUESTIONS

1. Petronius' poem describes a remembered peacefulness. Thus it is similar to Tiberianus' poem; but certain differences between the two poems appear. Carefully examine what effect the tenses of the verbs have in this poem. *Peruixi*, for example, is in a dominant

position at the beginning of a verse. What purpose do the tense and position of the verb serve? Why are the verbs describing the shore and sea in the present tense, but the other verbs with different subjects in one of the past tenses or the future?

2. What effect does the person of the verbs have in this poem? How does this fact indicate a difference from the *euntem* (19) of Tiberianus' poem? Explain the function of *fortuna* (7) in Petronius' poem. Is there any such figure in Tiberianus' poem? If so, how is the notion handled?

3. Write an essay comparing Petronius' poem with the poem of Tiberianus.

⋅⊰§⊱⋅

Petronius Arbiter (d. 66 A.D.)
Lecto compositus
Fragment 38 (Anth. Lat. 698 R.)

Lecto compositus uix prima silentia noctis
    carpebam et somno lumina uicta dabam:
cum me saeuus Amor prensat sursumque capillis
    excitat et lacerum peruigilare iubet.
5 "tu famulus meus," inquit, "ames cum mille puellas,
    solus, io, solus, dure, iacere potes?"
exsilio et pedibus nudis tunicaque soluta
    omne iter incipio, nullum iter expedio.
nunc propero, nunc ire piget, rursumque redire
10   paenitet et pudor est stare uia media.
ecce tacent uoces hominum strepitusque uiarum
    et uolucrum cantus turbaque fida canum:
solus ego ex cunctis paueo somnumque torumque
    et sequor imperium, magne Cupido, tuum.

NOTES

Meter: Elegiac Couplet
  3. *sursum*—an adverb.

QUESTIONS

1. Examine the meter and the metrics of this poem.

2. The poem is primarily concerned with establishing a mood through the use of description. Explain how the mood is brough⸱ about and how successfully it is accomplished.

⊸§§∾

Quintus Horatius Flaccus (65–8 B.C.)

Ode III.13

O fons Bandusiae splendidior uitro
dulci digne mero non sine floribus,
    cras donaberis haedo,
        cui frons turgida cornibus

5 primis et uenerem et proelia destinat;
frustra: nam gelidos inficiet tibi
    rubro sanguine riuos
        lasciui suboles gregis.

te flagrantis atrox hora Caniculae
10 nescit tangere, tu frigus amabile
    fessis uomere tauris
        praebes et pecori uago.

fies nobilium tu quoque fontium,
me dicente cauis impositam ilicem
15   saxis, unde loquaces
        lymphae desiliunt tuae.

NOTES

Meter: Fourth Asclepiadean.

  2. *non sine—litotes* (see glossary).

  3. *haedo—*i.e., as a sacrifice.

  4. *cui—*dative of possession.

  9. *Caniculae—*although a diminutive, it is used of Sirius, the Greater Dog constellation. It rises on 26 July around which time the hot season begins; hence, summer.

  13. *nobilium fontium—*genitive of the whole, in predicate. The reference is probably to such places as Castalia, Dirce, etc.

  14. *me dicente—*note how the ablative absolute can suggest many ambiguities. Here it can have causal force or at the other extreme,

{54}

perhaps, adversative force. Probably it is best construed simply as "attendant circumstances."

QUESTIONS

1. The poem describes in some detail the kid which is to be sacrificed at the fountain. Is the length of this passage out of proportion in the poem? What is the purpose of the sacrifice? How was animal sacrifice used in ancient Rome? (Look this matter up in some standard handbook on Roman religion.) Is there anything else in the poem which suggests the notion of sacrifice?

2. Carefully examine the organization of the descriptive elements of the poem. What part do the tenses of the verbs play in this organization? What purpose is served by the emphasis of *me dicente* in v. 14? Why is the introduction of the *me* delayed so long? After all, we can infer from earlier stanzas that probably the poet will do the sacrificing. Is the *me dicente* intrusive in the poem? Is it presumptuous?

3. What is the function of the dramatic situation of the poem? How closely is it connected with the descriptive parts?

4. Examine the caesuras of the poem, and indicate what role they serve in the total effect of the poem. What part do metrics play in the poem?

◆§§◆

Gaius Valerius Catullus (c.84–54 B.C.)

II

Passer, deliciae meae puellae,
quicum ludere, quem in sinu tenere,
cui primum digitum dare appetenti
et acris solet incitare morsus,
5 cum desiderio meo nitenti
carum nescio quid lubet iocari,
et solaciolum sui doloris,
credo, ut tum grauis acquiescat ardor:
tecum ludere sicut ipsa possem
10 et tristis animi leuare curas!

NOTES

Meter: Phalaecean or Hendecasyllabic.

1. *passer*—probably a sparrow. According to Sappho, the bird was sacred to Aphrodite.

2. *quicum—qui* is ablative.

3. *primum digitum*—"finger tip."

6. *carum*—modifies *nescio quid*, the object of *iocari*, a kind of cognate accusative. The word *iocari* is subject of *lubet* (*libet*).

7. *et solaciolum*—an appositive to subject of *libet*.

9. *possem*—the subjunctive used for the Greek optative in an unfulfilled wish.

QUESTIONS

1. The poem describes the sparrow of his mistress. What are the details of the description? Is there personification of the sparrow? Does the sparrow have qualities of a human being? Justify your answer.

2. Explain the use of *possem* (9). What is the effect of this verb? How has this effect been anticipated in the poem?

3. Look up the various meanings of *desiderium*. What are they, and what function do they have here?

4. What are the *tristis . . . curas* of line 10?

5. Write a comment on this poem in which you explain what the poem signifies.

❧

Gaius Valerius Catullus (c.84–54 B.C.)

IV

Phasellus ille, quem uidetis, hospites,
ait fuisse nauium celerrimus,
neque ullius natantis impetum trabis
nequisse praeterire, siue palmulis
5   opus foret uolare siue linteo.
et hoc negat minacis Hadriatici
negare litus insulasue Cycladas
Rhodumque nobilem horridamque Thraciam
Propontida trucemue Ponticum sinum,

10 ubi iste post phasellus antea fuit
    comata silua; nam Cytorio in iugo
    loquente saepe sibilum edidit coma.
    Amastri Pontica et Cytore buxifer,
    tibi haec fuisse et esse cognitissima
15 ait phasellus: ultima ex origine
    tuo stetisse dicit in cacumine,
    tuo imbuisse palmulas in aequore,
    et inde tot per impotentia freta
    erum tulisse, laeua siue dextera
20 uocaret aura, siue utrumque Iuppiter
    simul secundus incidisset in pedem;
    neque ulla uota litoralibus deis
    sibi esse facta, cum ueniret a mari
    nouissimo hunc ad usque limpidum lacum.
25 sed haec prius fuere: nunc recondita
    senet quiete seque dedicat tibi,
    gemelle Castor et gemelle Castoris.

NOTES

Meter: Iambic Trimeter.

2. *celerrimus*—the nominative here, where Latin would ordinarily show the accusative, is a grecism. Apparently Catullus first began such usage. Note too that the gender is also attracted from that of *nauium* to that of *phasellus*.

6. *hoc*—the object of *negare*.

10. *post, antea*—the use of an adverb with a substantive is another grecism, though this too became common in later Latin poetry.

11. *silua*—rarely used of a single tree.

13. *Amastri*—the city of Amastris, named for its founder, the wife of Dionysius, tyrant of Pontic Heraclea, was situated on the Paphlagonian coast of the Euxine Sea not far from Mount Cytorus.

    buxifer—used only here.

18. *impotentia*—the connotation is "raging," "lacking in self-control."

19–20. The ship went straight ahead, not veering to either side.

2 1. *pedem*—the sheets, or ropes, more properly, attached to each lower corner of a square sail, were used to hold it taut. Here *pedem* stands for the halves of the sail itself which was filled only when the vessel was sailing before the wind.

2 3. *sibi*—dative of agent.

2 6. *senet*—an archaism for *senescit*.

2 7. Sailors invoked the Dioscuri as dispellers of storms.

QUESTIONS

1. This poem, like the previous one, describes not a scene or a place, but an object, in this instance a sailing ship. Boats or ships do not usually speak. Why, then, should this one? Is there a justification for this fiction, or does it seem arbitrary and therefore sentimental? What function then does the first line perform?

2. The poem begins with a construction derived from Greek and unusual in Latin: *celerrimus* rather than *celerrimum* with *se* in normal indirect statement. Is there any purpose in using such a construction? Where else is this same device used in the poem? What is its cumulative effect?

3. Is there any pattern to the geographical references? (Look up the places mentioned.) What does the pattern, if there is one, contribute to the effect of the whole poem?

4. Explain the last two lines of the poem.

5. Describe the mood of the poem. How is it sustained or worked out?

6. What effect does this poem have? Does it show us something new? Does it give us a different view of human experience? What values does it imply or represent? What is the "human event" of the poem?

⋅⸨§⸩⋅

Gaius Valerius Catullus (c.84–54 B.C.)

XXXI

Paene insularum, Sirmio, insularumque
ocelle, quascumque in liquentibus stagnis
marique uasto fert uterque Neptunus,
quam te libenter quamque laetus inuiso,

5 uix mi ipse credens Thyniam atque Bithynos
   liquisse campos et uidere te in tuto.
   o quid solutis est beatius curis,
   cum mens onus reponit, ac peregrino
   labore fessi uenimus larem ad nostrum
10 desideratoque acquiescimus lecto?
   hoc est quod unum est pro laboribus tantis.
   salue, o uenusta Sirmio, atque ero gaude;
   gaudete uosque, o Lydiae lacus undae;
   ridete quidquid est domi cachinnorum.

NOTES

Meter: Choliambic.

1. *paene*—used adjectivally; a grecism.
   Sirmio—the modern Sermione at the southern end of Lago di Garda.
3. *uterque*—i.e., as god of *stagna* and *mare*.
5. *Thyniam*—the Thyni, a people from Thrace who settled near the Thracian Bosphorus in Bithynia. The distinction between the two, Thyni and Bithyni, is a learned one.
9. *larem*—the singular; subsequently the plural became common.
11. *hoc . . . est*—"This is itself reward enough."
14. *quidquid . . . cachinnorum*—partitive genitive.

The "human event" of the poem is the joy of homecoming. Catullus has returned home to Sirmio, the peninsula jutting into Lago di Garda. The poem is not an elaborate description of Sirmio. Indeed, the only thing we know about it is that it is almost an island. The fact that it is Sirmio, a particular spot, is not of great concern in the poem; that it is home is. The poem communicates a joyful feeling of return, a feeling we can recognize from our own experience of going home after a long absence. How the poet achieves this mood is of interest to us as students of poetry, and it is worthwhile to attempt to understand some of the means whereby this feeling is awakened.

One of the means is that of contrast. In the first six lines Catullus contrasts Sirmio's peninsular location with the plains of Bithynia. The water of Sirmio is emphasized by the comparison in the first three lines and by the contrast in vv. 4–6. From this setting the poem moves to a general reflection on home as a place for the resolution of cares, for the recovery from travel, and for rest in one's familiar bed. Verse 11 echoes the thought of v. 7. Verses 12–14 echo the delight in Sirmio and its waters.

The poem thus is in three parts which are interestingly connected. The connection can be illustrated by examining vv. 5–6 and 8–9. The word *uix* in v. 5 conveys the sense of weariness which comes from a long sojourn away when one begins to despair of ever returning home. The appropriateness of the word and its position of emphasis to underscore the effect can be tested by substituting such a word as *nunc* in the line. Observe how the verse is changed, and how it no longer conveys the same ideas. Further, *uix* and the rest of vv. 5–6 look forward to vv. 8–9. In the first couplet the poem suggests the common feeling of disbelief that the weariness of travel is actually over. In the second couplet the feeling has dissipated. The fact that travel is frequently an exhausting business is now asserted as a reason for the joy of homecoming. In keeping with the organization of vv. 1–6 and 7–11, feeling is emphasized in one, statement in the other.

A further indication of the poem's skillful organization to effect the mood can be seen in the relationship of the first and third sections with the middle one. The first and last parts are specifically concerned with Sirmio and Catullus' pleasure at returning there; the middle, with an almost philosophical reflection on homecoming. The first and third form a ring of sentiment around the intellectual quality of the second, just as water almost surrounds Sirmio. Thus the reference to water in vv. 13–14 not only echoes vv. 1–3 but underscores the arrangement of the poem's ideas.

QUESTIONS

1. In the light of what has been said, see if there are other con-

nections between vv. 1–6 and 7–11. Carefully examine v. 10 to see whether it bears any relationship to vv. 2–3.

2. What differences exist in the use of water in vv. 2–3 and 13–14? What is the reason for such differences?

❧

Gaius Valerius Catullus (c.84–54 B.C.)

CI

Multas per gentes et multa per aequora uectus
    aduenio has miseras, frater, ad inferias,
ut te postremo donarem munere mortis
    et mutam nequiquam alloquerer cinerem.
5 quandoquidem fortuna mihi tete abstulit ipsum,
    heu miser indigne frater adempte mihi,
nunc tamen interea haec, prisco quae more parentum
    tradita sunt tristi munere ad inferias,
accipe fraterno multum manantia fletu
10   atque in perpetuum, frater, aue atque uale.

NOTES

Meter: Elegiac Couplet.

2. *ad inferias*—Servius on Vergil, *Aen.* X.519 says: *inferiae sunt sacra mortuorum, quod inferis soluuntur.*

10. *aue atque uale*—the conclusion is the final farewell which would have been spoken at the burial.

The mood of the poem is elegiac. The comments which follow suggest some of the ways in which this mood is created; for Catullus has chosen to concentrate on his own sense of loss, not on any specific qualities or characteristics of his brother.

The fact of the fraternal relationship is claim enough for his attention and ours. The poem begins by referring to the distance Catullus has had to travel to reach his brother's grave to pay his last respects. The repetition of *multas . . . multa . . .* emphasizes the distance; *miseras ad inferias* emphasizes the sadness. The notion of loss is further stressed by the action performed and the muteness of the ashes, which in themselves suggest the idea of irrevocable loss in that Catullus cannot address even his brother's corpse. The following verses (5–6) make clear that the sense of loss is what we are concentrating on. The final four verses describe the action of Catullus as though he had been able to be at the burial itself, for he performs the ancient rite of Roman mourners. The sense of loss is thus emphasized by the irony of the final line, especially *aue atque uale*. He arrived only to bid farewell. The notion is further strengthened by the phrases *fraterno fletu, in perpetuum*, and the verbal echo of *multum manantia* from v. 1.

QUESTIONS

1. Explore the reference to burial rites in the poem. How do they fit in with the dramatic quality of the poem?

2. What does *haec* (v. 7) refer to?

3. Explain the role of metrics in the poem.

IMAGERY AND FIGURATIVE LANGUAGE

4

Our foregoing discussions of poems have clearly indicated that drama, metrics, and description are not the only parts of a poem needing consideration. Repeated references have been made to an image or a metaphor within individual poems. For example, Catullus' poem on Sirmio shows how the form of the poem can shape the meaning and affect the mood and response we have to the poem. The use of water as the "bed" for the land is comparable to the longed-for bed of the weary traveler. Furthermore, mention has been made of how emphasis is achieved by the position of the words in a line or stanza.

The successful poem is an organic whole in which all the parts function together naturally. Tiberianus' description of the riverside illustrates this point, as do the other poems so far discussed. Imagery and figurative language are functional parts.

We are all familiar with imagery from our acquaintance with English poetry. We have also seen it used in Catullus' lament for his brother, as well as in Tiberianus' description of the river. In its broadest definition imagery is the representation of any sense experience. Poetry appeals to the senses, but not in an irrelevant or mechanical fashion; that is, not merely for the sake of the sensation. Through comparisons, through images, the poet makes his statements and conveys his ideas. This is the way, we can say, a poet thinks. The object of poetry is to communicate insight about the world and its effect upon us, and the poet uses imagery as one of the means to give us this insight.

The most familiar varieties of imagery or figurative language are simile and metaphor. The first is an explicit comparison which is often announced in Latin by some word such as *uelut*. The second is an implied comparison. The important point, however, in that comparison is the method whereby the insight is communicated. Symbol is a variety of metaphor, but in it the first member is inferred. Metaphor or simile emphasizes the *transfer*; symbol emphasizes the fact that one object is used for another. Allegory is an extended metaphor whereby objects and persons in the poem are equated with something outside the poem itself.

Personification is a frequent device of allegory and yet another form of imagery. It is the representation of an abstract idea in the guise of a human or divine being. For example, when we speak of a ship as a girl, we are personifying the ship.

Figurative language varies from poem to poem. In some it is subtle and complex, suggesting a variety of meanings; in others direct and blunt. Catullus' poem about the sparrow (II) is a rather subtle one, for we gradually perceive that the sparrow is in some way analogous to what Catullus wishes himself to be without saying so directly, because the sparrow can do what is denied Catullus. Tiberianus' poem is also subtle in that we infer from his description that what he longs for is a lost idyllic place. But the thing we should ask of figurative language, whether subtle or direct, is that it make sense in the poem and not be merely decorative, that it further the insight the poet wants to communicate. How effective figurative language is can be judged only in the context of the particular poem.

In the following poems attention is concentrated on the way figurative language is used, but it should be remembered that this is only one aspect of poetry. How the context affects and is affected by the imagery should never be lost sight of.

❧

Gaius Valerius Catullus (c.84–54 B.C.)

V

Viuamus, mea Lesbia, atque amemus,

rumoresque senum seueriorum
omnes unius aestimemus assis!
soles occidere et redire possunt:
5 nobis, cum semel occidit breuis lux,
nox est perpetua una dormienda.
da mi basia mille, deinde centum,
dein mille altera, dein secunda centum,
deinde usque altera mille, deinde centum,
10 dein, cum milia multa fecerimus,
conturbabimus illa, ne sciamus,
aut ne quis malus inuidere possit,
cum tantum sciat esse basiorum.

NOTES

Meter: Phalaecean or Hendecasyllabic.

3. *unius . . . assis*—"at a single *as*," i.e., at nothing.
7ff. *deinde, dein*—the *ei* regularly contracts into a single syllable.
9. *usque*—"straight away," "straight on."

The dramatic situation of the poem lies in Catullus' exhortation to Lesbia to kiss and kiss again. The central character is Catullus himself. His exhortation is advanced against her implied objection (vv. 5–6), which is that she will lose her reputation by becoming an object of gossip to old men. To this feeling on Lesbia's part Catullus opposes his rationale of the brevity of life beside which the gossip of old men is worth extremely little—one *as*. Rushing on, as though she had consented, he offers something more, the possibility of a thousand, then a hundred kisses and thousands more with the promise of confusing the account through still more so that, even if someone were to keep track of the kisses, he would find his tally confused. The poet in effect pleads with his mistress for love and life. His plea uses a metaphor based on counting and weighing which suggests several things in this poem. First, the scene is that of an argument in which reasons are offered and weighed in comparison with one another, even as when one shops for the best bargains. Further, old men are traditionally associated with the concerns of counting and estimating, in short, with money. By them money is regarded as the foundation of reputation and thus as a symbol of responsibility. Youth, on the other hand, is traditionally opposed to such notions. Hence to the responsible man youth appears reckless, foolish, and without sufficient gravity for responsibility. Catullus' point of view is that of youth, for he recognizes that the joys of youth are denied the old men who, as a result, are occupied with such matters as reputation and calculating and weighing. Catullus casts his argument in the very language of those he would answer since he also recognizes that the desire for passion remains and often works itself out among those no longer capable of passion in the vicarious pleasure of keeping track of what others do. Furthermore, he implies in his promise to confuse the accounts that kisses are not really material things like coins which can be weighed and counted, and so such terms are irrelevant. By mocking those who think such pleasure is measurable he demonstrates that kisses far outweigh the gossip of the envious. His argument has validity, for awareness of sensual pleasure gives an insight into its brevity and into the brevity of life itself. That insight is denied those who place their faith in money with its specious illusion of eternity. Death itself makes the final mockery of money, reputation, and pleasure. Hence when the choice lies between kisses and reputation, kisses, properly, win, for the brief sensual life is to be prized above all else. This the young know and so dismiss the false respectability of the aged. The dramatic aspect of the poem with its outweighing of Lesbia's objection emphasizes the point and permits Catullus' argument.

QUESTIONS

1. Explain how the clause *ne sciamus* (11) functions in the poem.

2. What construction is *basiorum* in v. 13, and how does that further the concerns of the poem?

The metrics of the following poem have already been commented on. Reread the poem and the discussion on the imagery, then return to the earlier discussion of the metrics to see how closely the two aspects of the poem, metrics and imagery, function in making the poem an organic unit.

❧

Quintus Horatius Flaccus (65–8 B.C.)
Ode I.30
O Venus, regina Cnidi Paphique,
sperne dilectam Cypron et uocantis
ture te multo Glycerae decoram
transfer in aedem.
5 feruidus tecum puer et solutis
Gratiae zonis properentque Nymphae
et parum comis sine te Iuuentas
Mercuriusque.

NOTES

Meter: Sapphic Stanza.

1. *Cnidi Paphique*—Cnidos, a Doric city of Caria; Paphos is on the western coast of Cyprus. Both are cities where Venus (Aphrodite) was worshiped.

2. *Cypron*—a Greek accusative.

In Horace's ode again a little drama is being performed. The poet, or what one might call the "I" of the poem, prays to Venus to come with her attendants to Glycera. The "action" of the poem is simple and presupposes only our awareness that to pray is to perform an action. The reason for the prayer is implied in vv. 3 and 4, for Glycera herself has been invoking Venus, and the poet adds his prayer. Verses 5–8 further imply the poet's reason for his action. The specific locale is not mentioned; all that is implied is that it is not Cyprus. Possibly it is some altar of Glycera herself, though we are not told so. Such details for this poem are irrelevant, and by their suppression our attention is concentrated exclusively on the action and on the reasons for the action. Here, however, there is a profusion of names: Venus, Glycera, Puer, Graces,

Nymphs, Youth, Mercury. Distinctions or similarities are to be observed in the mention of each name. Venus, the goddess of love, is obviously referred to because the prayer is addressed to her. Glycera is named, for it is in her interest that Venus is to come. *Puer* (Cupid) and the Graces and Nymphs are attendants of Venus who help inspire her actions. But *Iuuentas* is a generalized term, a personification, of a quality which achieves a character in this poem, not simply because it is capitalized but because it pointedly refers to Glycera who is the young girl here. *Iuuentas* is a characteristic of Glycera, but a personified characteristic. If this is so of *Iuuentas*, so must it be of *Mercurius*. Mercury is both a god and thus like Venus, but also a kind of personification, for he is joined with *Iuuentas*. The syntax of the sentence indicates that *Iuuentas* and *Mercurius* are in the same relationship, but that the relationship is different from the one binding Cupid, the Graces, and the Nymphs together. Among other attributes of Mercury is that of the patron of eloquence, dexterity, and thievery.[1] What then does the patron god of such qualities have to do with the prayer, for the poem states clearly that without Venus, *Mercurius*, like *Iuuentas*, has too little charm? To answer this question, we should return to the poem to see what clues it gives. The reference is connected in some way to Glycera, for it is for her that the poet prays to Venus. The answer is to be found in the name Glycera. The name in Greek means "sweet," and is frequently used in the *Odes* of Horace to refer to young girls who are courtesans. Glycera is a youthful and persuasive girl, apparently, in attracting men, as the compressed statement of vv. 7–8 implies. Nevertheless, she needs Venus' aid to make her completely lovable. Youth and eloquence are not enough, for if a girl has only those attributes she frequently serves not love but herself.

Such seems to be the case with Glycera. If so, then, perhaps the first stanza takes on an ambiguous connotation. Horace like Glycera prays to Venus, but they pray with different intentions:

[1] When one sees such a reference as this to a god in a poem, it is wise to examine all the attributes of the deity to discover which are relevant. Here, for example, the reference would not be to Mercury, the conductor of dead souls.

Glycera, so that she may capture young men; Horace, so that Glycera may be captured by love. Glycera seems to pray for Venus' aid but only as a means to an end; Horace prays for love as the end itself.

QUESTIONS

1. The handbooks of Latin prose composition tell us that the conjunction -*que* is not used as it appears in v. 6, i.e., it joins coordinate words. But in v. 6 the -*que* is attached not to the second noun but to the verb common to each. What is the purpose of such a usage in this poem? Does it have any effect on the meaning of the passage?

2. Explain the number of *comis* in v. 7. Comment on its usage.

3. In the light of what has been said about *Iuuentas* and *Mercurius*, comment on Venus as she appears in this poem. Is she a goddess with a personality such as we find in the *Aeneid*? How does she differ from the goddess of Vergil's poem?

‍ঙ১৪৯

Quintus Horatius Flaccus (65–8 B.C.)
Ode I.9
Vides ut alta stet niue candidum
Soracte, nec iam sustineant onus
 siluae laborantes, geluque
  flumina constiterint acuto.

5 dissolue frigus ligna super foco
large reponens atque benignius
 deprome quadrimum Sabina,
  o Thaliarche, merum diota:

permitte diuis cetera, qui simul
10 strauere uentos aequore feruido
 deproeliantis, nec cupressi
  nec ueteres agitantur orni.

quid sit futurum cras fuge quaerere et
quem Fors dierum cumque dabit lucro

15   appone, nec dulcis amores
          sperne puer neque tu choreas,

    donec uirenti canities abest
    morosa. nunc et campus et areae
        lenesque sub noctem susurri
20   composita repetantur hora,

    nunc et latentis proditor intimo
    gratus puellae risus ab angulo
        pignusque dereptum lacertis
          aut digito male pertinaci.

NOTES

Meter: Alcaic Stanza.

The first two stanzas are based on an ode of Alcaeus (*Frag.* 34).

1. *ut*—"how"; introduces indirect question.
2. *Soracte*—a mountain north of Rome and visible from it.
4. *constiterint*—i.e., are frozen.
7. *deprome*—"draw off" from the jar.
8. *Thaliarche*—"master of the feast."
   diota—"two-eared."
11. *deproelior*—found only here in Latin poetry.
14. *quem . . . cumque*—tmesis.
    dierum—a partitive genitive dependent on *quemcumque*.
15. *nec*—for the more normal and prosy *neue* (*neu*).
17. *donec*—"while," "as long as."
21. *et*—"also," a grecism.
22. *risus, pignus*, as well as *susurri* (19), are subjects of *repetantur*.
24. *male*—a kind of weak *non*, but the usual meaning also applies.

Horace's ode is a more complex poem of description than those we have so far considered. The first three stanzas describe a wintry scene and contrast it with the indoor cheer. Had the poem ended at v. 12, it would have been a skillful, although a somewhat simple, description. But as we have seen, even simple descriptions evoke moods and attitudes which themselves are often complex and suggest different ways of regarding the world around us. In this poem Horace elaborates the contrast between the chill of age and the warmth of youth. The final three stanzas emphasize the notion implicit in the first three.

The wintry landscape of vv. 1–4 forms a contrast to the indoor pleasures of vv. 5–8. The pleasures, however, are those which are enforced by the natural world. In a country such as Italy pleasure is naturally found out of doors. One puts up with the indoors when it is winter, but one would prefer to be elsewhere. The tone in these verses is one of resignation, especially in vv. 9–12. We have little control over these matters which are in the hands of the gods.

The following stanzas pursue this theme of accepting what is given and enjoying it as best one may. By a slight shift in vv. 17ff. this notion becomes one of enjoying the sensual world about us, especially that of dalliance. But such enjoyment is also conditioned. Verses 17–18 convey clearly that the sensual pleasure of love is one that occurs only in youth. Youth is, by implication, fleeting; it too will change into hoary old age. Therefore, count all the time at your disposal as so much gain. But old age brings other pleasures, which are accepted as substitutes for those of youth; for example, wine-drinking. They are palliatives against the cold of age even as the indoor fire comforts against the wintry blasts.

From the organization of the poem we can observe that the first four lines acquire a symbolic meaning within the poem. The wintry scene portrayed is comparable to old age, which is white haired, laboring under its burden of years, and held by coldness. The poet does not state that the snow-capped Soracte is an old man or even is like an old man. He employs neither simile nor allegory. The snow-capped mountain in the poem remains a snow-capped mountain. The laboring trees remain trees weighted with ice, and the river is a frozen river. But, through the employment of other details of the poem, we make the connection ourselves; we perceive how the wintry landscape comes to symbolize old age.

There is nothing strange or cryptic about symbols. They are common phenomena in everyday speech, for even words or signs are in a sense symbols. Snow-covered mountains are not always, however, symbols for old age. There is in poetry not a simple one-to-one relationship. That which is symbolic in one poem may not be so in another. All the details of the poem must be taken into consideration, as we have seen in the comment on this poem.

QUESTIONS

1. What purpose does *Vides* serve? Why is it second person singular? Are there any connotations the word acquires as one reads the poem? What is the function of the vocative, *o Thaliarche*, in v. 8? Does it conflict with the *uides*? Is it important for the poem? What about the *puer* of v. 16? Does this shift the emphasis from the *uides*? Who is being addressed in the poem?

2. Carefully examine the effect of the prominent position of the following phrases: *permitte diuis cetera* (9), *quid sit futurum . . .* (13), *donec . . . morosa* (17–18), and *nunc* (21). Each begins the stanza of which it is a member. Does each contribute to the effect of the stanza and of the whole poem?

3. What is the effect of the parallelism of words in vv. 21–22?

4. What is the *pignus* of v. 23? What are we to understand about vv. 21–24? Are they effective as a conclusion to the poem? Do they have any relationship to what has gone before? How and why?

❦

Quintus Horatius Flaccus (65–8 B.C.)

Ode I.4

Soluitur acris hiems grata uice ueris et Fauoni,
    trahuntque siccas machinae carinas,
ac neque iam stabulis gaudet pecus aut arator igni,
    nec prata canis albicant pruinis.
5 iam Cytherea choros ducit Venus imminente Luna,
    iunctaeque Nymphis Gratiae decentes

alterno terram quatiunt pede, dum grauis Cyclopum
    Vulcanus ardens uisit officinas.
nunc decet aut uiridi nitidum caput impedire myrto
10   aut flore terrae quem ferunt solutae;
nunc et in umbrosis Fauno decet immolare lucis,
    seu poscat agna siue malit haedo.
pallida Mors aequo pulsat pede pauperum tabernas
    regumque turris. o beate Sesti,
15 uitae summa breuis spem nos uetat incohare longam.
    iam te premet nox fabulaeque Manes
et domus exilis Plutonia; quo simul mearis,
    nec regna uini sortiere talis,
nec tenerum Lycidan mirabere, quo calet iuuentus
20   nunc omnis et mox virgines tepebunt.

Notes

Meter: Fourth Archilochian Stanza.

1. *solvitur*—i.e., in the sense of breaking up; winter has loosed its grip on the earth.

2. *carinas*—"keels"; an example of the rhetorical figure, synecdoche, the part for the whole.

5. *Cytherea*—from island of Cythera, near which Aphrodite rose from the sea. She is identified with Venus who presides over gardens and fruits; hence Spring.

6. *Nymphis*—the ablative of association which is found with verbs of joining, mixing, changing. Also interpreted sometimes as an ablative of accompaniment without *cum* (Allen and Greenough, § 413 a, note). The dative with these verbs occurs in later writing, although it would be difficult to tell why this instance could not be a dative.

9. *nitidum*—i.e., with perfumed oil.
    impedire—i.e., *cingere* or *uincere*.
    myrto—sacred to Venus.

11. *et*—like "*etiam*"; a grecism for καί.
    lucis—used by Horace to refer to sacred groves.

12. *agna, haedo*—*sibi immolari* is to be understood.

13. *pulsat pede*—an ancient way of knocking at a door.
17. *simul*—for *simul ac*.

QUESTIONS

1. Explain how the poet employs the seasons of spring and winter in the poem? What imagery is connected with each season? Is the imagery natural, or does it seem forced and merely decorative?

2. What use is made of personification in the poem? Is it effective? Does it seem tightly connected with the poem as a whole? Are the gods who are mentioned in the poem regarded as deities, or do they serve a different purpose? Do they give an effect of concrete detail? If so, how? If not, why not?

3. Is there any imagery in vv. 17–20? How are these verses related to the rest of the poem?

4. What is the purpose of "*o beate Sesti*" in v. 14?

5. Show what effect alliteration has on the poem.

6. How does the meter help the intention of the poem?

&§&

Quintus Horatius Flaccus (65–8 B.C.)
Ode IV.7

Diffugere niues, redeunt iam gramina campis
    arboribusque comae;
mutat terra uices, et decrescentia ripas
    flumina praetereunt;
5 Gratia cum Nymphis geminisque sororibus audet
    ducere nuda choros.
immortalia ne speres, monet annus et almum
    quae rapit hora diem:
frigora mitescunt Zephyris, uer proterit aestas
10   interitura simul
pomifer Autumnus fruges effuderit, et mox
    bruma recurrit iners.
damna tamen celeres reparant caelestia lunae:
    nos ubi decidimus

15 quo pater Aeneas, quo Tullus diues et Ancus,
    puluis et umbra sumus.
quis scit an adiciant hodiernae crastina summae
    tempora di superi?
cuncta manus auidas fugient heredis, amico
20   quae dederis animo.
cum semel occideris et de te splendida Minos
    fecerit arbitria,
non, Torquate, genus, non te facundia, non te
    restituet pietas;
25 infernis neque enim tenebris Diana pudicum
    liberat Hippolytum,
nec Lethaea ualet Theseus abrumpere caro
    uincula Perithoo.

NOTES

Meter: First Archilochian Stanza.

3. *uices*—accusative of "inner object" with *mutat*; a grecism.

4. *praetereunt*—i.e., within their banks.

7. *immortalia ne speres*—clause is object of *monet*.

15. *Ancus*—Ancus Martius, fourth king of Rome.

17. *an*—"whether."

    hodiernae summae—i.e., to the number you now have.

20. *dederīs . . . occiderīs*—the *-i* is long, perhaps following the analogy of the archaic perfect subjunctive, though these seem to be future perfects which show short *-i* in the second person.

21. *Minos*—legendary king at Cnossos in Crete; honored by Zeus; after his death made a judge of shades of the underworld with Aeacus and Rhadamanthus. The name probably means simply "judge."

23. *Torquate*—possibly an orator friend of Horace, who belonged to the Manilian *gens*. The insigne of the Torquati was the *torques* or neck chain taken by an ancestor from a gigantic Gaul in single combat.

25. *Hippolytum*—son of Theseus and Hippolyte, the Amazon. Phaedra, a subsequent spouse of Theseus, fell in love with him;

Hippolytus rejected her advances whereupon to Theseus she falsely accused him of improprieties. Theseus, enraged, had him destroyed by means of a bull sent by Poseidon, Theseus' own father. Diana (Artemis) abandons him to his fate. So Euripides. Vergil says (*Aen.* VII.761ff.) that Diana saved Hippolytus.

The poem is based on the rhetorical device of antithesis, from which comes the dominant pattern of images. *Diffugere niues* may be divided, for purposes of analysis, at v. 13 (*tamen*). The first part of the poem expresses an exuberance in the springlike qualities of growth and vigor, e.g., *decrescentia ripas/ flumina praetereunt* (3–4), and the very lovely image of the Nymphs and Graces in vv. 5–6. But none of this feeling appears in the latter portion, where all is narrow, frugal, dark, and constricted, for the world ends in the darkness of death. A contrast thus exists between two parts.

A discussion of the verbs Horace uses can demonstrate this point. From the beginning the motif of contrast brought about by change appears: *Diffugere* opposed by *redeunt*. The next lines further elaborate the motif with *mutat* and *praetereunt*. The idea continues with *rapit* (8), *mitescunt, proterit* (9), *interitura* (10), *effuderit* (11), and *recurrit* (12) and *reparant* (13). These seven lines explore the image of change through the very verbs they contain. But the change is a particular kind in that it is cyclic, i.e., the snows have fled but they will return. Of this recurring or circular imagery the subject is the natural world; that is, the world without mankind: snow, grass, earth, rivers, winds, stars, spring, summer, autumn, winter, even the Graces and Nymphs, but not man. Verses 7 and 8 specifically warn against the idea of man's being a part of this cycle: *immortalia ne speres, monet annus et almum/ quae rapit hora diem*, in which the tessellated word order underlines the point. However, though the condition is stated here, it is not expanded until v. 14. *Tamen* in v. 13 emphasizes the contrast between man and nature. Although nature continues in the fashion described in vv. 1–13, man can endure only one cycle of growth, decay, and death; he is doomed to become dust and shade. The verbs used in this latter portion contain the image of change but in a different aspect: the change that comes from descent, from falling away with no possibility of returning. The verb pattern that begins in *decidimus* (14), continues with *fugient* (19), *occideris* (21), *restituet* (24), *neque . . . liberat* (25–26), and ends with *nec . . . abrumpere* (27). Nothing of man can ever return to its original state (21–24). This immutable condition of human life prevails despite wealth or deeds or even the intercession of gods and heroes.

The passage from vv. 7ff. creates the effective transition between the two parts of the poem. Immediately after *immortalia ne speres*, Horace shows the seasons of the year hastening upon each other, ending significantly with winter. These verses (9–12) explain *monet annus et almum/ quae rapit hora diem.* But they offer a comment as well on man's condition: spring once past for man can never return, for his own life does not follow nature's pattern. This passage demonstrates how Horace can make an image work for him without his succumbing to its mastery. After showing the recurrent character of nature, he then uses a single aspect of that image to effect his transition to man.

The poem thus sets up a dichotomy between the natural world and the world of man. From this dichotomy arises man's frustration, for man is involved in, but is not a part of, the natural world. Horace makes this point when he inserts *immortalia ne speres* in the midst of the elaborate passage on nature's recurring changes. He drives the point home by his use of *almum* (7) to describe nature's (*diem*) care for man. Hence man, however much he might strive, can never achieve an identity with nature. Horace makes no statement of this theme anywhere in the poem. But he leads us to make the judgment to enjoy nonetheless whatever we may of this world. His observations allow the inference. The contrast in the imagery in the two parts of the poem and the pattern created by the verbs participate in creating the poem whose theme is the irreconcilable rift in the universe between man and nature.

QUESTIONS

1. Compare the meter of this poem with that of *Ode* I.4. What are the metrical qualities of this poem? How do they affect the poem?

2. Write an essay comparing *Ode* I.4 and *Ode* IV.7, examining in detail the imagery of both poems.

⋙⋘

Incertus Auctor

Dic quid agis

Dic quid agis, formosa Venus, si nescis amanti
ferre uicem? perit omne decus, dum deperit aetas,
marcent post rorem uiolae, rosa perdit odorem,
lilia post uernum posito candore liquescunt.
5   haec metuas exempla precor et semper amanti
redde uicem, quia semper amat, qui semper amatur.

NOTES

Meter: Dactylic Hexameter.

1. *Dic*—note that the *dic* is treated as an interjection so that *agis* is in the indicative and not the expected subjunctive. The phenomenon is common in early Latin and occurs in classical poetry.

5. *metuas . . . precor*—note that *ut* is omitted after *precor*.

QUESTIONS

1. How does the last verse beginning with *quia semper* and continuing to the end contrast with the metaphors of vv. 3–4?

2. What, in turn, is implied then in the last line?

⋙⋘

Gaius Valerius Catullus (c.84–54 B.C.)

L

Hesterno, Licini, die otiosi
multum lusimus in meis tabellis,
ut conuenerat esse delicatos.
scribens uersiculos uterque nostrum

{78}

5 ludebat numero modo hoc modo illoc,
  reddens mutua per iocum atque uinum.
  atque illinc abii tuo lepore
  incensus, Licini, facetiisque,
  ut nec me miserum cibus iuuaret
10 nec somnus tegeret quiete ocellos,
  sed toto indomitus furore lecto
  uersarer, cupiens uidere lucem,
  ut tecum loquerer simulque ut essem.
  at defessa labore membra postquam
15 semimortua lectulo iacebant,
  hoc, iucunde, tibi poema feci,
  ex quo perspiceres meum dolorem.
  nunc audax caue sis, precesque nostras,
  oramus, caue despuas, ocelle,
20 ne poenas Nemesis reposcat a te.
  est uehemens dea: laedere hanc caueto.

NOTES

Meter: Phalaecean or Hendecasyllabic.

1. *Licini*—C. Licinius Macer Calvus, son of annalist Licinius Macer, born 28 May 82 B.C., and died c.47 B.C. He was an orator, writer of epic and lyric poetry and of epigrams; an intimate friend of Catullus. Extant fragments of his writing may be found in the editions of Catullus by Lachmann and L. Müller.

2. *lusimus*—used especially of the composition of amatory verse.

3. *conuenerat*—impersonal, but translate as personal.
   esse delicatos—i.e., to compose verses.

14. *postquam*—note the imperfect used in this clause, a usage more familiar in prose.

21. *uehemens*—dissyllabic.

Catullus in this poem writes what is, in effect, a thank-you note to his friend Licinius who, supposedly, receives it the next morning. Catullus describes the effect on himself of the previous day's pleasure, and indicates his hope for a repetition of the encounter, and he utters an exaggerated curse against Licinius if the latter should not comply. The dramatic quality of the poem arises from the excitement Catullus felt in composing verses with Licinius and from his response to that excitement.

The first six verses would be otiose were the poem simply a thank-you note, but as we read, we see that they perform the useful function of indicating the cause of Catullus' excitement. Keyed up by his friend's wit, Catullus returned home to find no pleasure in his supper nor rest in his bed. When we examine the language beginning in v. 6, we find that it amplifies and clarifies the meaning of *lusimus* in v. 2 and *delicatos* in v. 3. The writing is not simply verses, but refined, sharpened verses, perhaps about love. Catullus describes his return: he was *incensus*, then *miserum*; he could not sleep; in bed he was overcome by *furor*; he needs to see the light so that he can see his friend; his *membra* are *defessa* and finally *semimortua*; to indicate his *dolorem* he sends his poem; and concludes with a prayer in the midst of which he refers to his friend as *ocelle*. The description is of Catullus' restlessness, yet the language is that of a confused lover. But that language is applied not to an actual love affair but to the much more intellectual business of writing poetry. Catullus makes us aware that writing poetry can be as passionately exciting as love-making. The interruptions, the cessation, are frustrating in both; the desire to begin again as strong. Catullus communicates the excitement and the intensity of his perception by applying a vocabulary, commonly used to describe love, to another matter which is not usually regarded in such terms, i.e., the writing of poetry. By this transposition he has presented us with a new way of regarding the experience.

Furthermore, Catullus demonstrates his insight through a particular incident, described in its essential detail. We know only that the two men drank and wrote poems. We know nothing else about their day: whether it was hot, sunny, cloudy; whether they took a walk, had a feast, saw some pretty girls; we do not even know what Licinius is like physically. The poet isolates the one aspect he wishes to emphasize, the writing of poetry with a witty friend. He then describes through concrete details what happened upon his leaving his friend. We see here how poetry uses concrete details to achieve a new way of looking at an experience. The dramatic nature of the poem allows us to see Catullus' perception. As the poem unfolds, we too perceive the essential similarity of the two things compared.

QUESTIONS

1. Explore the ramifications of the comparison of writing poetry with love-making. In what ways are they alike? How do they differ? What purpose does another human being serve in each? Is another person really necessary for each? Are there ways in which the comparison breaks down? What limits, if any, are implied in the poem?

2. What would happen to the poem if the last four verses were removed? How would the poem be changed? Would it be a change for the better?

ఆర్గ్యా

Publius Ovidius Naso (43 B.C.–18 A.D.)
Amores II.12

Ite triumphales circum mea tempora laurus!
    uicimus: in nostro est, ecce, Corinna sinu,
quam uir, quam custos, quam ianua firma, tot hostes
    seruabant, nequa posset ab arte capi.
5 haec est praecipuo uictoria digna triumpho,
    in qua, quaecumque est, sanguine praeda caret.
non humiles muri, non paruis oppida fossis
    cincta, sed est ductu capta puella meo.
Pergama cum caderent bello superata bilustri,
10   ex tot in Atridis pars quota laudis erat?
at mea seposita est et ob omni milite dissors
    gloria, nec titulum muneris alter habet:
me duce ad hanc uoti finem, me milite ueni;
    ipse eques, ipse pedes, signifer ipse fui.
15 nec casum fortuna meis inmiscuit actis:
    huc ades, o cura parte Triumphe mea!

nec belli est noua causa mei: nisi rapta fuisset
    Tyndaris, Europae pax Asiaeque foret;
femina siluestris Lapithas populumque biformem
20   turpiter adposito uertit in arma mero;
femina Troianos iterum noua bella mouere
    inpulit in regno, iuste Latine, tuo;
femina Romanis etiamnunc urbe recenti
    inmisit soceros armaque saeua dedit.
25 uidi ego pro niuea pugnantes coniuge tauros:
    spectatrix animos ipsa iuuenca dabat.
me quoque, qui multos, sed me sine caede, Cupido
    iussit militae signa mouere suae.

NOTES

Meter: Elegiac Couplet.

17. *Tyndaris*—i.e., Helen.

19. Refers to the battle between the Lapithae and Centaurs at the marriage of Hippodameia and Perithoos.

21. Refers to Lavinia, daughter of Latinus, who although desired by Turnus married Aeneas, after the latter had killed the former, as we know from the *Aeneid*.

QUESTION

1. Examine the metaphor of war in this poem, showing how it is used in the organization of the poem.

Gaius Valerius Catullus (c.84–54 B.C.)

XI

Furi et Aureli, comites Catulli,
siue in extremos penetrabit Indos,
litus ut longe resonante Eoa
    tunditur unda,

5   siue in Hyrcanos Arabasue molles,
seu Sacas sagittiferosue Parthos,

siue quae septemgeminus colorat
    aequora Nilus,

siue trans altas gradietur Alpes,
10 Caesaris uisens monimenta magni,
    Gallicum Rhenum, horribile aequor, ulti-
        mosque Britannos,

omnia haec, quaecumque feret uoluntas
    caelitum, temptare simul parati,
15 pauca nuntiate meae puellae
        non bona dicta.

cum suis uiuat ualeatque moechis,
    quos simul complexa tenet trecentos,
    nullum amans uere, sed identidem omnium
20   ilia rumpens;

nec meum respectet, ut ante, amorem,
    qui illius culpa cecidit uelut prati
    ultimi flos, praetereunte postquam
        tactus aratro est.

Notes

Meter: Sapphic Stanza.

1. *comites*—technical word for members of a provincial governor's *cohors*.

3. *ut*—"where," a rare locative usage.

Eoa unda—i.e., the ocean stream of the extreme East.

5. *Hyrcanos*—a people dwelling by the southern end of the Caspian Sea.

6. *Sacas*—a nomadic people living northeast of Parthia and Bactria; the Scythians.

11. *Gallicum*—Rhine is so called because it was the boundary of Caesar's conquests.

horribile aequor—i.e., the English Channel.

Questions

1. What purpose do the first fourteen verses serve in this poem?

2. Explain the usage of *molles* (5), *sagittiferos* (6), and *monimenta* (10). How do these words aid the poem?

3. Carefully examine the simile in vv. 22–24. How is such an image prepared for in the poem? How does it function to help unify the poem? Or does it? Explain its ambiguities. The figure is also found in Vergil's *Aeneid* IX.435f.:

> *purpureus ueluti cum flos succisus aratro*
> *languescit moriens . . .*

How does Catullus' image differ? What difference is there between *tactus* and *succisus*?

4. Comment on the metrics of this poem, and compare them with one of Horace's poems in the same meter.

❧

Publius Ovidius Naso (43 B.C.–18 A.D.)

Amores I.1

Arma graui numero uiolentaque bella parabam
    edere, materia conueniente modis.
par erat inferior uersus: risisse Cupido
    dicitur atque unum surripuisse pedem.
5 "quis tibi, saeue puer, dedit hoc in carmina iuris?
    Pieridum uates, non tua, turba sumus.
quid, si praeripiat flauae Venus arma Mineruae,
    uentilet accensas flaua Minerua faces?
quis probet in siluis Cererem regnare iugosis,
10   lege pharetratae uirginis arua coli?
crinibus insignem quis acuta cuspide Phoebum
    instruat, Aoniam Marte mouente lyram?
sunt tibi magna, puer, nimiumque potentia regna:
    cur opus adfectas, ambitiose, nouum?
15 an, quod ubique, tuum est? tua sunt Heliconia tempe?
    uix etiam Phoebo iam lyra tuta sua est?
cum bene surrexit uersu noua pagina primo,
    attenuat neruos proximus ille meos.

nec mihi materia est numeris leuioribus apta,
20   aut puer aut longas compta puella comas."
questus eram, pharetra cum protinus ille soluta
      legit in exitium spicula facta meum
lunauitque genu sinuosum fortiter arcum
      "quod" que "canas, uates, accipe," dixit, "opus!"
25 me miserum! certas habuit puer ille sagittas:
      uror, et in uacuo pectore regnat Amor.
sex mihi surgat opus numeris, in quinque residat;
      ferrea cum uestris bella ualete modis!
cingere litorea flauentia tempora myrto,
30   Musa per undenos emodulanda pedes!

Notes

Meter: Elegiac Couplet.

2. *modis*—dative with adjectives.

5. *iuris*—genitive of the whole, used here with the singular neuter accusative of the pronoun.

12. *Aoniam*—part of Boeotia in which is Mount Helicon, home of the Muses.

15. *quod ubique*—understand *est.*

18. *neruos*—metonomy (see glossary).

24. *canas*—subjunctive of characteristic.

Questions

1. In what ways does the poet describe the formation of the elegiac couplet? What purpose does he have in doing so?

2. The poem plays with the conceit, or extended metaphor, of the poet who wishes to write of wars but is forced into writing of other matters, for example love. What, however, is meant by "love" in this poem? What is the purpose of the address by the "I" of the poem in vv. 5–18? What, finally, is the subject of the poem?

3. Ovid is a witty, skillful poet. Such a poet is often praised for treating serious matters lightly. How does Ovid merit this sort of praise? In what way can he be said to take serious matters lightly in this poem?

Albius Tibullus (c.55–19 B.C.)

Elegy II.4

Hic mihi seruitium uideo dominamque paratam:
    iam mihi, libertas illa paterna, uale.
seruitium sed triste datur, teneorque catenis,
    et numquam misero uincla remittit Amor,
5 et seu quid merui seu nil peccauimus, urit.
    uror, io, remoue, saeua puella, faces.
o ego ne possim tales sentire dolores,
    quam mallem in gelidis montibus esse lapis,
stare uel insanis cautes obnoxia uentis,
10   naufraga quam uasti tunderet unda maris!
nunc et amara dies et noctis amarior umbra est:
    omnia nam tristi tempora felle madent.
nec prosunt elegi nec carminis auctor Apollo:
    illa caua pretium flagitat usque manu.
15 ite procul, Musae, si non prodestis amanti:
    non ego uos, ut sint bella canenda, colo,
nec refero Solisque uias et qualis, ubi orbem
    compleuit, uersis Luna recurrit equis.
ad dominam faciles aditus per carmina quaero:
20   ite procul, Musae, si nihil ista ualent.
at mihi per caedem et facinus sunt dona paranda,
    ne iaceam clausam flebilis ante domum:
aut rapiam suspensa sacris insignia fanis:
    sed Venus ante alios est uiolanda mihi.
25 illa malum facinus suadet dominamque rapacem
    dat mihi: sacrilegas sentiat illa manus.
o pereat quicumque legit uiridesque smaragdos
    et niueam Tyrio murice tingit ouem.
addit auaritiae causas et Coa puellis
30   uestis et e rubro lucida concha mari.
haec fecere malas: hinc clauim ianua sensit
    et coepit custos liminis esse canis.
sed pretium si grande feras, custodia uicta est

nec prohibent claues et canis ipse tacet.
35 heu quicumque dedit formam caelestis auarae,
    quale bonum multis attulit ille malis!
hinc fletus rixaeque sonant, haec denique causa
    fecit ut infamis sic deus esset Amor.
at tibi quae pretio uictos excludis amantes,
40   eripiant partas uentus et ignis opes:
quin tua tunc iuuenes spectent incendia laeti,
    nec quisquam flammae sedulus addat aquam.
seu ueniet tibi Mors, nec erit qui lugeat ullus,
    nec qui det maestas munus in exsequias.
45 at bona quae nec auara fuit, centum licet annos
    uexerit, ardentem flebitur ante rogum:
atque aliquis senior ueteres ueneratus amores
    annua constructo serta dabit tumulo
et "bene," discedens dicet, "placideque quiescas,
50   terraque securae sit super ossa leuis."
uera quidem moneo, sed prosunt quid mihi uera?
    illius est nobis lege colendus amor.
quin etiam sedes iubeat si uendere auitas,
    ite sub imperium sub titulumque, Lares.
55 quidquid habet Circe, quidquid Medea ueneni,
    quidquid et herbarum Thessala terra gerit,
et quod, ubi indomitis gregibus Venus adflat amores,
    hippomanes cupidae stillat ab inguine equae,
si modo me placido uideat Nemesis mea uultu,
60   mille alias herbas misceat illa, bibam.

NOTES

Meter: Elegiac Couplet.

  2. *mihi*—"ethical" dative.

 12. *madent*—used to describe effect of a great amount of wine.

 14. *caua manu*—i.e., the beggar's gesture.

 16. *ut sint canenda*—i.e., not "to write epic."

 18. *recurrit*—although the subjunctive is supposedly the rule, in such indirect questions the indicative is frequently found in Old

Latin and in poetry of the classical period; it grows common in Silver Latin and becomes the rule in Late Latin.

28. *ouem*—synecdoche; but here the whole is used for the part.

35. *caelestis*—the use of this adjective as a substantive in the nominative singular seems unique.

38. *ut*—common in pre-Augustan literature; an archaism perhaps.

47. *aliquis*—a substantive in apposition with *senior*.

54. *sub imperium etc.*—i.e., an auction; *imperium* is magisterial authority, reference is to a custom dating from the time when an *auctio* was the public sale of war booty.

60. *misceat*—note omission of conditional sign for this verb.

QUESTIONS

1. The basic metaphor of the poem is that of the slave of love. The device is found in Greek literature, but it is more common in Roman love poetry. In this poem examine how the metaphor functions. What are the details of the slavery, and what are the causes? What are the limits of the slavery?

2. How does the poet maintain a distance within the conceit? That is, how is the reader made aware of the fact that there is a difference between the slavery in love and the actual slavery which was practiced in Rome? What attitude results from the maintaining of this distance? How then do we regard the theme of the "slave of love"? How does it affect our understanding of love and of the poem?

Gaius Valerius Catullus (c.84–54 B.C.)

XLVI

Iam uer egelidos refert tepores,
iam caeli furor aequinoctialis
iucundis Zephyri silescit aureis.
linquantur Phrygii, Catulle, campi
5 Nicaeaeque ager uber aestuosae:
ad claras Asiae uolemus urbes.
iam mens praetrepidans auet uagari,

iam laeti studio pedes uigescunt.
o dulces comitum ualete coetus,
10 longe quos simul a domo profectos
diuersae uariae uiae reportant.

NOTES

Meter: Phalaecean or Hendecasyllabic.

2. *furor aequinoctialis*—it is commonly noted that storms accompany the vernal and autumnal equinoxes.

3. *Zephyri*—the spring wind of Rome.

5. *aestuosae*—frequently the summer is unpleasant and often unhealthy at Rome.

9. *comitum*—i.e., members of a governor's *cohors*.

QUESTIONS

1. What is the effect of the address to Catullus?

2. What patterns of imagery are found in the poem? Which pattern is most important? How does it affect our understanding of the poem? What part in the poem do other images play?

⋘§⋙

Quintus Horatius Flaccus (65–8 B.C.)

Ode III.26

Vixi puellis nuper idoneus
et militaui non sine gloria;
    nunc arma defunctumque bello
        barbiton hic paries habebit,
5 laeuum marinae qui Veneris latus
custodit. hic, hic ponite lucida
    funalia et uectis et arcus
        oppositis foribus minaces.
o quae beatam diua tenes Cyprum et
10 Memphin carentem Sithonia niue,
    regina, sublimi flagello
        tange Chloen semel arrogantem.

Notes

Meter: Alcaic Stanza.

4. *hic paries*—used perhaps for decorative, commemorative purposes.

8. *oppositis foribus*—dative with *minaces*; *oppositis*, i.e., barred.

10. *Memphin*—in Egypt.

Sithonia—i.e., Thracian; Sithonii were a Thracian tribe.

12. *Chloen*—a Greek accusative.

Questions

1. What is the source of the metaphor in vv. 1–4? Is this metaphor used well in this poem?

2. Verses 5–8 employ a different pattern of metaphors. What is it? What do you make of *laeuum . . . custodit*? Who or what is the subject? What is meant by the phrase *laeuum marinae Veneris latus*? Why *marinae*? How are the matters mentioned in v. 7 appropriate in this context? In what sense are they *minaces*? What is meant by *oppositis foribus*? Explain how this stanza and its imagery are connected with the first, if they are.

3. Does stanza three continue any of the image patterns of the earlier stanzas? What significance do you attach to *beatam Cyprum* and to all of v. 10? What does the name *Chloe* mean? What connection, if any, do vv. 11 and 12 have with what has gone before?

4. What is the dramatic situation of the poem? How does it function in the poem? What connection, if any, does it have with the imagery?

5. Write an essay analyzing the unity of this poem.

❧

Gaius Valerius Catullus (c.84–54 B.C.)

LI

Ille mi par esse deo uidetur,
ille, si fas est, superare diuos,
qui sedens aduersus identidem te
 spectat et audit

5   dulce ridentem, misero quod omnis
     eripit sensus mihi: nam simul te,
     Lesbia, adspexi, nihil est super mi

     . . . .

     lingua sed torpet, tenuis sub artus
10 flamma demanat, sonitu suopte
     tintinant aures, gemina teguntur
       lumina nocte.

     otium, Catulle, tibi molestum est:
     otio exsultas nimiumque gestis:
15 otium et reges prius et beatas
       perdidit urbes.

NOTES

Meter: Sapphic Stanza. After v. 7 a verse has been lost.

  2. *si fas est*—a common religious and legal expression.

13. *molestum*—often used of a disease.

QUESTIONS

  1. As is clear from vv. 1–8, the presence of Lesbia makes the spectator divine. The implication is that Lesbia is herself so awesome that she can confer divinity. What imagery is involved in these first eight verses? What then is the effect of the next stanza? How does it continue the imagery begun in the first two?

  2. Up to v. 12 what has inspired the attitude? What happens in vv. 13–16? Why is there a change of address? What does it signify for the first three stanzas? What is meant by *otium*?

  3. The poem is, as we see, a meditation on love. It is an adaptation of a poem by Sappho. Compare it then with Sappho's poem. What changes have been made? What is achieved by those changes?

❦

Sappho

Fragment 31

φαίνεταί μοι κῆνος ἴσος Θέοισιν
ἔμμεν᾽ ὤνηρ, ὄττις ἐνάντιος τοι

ἰσδάνει καὶ πλάσιον ἆδυ φωνεί-
σας ὑπακούει

5 καί γελαίσας ἰμέροεν, τό μ' ἦ μὰν
καρδίαν 'εν στήθεσιν ἐπτόαισεν
ὡς γὰρ ἔς σ' ἴδω βρόχε', ὥς με φώναι-
σ' οὐδ' ἒν ἔτ' εἴκει
ἀλλ' ἄκαν μὲν γλῶσσα † ἔαγε †, λέπ τον

10 δ'αὔτικα χρῷ πῦρ ὑπαδεδρόμηκεν
ὀππάτεσσι δ' οὐδ' ἒν ὄρημμ', ἐπιρρόμ-
βεισι δ'ἄκουαι,
κὰδ δέ μ' ἴδρως ψῦχρος ἔχει τρομός δε
παῖσαν ἄγρει, χλωροτέρα δε ποίας

15 ἔμμι, τεθνάκην δ'ὀλίγω 'πιδεύης
φαίνομαι †
ἀλλὰ πὰν τόλματον, ἐπεὶ † καὶ πένητα

Fortunate as the gods he seems to me, that man who sits opposite
you, and listens nearby to your sweet voice
And your lovely laughter; that, I vow, has set my heart within my
breast a-flutter. For when I look at you a moment, then I
have no longer power to speak,
But my tongue keeps silence, straightway a subtle flame has stolen
beneath my flesh, with my eyes I see nothing, my ears are
humming,
A cold sweat covers me, and a trembling seizes me all over, I am
paler than grass, I seem to be not far short of death. . . .
But all must be endured, since . . .[2]

◆§§◆

Albius Tibullus (c.55–19 B.C.)
Elegy I.5
Asper eram et bene discidium me ferre loquebar:
    at mihi nunc longe gloria fortis abest.
namque agor ut per plana citus sola uerbere turben
    quem celer adsueta uersat ab arte puer.

[2] Denys L. Page, *Sappho and Alcaeus* (Oxford University Press, 1955), 19–20.

5 ure ferum et torque, libeat ne dicere quicquam
        magnificum post haec: horrida uerba doma.
   parce tamen, per te furtiui foedera lecti,
        per uenerem quaeso compositumque caput.
   ille ego, cum tristi morbo defessa iaceres,
10   te dicor uotis eripuisse meis:
   ipseque te circum lustraui sulfure puro,
        carmine cum magico praecinuisset anus;
   ipse procuraui ne possent saeua nocere
        somnia, ter sancta deueneranda mola;
15 ipse ego uelatus filo tunicisque solutis
        uota nouem Triuiae nocte silente dedi.
   omnia persolui: fruitur nunc alter amore,
        et precibus felix utitur ille meis.
   at mihi felicem uitam, si salua fuisses,
20   fingebam demens, sed renuente deo.
   rura colam, frugumque aderit mea Delia custos,
        area dum messes sole calente teret,
   aut mihi seruabit plenis in lintribus uuas
        pressaque ueloci candida musta pede,
25 consuescet numerare pecus, consuescet amantis
        garrulus in dominae ludere uerna sinu.
   illa deo sciet agricolae pro uitibus uuam,
        pro segete spicas, pro grege ferre dapem.
   illa regat cunctos, illi sint omnia curae:
30   at iuuet in tota me nihil esse domo.
   huc ueniet Messalla meus, cui dulcia poma
        Delia selectis detrahat arboribus:
   et tantum uenerata uirum, hunc sedula curet,
        huic paret atque epulas ipsa ministra gerat.
35 haec mihi fingebam, quae nunc Eurusque Notusque
        iactat odoratos uota per Armenios.
   saepe ego temptaui curas depellere uino:
        at dolor in lacrimas uerterat omne merum.
   saepe aliam tenui: sed iam cum gaudia adirem,
40   admonuit dominae deseruitque Venus.

tunc me discedens deuotum femina dixit,
    a pudet, et narrat scire nefanda meam.
non facit hoc uerbis, facie tenerisque lacertis
    deuouet et flauis nostra puella comis.
45   talis ad Haemonium Nereis Pelea quondam
    uecta est frenato caerula pisce Thetis.
haec nocuere mihi. quod adest huic diues amator,
    uenit in exitium callida lena meum.
sanguineas edat illa dapes atque ore cruento
50   tristia cum multo pocula felle bibat:
hanc uolitent animae circum sua fata querentes
    semper, et e tectis strix uiolenta canat:
ipsa fame stimulante furens herbasque sepulcris
    quaerat et a saeuis ossa relicta lupis;
55   currat et inguinibus nudis ululetque per urbes,
    post agat e triuiis aspera turba canum.
eueniet; dat signa deus: sunt numina amanti,
    saeuit et iniusta lege relicta Venus.
at tu quam primum sagae praecepta rapacis
60   desere: nam donis uincitur omnis amor.
pauper erit praesto tibi semper: pauper adibit
    primus et in tenero fixus erit latere:
pauper in angusto fidus comes agmine turbae
    subicietque manus efficietque uiam:
65   pauper ad occultos furtim deducet amicos
    uinclaque de niueo detrahet ipse pede.
heu canimus frustra, nec uerbis uicta patescit
    ianua, sed plena est percutienda manu.
at tu, qui potior nunc es, mea furta timeto:
70   uersatur celeri Fors leuis orbe rotae.
non frustra quidam iam nunc in limine perstat
    sedulus ac crebro prospicit ac refugit
et simulat transire domum, mox deinde recurrit
    solus et ante ipsas exscreat usque fores.
75   nescio quid furtiuus amor parat. utere quaeso,
    dum licet: in liquida nam tibi linter aqua.

Notes

Meter: Elegiac Couplet.

3. *sola*—plural because the top skips from one spot to another. *turben*—an archaic nominative form.

4. *ab arte*—unusual but acceptable of the preposition.

9. *ille*—probably in apposition to *ego*, "that self of other times."

13. *procuraui—prŏcuraui*, a word found usually in a religious context.

15. *uelatus filo*—head covering worn by priest; although commonly used in the ceremonial of many Roman sacrifices, the *filum* was generally worn by *flamines* or *fetiales*.

tunicis solutis—usually so worn in any service to a god.

16. *nouem*—ritualistic and often associated with Hecate.

25–34. Note anaphora (see glossary).

27. *deo*—a dative with a verb of motion.

28. *segetē*—the ultima is long.

32. *arboribus*—when no personal interest in involved, Tibullus uses the ablative with or without a preposition, as here; otherwise he uses a dative.

33. *uirūm hunc*—hiatus with a syllable in *m* is rare.

35. *Eurusque Notusque*—in imitation of the Homeric combination.

36. *Armenios*—for the more usual Assyrios, perhaps because Armenia is high and windy.

40. *admonuit dominae—me* is understood; omission of an object is rare in a construction with *admoneo*.

42. *meam*—this use of the possessive is characteristic of colloquial speech.

45. Nerēis.

47–56. The *diues amator* and his crony, the *lena*, are types common in comedy.

52. *e tectis . . . canat*—i.e., exceptionally ominous.

53. *herbasque sepulcris*—i.e., sacrilege is being committed, the punishment for which will ensue.

56. *post*—adverbial and local.

66. *uincla*—sandals were regularly removed at dinner.

68. *plena manu*—ambiguity exists here.

75. *utere*—object is implied from the previous sentence.

QUESTIONS

1. The general organization of the poem is based on antithesis. Examine how antithesis operates throughout the poem.

2. Within such an organization two images are used to explore the meaning of that antithesis: the "top" as seen in vv. 3–4 and its opposite, the top at rest. Examine how the image of the top moves throughout the poem. What parts are connected to it? Is it always a top or does the top become emblematic of other matters as well?

3. Explain how the poet suggests the contrary of the whirlwind effect of the top in vv. 7–20. What has been the occasion of the poem? How does this occasion relate to the two images discussed?

4. In v. 20 the words *fingebam demens* occur and then a descriptive scene from v. 21 to v. 34 follows, after which in v. 35 *fingebam* again occurs. What is the effect of the scene? What is the purpose of the tenses and the moods of the verbs in the scene? How do they form a contrast with the "framing word" *fingebam*?

5. The first portion of the poem has ended. What happens in the second half of the poem, from vv. 37ff.? Carefully examine the imagery of this section, and indicate how it is related to the first half of the poem. Who is responsible for the lover's plight? What does the lover do to counteract the effect of the *diues amator*?

6. Carefully examine vv. 70–76. How do they form a recapitulation of the ideas and the imagery used previously in the poem?

7. In the light of the entire poem, write a careful account of the significance of v. 1.

❧

Quintus Horatius Flaccus (65–8 B.C.)

Ode II.14

Eheu fugaces, Postume, Postume,
labuntur anni nec pietas moram
   rugis et instanti senectae
      adferet indomitaeque morti:

5   non si trecenis quotquot eunt dies,
amice, places illacrimabilem
     Plutona tauris, qui ter amplum
        Geryonen Tityonque tristi

compescit unda, scilicet omnibus,
10 quicumque terrae munere uescimur,
     enauiganda, siue reges
        siue inopes erimus coloni.

frustra cruento Marte carebimus
fractisque rauci fluctibus Hadriae,
15   frustra per autumnos nocentem
        corporibus metuemus Austrum:

uisendus ater flumine languido
Cocytos errans et Danai genus
     infame damnatusque longi
20   Sisyphus Aeolides laboris:

linquenda tellus et domus et placens
uxor, neque harum quas colis arborum
     te praeter inuisas cupressos
        ulla breuem dominum sequetur:

25 absumet heres Caecuba dignior
seruata centum clauibus et mero
     tinget pauimentum superbo,
        pontificum potiore cenis.

NOTES

Meter: Alcaic Stanza.

1. *fugaces*—predicate adjective with *anni.*

5. *quotquot eunt dies*—"every day that passes by"; also observe the hyperbole in *trecenis . . . tauros.*

6. *places*—the verb has a conative force.
illacrimabilem—active in meaning, i.e., relentless.

7. *ter amplum Geryonen*—Geryon was a Spanish giant with

three bodies, whom Hercules slew and from whom Hercules also stole cattle.

8. *Tityon*—son of Earth; insulted Latona, whose children, Apollo and Diana, slew him. In Tartarus he covers nearly six acres with his vast body.

tristi . . . unda—i.e., the Styx.

9. *scilicet*—"surely," "indeed."

11. *enauiganda*—as a transitive verb *enauigare* is first found in Horace.

reges—i.e., men of wealth, though also, of course, "kings."

13. *carebimus*—i.e., in the sense of escape.

16. *corporibus*—with both *nocentem* and *metuemus*. Note in vv. 13–16 the skillful use Horace makes of the common endings for ablative and dative.

18. *Cocytos*—the river of Lamentation, from the Greek.

Danai genus infame—the fifty daughters of Danaus, except Hypermnestra, destroyed their husbands on their wedding night. As a result the maidens were condemned to carry water endlessly in leaky vessels.

19. *longi*—i.e., ceaseless.

20. *Sisyphus*—son of Aeolus, king of Corinth, who was punished for his avarice and deceit by being condemned to roll uphill a huge stone, which immediately rolled down again.

laboris—genitive of charge.

24. *ulla*—understand "*arbor*."

Caecuba—a good wine.

28. *pontificum potiore cenis*—i.e., superior to that used at banquets of the priests, which were supposed to be magnificent affairs.

QUESTIONS

1. In vv. 3 and 4, what is the significance of the order of *rugis . . . senectae . . . morti?*

2. Explain the imagery in the poem. What purpose does the imagery serve?

3. What purpose do the common endings of the dative and ablative cases serve in vv. 13–16?

4. Carefully examine the last stanza, and then analyze with what justification it concludes the poem.

5. Examine the metrics of the poem.

❧

Gaius Valerius Catullus (c.84–54 B.C.)

XXIX

Quis hoc potest uidere, quis potest pati,
nisi impudicus et uorax et aleo,
Mamurram habere quod Comata Gallia
habebat uncti et ultima Britannia?

5   cinaede Romule, haec uidebis et feres?
et ille nunc superbus et superfluens
perambulabit omnium cubilia,
ut albulus columbus aut Adoneus?
cinaede Romule, haec uidebis et feres?

10 es impudicus et uorax et aleo.
eone nomine, imperator unice,
fuisti in ultima occidentis insula,
ut ista uestra diffutata mentula
ducenties comesset aut trecenties?

15 quid est alid sinistra liberalitas?
parum expatrauit an parum elluatus est?
paterna prima lancinata sunt bona,
secunda praeda Pontica, inde tertia
Hibera, quam scit amnis aurifer Tagus:

20 nunc Galliae timetur et Britanniae.
quid hunc malum fouetis? aut quid hic potest
nisi uncta deuorare patrimonia?
eone nomina† urbis opulentissime†
socer generque, perdidistis omnia?

NOTES

Meter: Iambic Trimeter.

3. *Mamurra*—an *eques* of Formiae and *praefectus fabrum* of Caesar in Gaul. He was the first to encrust the entire walls of his

house with marble and to have solid marble columns in his home. He was an intimate friend of the dictator. The first syllable of the name may be long.

Comata Gallia—transalpine Gaul where the men wore long hair.

8. *columbus*—a favorite bird of Venus.

Adoneus—another form of Adonis.

11. *eo nomine*—"on this account." The term is borrowed from accounting.

21. *fouetis*—understand Caesar and Pompey, and also with *perdidistis* in v. 24. The reference is to the marriage of Caesar's daughter to Pompey after the meeting at Luca in 56 B.C.

QUESTIONS

1. Examine the figurative language of this poem. How does it help illuminate the thought Catullus communicates?

2. Explain the change of address which occurs in the poem. Does this contribute to the effectiveness of the poem? Is it relevant? Although the note tells us that we are to understand Caesar and Pompey as the subject of *fouetis* in v. 21, what evidence in the poem justifies this assertion? Why are they referred to obliquely? Is this effective in the poem? How does the matter of the address interact with the imagery of the poem?

⋅⧵⧸⋅

Quintus Horatius Flaccus (65–8 B.C.)

Epode VII

Quo, quo scelesti ruitis? aut cur dexteris
    aptantur enses conditi?
parumne campis atque Neptuno super
    fusum est Latini sanguinis,
5 non, ut superbas inuidae Carthaginis
    Romanus arces ureret,
intactus aut Britannus ut descenderet
    Sacra catenatus uia,
sed ut secundum uota Parthorum sua

10   urbs haec periret dextera?
neque hic lupis mos nec fuit leonibus
    umquam nisi in dispar feris.
furorne caecus, an rapit uis acrior,
    an culpa? responsum date!
15   tacent et albus ora pallor inficit
    mentesque perculsae stupent.
sic est: acerba fata Romanos agunt
    scelusque fraternae necis,
ut immerentis fluxit in terram Remi
20   sacer nepotibus cruor.

NOTES

Meter: Iambic Stanza.

3. *Neptuno super—super* follows its noun; *Neptuno* by metonomy for *mari*.

5. *inuidae*—i.e., of Rome's power.

7. *ut descenderet*—the Sacra Via sloped considerably as it approached the Forum, after which it rose sharply at the Capitoline Hill. There it joined the *Cliuus Capitolinus* which led to the *Capitolium*, the temple of Jupiter.

8. *catenatus*—predicate adjective.

12. *dispar*—used as a substantive.

13. *uis acrior*—some force beyond human control. The same connotation occurs in v. 17, *acerba fata*.

20. *nepotibus*—depends on *sacer*.

QUESTIONS

1. Explain vv. 11 and 12 and their relationship to the rest of the poem. How do they serve as a focal point of the poem?

2. Write an essay analyzing the imagery of this poem.

RHETORICAL FIGURES
IN POETRY
5

So far we have talked about the dramatic situation, the function of description, and the use of figurative language or imagery in a poem. As we have seen, poetry conveys much of its meaning through images which help to organize a poem and its effect. Another part of the organizing process is the tone or attitude the author adopts towards his material. In our earlier discussions the idea of tone has been implicit. In Catullus' lament for his brother the tone of sadness dominates the poem; on the other hand Horace's tone towards his material in *Ode* III.9 is that of amused detachment.

The manipulation of tone in poetry is naturally more difficult than in conversation. In conversation the "tone" or the attitude we want to suggest is conveyed by the voice, the face, gestures, and indeed, sometimes by the entire body. A poet has no such recourse. He has simply the words on a page whereby he can convey his attitude and arouse our response. Hence he is dependent on the arrangement of his words, his images, his ideas, his thoughts.

One means the poet has at his disposal is that of rhetorical figures of speech. Rhetorical figures in English prose and poetry are not unfamiliar to us. They may be called by different names, but they are still commonly employed for many purposes. The subject has already been touched on in the notes to various poems in the preceding sections. Metonomy, synecdoche, hyperbole, and anaphora have all been alluded to, and all are figures of speech. Metonomy is the use of the name of one thing to indicate another, e.g., *Neptuno* for *mari* in Horace's *Epode* VII.3. Synecdoche is the use of a name of a part to stand for the whole or of the whole for a part, e.g., sails for ships, or ships for sails. Horace, *Ode* I.4.2, uses the figure as does Tibullus in *Elegy* II.4.28. Hyperbole is exaggeration for the sake of emphasis, e.g., three hundred bulls where one would do as well as in Horace's *Ode* II.14.5. Anaphora is simply marked repetition, such as occurs in Tibullus' *Elegy* I.5.25-34. Such figures are commonly used to convey attitudes. When rhetorical figures are used well, they do not merely decorate, merely add to a poem something which if removed would not affect the poem. They help to create concreteness and to give intensity. They are part of the means of organization, and like imagery they contribute to the unity of the poem.

Rather than give an exhaustive list of rhetorical figures here, we shall examine various ones in individual poems, and refer to the poems which have already been discussed where such figures occur.

⁓§⁓

Marcus Valerius Martialis (c.40-104 A.D.)
Epigram I.32
Non amo te, Sabidi, nec possum dicere quare:
hoc tantum possum dicere, non amo te.

NOTES

Meter: Elegiac Couplet.

1. *amŏ*—ultima is short; at the time Martial wrote, any final *o* might be freely shortened except in inflectional forms of the second declension.

This poem depends largely upon the rhetorical figure of chiasmus which is the crosslike arrangement of contrasted pairs of words, phrases, clauses, or inflections and which thus gives an alternate stress to the members of the pairs. Examine this poem to see how such crosslike arrangement is used. Account for every word or phrase in these two verses. What particularly is the effect of *quare?* What effect does the poem achieve by the chiastic arrangement?

Observe in Horace's *Ode* IV.7.1 the use of chiasmus and explain how it functions.

❦

Marcus Valerius Martialis (c.40–104 A.D.)
Epigram I.95

Quod clamas semper, quod agentibus obstrepis, Aeli,
    non facis hoc gratis: accipis, ut taceas.

Meter: Elegiac Couplet.

QUESTIONS

1. Explain how the phrase *non facis hoc gratis* is affected by v. 1 and by the rest of v. 2.

2. What is the tone of the poem?

❦

Marcus Valerius Martialis (c.40–104 A.D.)
Epigram VII.51

Mercari nostras si te piget, Urbice, nugas
    et lasciua tamen carmina nosse libet,
Pompeium quaeres, et nosti forsitan, Auctum;
    ultoris prima Martis in aede sedet:
5 iure madens uarioque togae limatus in usu
    non lector meus hic, Urbice, sed liber est.
sic tenet absentes nostros cantatque libellos
    ut pereat chartis littera nulla meis:
denique, si uellet, poterat scripsisse uideri;
10   sed famae mauult ille fauere meae.
hunc licet a decuma (neque enim satis ante uacabit)
    sollicites, capiet cenula parua duos;
ille leget, bibe tu; nolis licet, ille sonabit:
    et cum "iam satis est" dixeris, ille leget.

NOTES

Meter: Elegiac Couplet.

4. *ultoris*—temple of Mars Ultor in Forum Augusti, where a considerable part of Rome's legal affairs was transacted.

sedet—i.e., in court.

11. *decuma*—understand *hora*.

QUESTIONS

1. What is the tone of this poem? How does Martial suggest it?

2. What is the source of humor? Is the humor malicious? dry? perceptive? understanding?

❦

Gaius Valerius Catullus (c.84–54 B.C.)

LXXXII

Quinti, si tibi uis oculos debere Catullum
aut aliud si quid carius est oculis,
eripere ei noli multo quod carius illi
est oculis seu quid carius est oculis.

NOTES

Meter: Elegiac Couplet.

3. *ei*—monosyllabic.

4. *seu*—for *uel si*.

QUESTIONS

1. How is chiasmus used in this poem? Is it as balanced as in Martial's epigrams? What variations do you observe? What is the effect of those variations?

2. Explain carefully the use of the word *oculi* in this poem. What does *oculos debere* mean? How is it employed in this poem? Why should *oculi* be the word so used? What connection do you find between this usage and the chiastic arrangement of the poem? Do they reinforce one another?

❦

Marcus Valerius Martialis (c.40–104 A.D.)

Epigram I.79

Semper agis causas et res agis, Attale, semper:

est, non est quod agas, Attale, semper agis.
   si res et causae desunt, agis, Attale, mulas.
   Attale, ne quod agas desit, agas animam.

NOTES

Meter: Elegiac Couplet.

2. *est, non est*—the statement forms a kind of protasis; *quod* is to be understood also with *agis*.

QUESTIONS

1. The previous poem showed a repeated use of one word, *oculi*; such repetition is also a figure of speech, anaphora. Examine in this poem the use of *ago*. What does it mean each time it is used? What is the effect of its repeated usage? What is the purpose of such a repetition?

2. Examine Tibullus' *Elegy* I.5.25–34 for the effect of anaphora.

✺

Marcus Valerius Martialis (c.40–104 A.D.)
Epigram VI.60

Laudat amat cantat nostros mea Roma libellos,
   meque sinus omnes, me manus omnis habet.
ecce rubet quidam pallet stupet oscitat odit.
   hoc uolo: nunc nobis carmina nostra placent.

NOTES

Meter: Elegiac Couplet.

2. *habet*—singular with nearer subject.

QUESTIONS

1. This poem illustrates well two other figures of speech, those of asyndeton and parataxis. Asyndeton occurs when there is an omission of connectives where two or more members would ordinarily be connected. How is it used in this poem?

2. Parataxis is the arrangement of clauses without subordination. Each clause is grammatically equal to the next. Frequently para-

{ 106 }

taxis is indicated by the repeated use of *et* or *-que*. How is it used in this poem?

3. The opposite of chiasmus is parallelism. Find illustrations of it in this poem. Compare the use of parallelism here with that found in Horace's *Ode* I.9.21–22.

4. What is the effect of asyndeton, parataxis, chiasmus, and parallelism in the poem? How do they help in the organization of the poem?

Irony is a tone familiar to all of us. Sarcasm or exaggeration or understatement, as well as paradox, are all varieties of irony. An ironical statement indicates a meaning contrary to the one it seems to give. An ironic event or situation is one in which a contrast exists between expectation and fulfillment. Both irony of statement and event may appear in a poem. Irony has a wide variety of shades and functions so that the way it is used differs from poem to poem, from subtlety to broadside. It can be conveyed by a single word, or by a sentence, or by a paragraph.

In the following poem explain how the irony of the poem depends on the name of the addressee.

❧§❧

Marcus Valerius Martialis (c.40–104 A.D.)
Epigram I.110
Scribere me quereris, Velox, epigrammata longa,
    ipse nihil scribis: tu breuiora facis.

Meter: Elegiac Couplet.

❧§❧

Marcus Valerius Martialis (c.40–104 A.D.)
Epigram VI.17
Cinnam, Cinname, te iubes uocari.
non est hic, rogo, Cinna, barbarismus?
tu si Furius ante dictus esses,
Fur ista ratione dicereris.

NOTES

Meter: Phalaecean or Hendecasyllabic.

1. *Cinname*—a pretentious name for a slave.
4. *fur*—branded on the forehead of a slave for stealing.

QUESTIONS

1. What is the effect of v. 2? How does it function to emphasize the irony of the poem?
2. Comment on the metrics of v. 3.
3. What pun is there in v. 4?

Oxymoron and paradox are varieties of irony. Oxymoron is the juxtaposition of words which are ordinarily contradictory; paradox is a statement which seems contradictory but in actuality is true. Both figures reveal an obscure truth though their form suggests contradiction. It is the contrast between the form of statement and its implication which makes both oxymoron and paradox part of the ironic mood. In the following poem observe how they function.

Marcus Valerius Martialis (c.40–104 A.D.)
Epigram XII.46
Difficilis facilis, iucundus acerbus es idem:
nec tecum possum uiuere nec sine te.

Meter: Elegiac Couplet.

Understatement is common enough to us. We use such phrases as "a rather good-looking girl" when we mean a beautiful one, or refer to an enormously big man as "Tiny." Both are understatements used to emphasize the disparity between the statement and the reality. In rhetoric the device is termed either meiosis or litotes. Precisely defined, litotes is a double negative used for a positive, e.g., a not unpleasant place. Meiosis is mere understatement.

The opposite of understatement is hyperbole or exaggeration. Both understatement and exaggeration, because of the disparity between the statement and the reality, lend themselves to ironic effects. The deliberate overstatement can be as utterly damning as the deliberate understatement. To make these matters clear and to show how important they are in Latin poetry, let us turn to a poem.

❧

Gaius Valerius Catullus (c.84–54 B.C.)

I

Cui dono lepidum nouum libellum
arido modo pumice expolitum?
Corneli, tibi: namque tu solebas
meas esse aliquid putare nugas
5   iam tum, cum ausus es unus Italorum
omne aeuum tribus explicare chartis
doctis, Iuppiter, et laboriosis!
quare habe tibi quidquid hoc libelli
qualecumque; quod, o patrona uirgo,
10   plus uno maneat perenne saeclo.

NOTES

Meter: Phalaecean or Hendecasyllabic.

2. *arido . . . pumice*—the reference is to the polishing of the end of the papyrus roll which contained the "book."

3. *Corneli*—apparently Cornelius Nepos, the historian, who wrote not only *De Viris Illustribus*, part of which is extant, but also other historical works.

4. *aliquid putare—aliquid* is predicate to *nugas*, and means "of some worth," "of some value," after such words as *putare, dicere,* etc.

8. *habe tibi*—a formula derived from legal terminology indicating the conveyance of rights in property.

quidquid hoc—understand *est.*

9. *qualecumque*—modifies the whole previous clause and has a deprecatory tone.

patrona uirgo—simply the Muse, the patron goddess; no specific one is necessarily meant.

{109}

This is apparently a dedicatory poem to a volume Catullus published. We learn from the poem that the book is small and elegant, *lepidum . . . libellum*, and we also learn that its cover is highly polished. Critics like to say that only the external characteristics are being talked about. But the poet who took himself seriously, as we have every right to believe he did, would hardly be concerned with the externals of the book were the internal matter not of importance to him. The polished papyrus roll by metonomy stands for the polished poems themselves. Thus the poet indirectly and by this ironic device calls attention to his own poetry.

The next two verses contain the dedication proper of the poem. The use of *nugas* in v. 4 suggests that understatement is involved. Upon reflection we see that the understatement has already been prepared for by the diminutive of the first verse and the metonomy of the second. It is the ironic mode which treats serious things lightly. The volume supposedly contains trifles, slight poems. *Nugae* has the connotation of inferior to superior, small to great, finished practice exercises in preparation for a *magnum opus*, but it may even on occasion mean a man's lifework. No necessarily pejorative idea exists. In the next two verses we can see why Catullus used *nugae* here. Cornelius has written a history of Italy in three volumes, long and learned. On the surface it appears that Catullus' efforts are mere trifles by comparison. He reinforces that notion in v. 8 in which he refers to his own book, in effect his life's work, again by the diminutive *libelli*. But this seemingly graceful diffidence on Catullus' part really has considerable force. By the deliberate use of understatement, juxtaposed and surrounding the description of Cornelius' own work, Catullus wants us to be aware of the irony. By such implications he suggests that there is something presumptuous about reducing *Italorum omne aeuum* to three books. Catullus underscores the idea by using *ausus es unus*. No one else would dare or had dared to lay out—*explicare*—the history of Italy in so short a compass. That there is an implied disparagement of Cornelius' attempt is further suggested by *doctis, Iuppiter, et laboriosis*! The tomes are learned and dull; they are not certainly *nugae*. Whether Cornelius' work was ponderous or not we do not know, but, for the purposes of the poem, we are to accept that idea. The use of such overstatement or exaggeration in this poem emphasizes the understatement with which Catullus describes his own work. If on one level Cornelius' work is not a trifle, on another, and more important one, neither is Catullus'. Furthermore, we should realize always that Catullus in a real sense is advertising his own works. In the last three verses the address to Cornelius becomes a prayer to the Muse of lyric poetry that Catullus' volume last indefinitely. Observe the ambiguity of reference in *tibi* in v. 8. The modest prayer in itself embraces two notions we have already seen in the poem: the use of understatement in regard to his work and the reference to time, *saeclo*, which Cornelius could reduce to *tribus chartis*. The change of address does two things in itself. By its comparison with the earlier address to Cornelius, the change emphasizes that Catullus is concerned not only with the present but with the future, and makes clear to which of the two the poet attaches more importance. By implication one suspects that Catullus might not have had much faith in Cornelius' enduring fame, nor indeed in his capacity to appreciate the real value of these *nugae*; the Muse, on the other hand, would know their worth.

By the end of the poem we are aware that Catullus has developed a more complex notion than would at first glance appear to be the case. It is an adroit poem in that it employs a cunning device to persuade us of what the poet himself believes. We are aware that only superficially are his poems *nugae*. They are, in his eyes, of much greater importance than Cornelius' labored efforts. Further, they are highly finished poems which he devoutly hopes will outlast his time, again in contrast to Cornelius' works. The form, the organization of the poem neatly enfold, and, one might add, overcome Cornelius' work. The dedication is two-edged. It gives Cornelius thanks for encouragement, but it neatly locates Catullus' own achievement in relation to that of his friend.

QUESTIONS

1. What function do the tenses of the verbs fulfill in the organization of the poem?

2. Comment on the role of metrics in this poem.

❧

Gaius Valerius Catullus (c.84–54 B.C.)
XXII

Suffenus iste, Vare, quem probe nosti,
homo est uenustus et dicax et urbanus,
idemque longe plurimos facit uersus.
puto esse ego illi milia aut decem aut plura
5 perscripta, nec sic, ut fit, in palimpsesto
relata: chartae regiae, noui libri,
noui umbilici, lora rubra membrana,
derecta plumbo et pumice omnia aequata.
haec cum legas tu, bellus ille et urbanus
10 Suffenus unus caprimulgus aut fossor
rursus uidetur: tantum abhorret ac mutat.
hoc quid putemus esse? qui modo scurra
aut si quid hac re scitius uidebatur,
idem infaceto est infacetior rure,
15 simul poemata attigit, neque idem umquam
aeque est beatus ac poema cum scribit:
tam gaudet in se tamque se ipse miratur.
nimirum idem omnes fallimur, neque est quisquam
quem non in aliqua re uidere Suffenum
20 possis. suus cuique attributus est error;
sed non uidemus manticae quod in tergo est.

Notes

Meter: Choliambic.

1. *Suffenus*—other than for his reputation as a bad poet, he has faded, properly, one supposes, into oblivion.

Vare—unknown, but may be Quintilius Varus who is mentioned in Catullus CI.

probe nosti—a colloquialism.

3. *longe*—before Catullus rarely used for *multo*, but *longe* for *multo* later became common.

4. *aut . . . aut*—second *aut* has the meaning of "or even"; an uncommon usage.

5. *palimpsesto*—a writing fabric from which previous writing has been erased so that the fabric may be used again for later writing.

6. *relata*—in writing refers to form as *prescripta* refers to fact.
chartae regiae—i.e., the best quality of paper.

9. *legas*—subjunctive used in a general statement; a grecism.

11. *rursus*—an adversative particle.
abhorret ac mutat—understand *a se.*

12. *modō*—final syllable is long.

15. *simul*—for *simul ac.*

QUESTIONS

1. How does the image of the published book function in this poem? What are the ambiguities of the image, and how does Catullus explore them?

2. How are the words *uenustas, dicax, urbanus* (v. 2) used? What are the distinctions between them?

3. Account for the shift in tone in vv. 18–21.

4. What effect does the meter have on this poem?

∾

Publius Papinius Statius (c.40 or 45–96 A.D.)
Siluae II.4
Psittacus   *Eiusdem*

Psittace, dux uolucrum, domini facunda uoluptas,
humanae sollers imitator psittace linguae,
quis tua tam subito praeclusit murmura fato?
hesternas, miserande, dapes moriturus inisti
5 nobiscum, et gratae carpentem munera mensae
errantemque toris mediae plus tempore noctis
uidimus. affatus etiam meditataque uerba
reddideras. at nunc aeterna silentia Lethes
ille canorus habes. cedat Phaethontia uulgi
10 fabula: non soli celebrant sua funera cygni.

a tibi quanta domus rutila testudine fulgens,
conexusque ebori uirgarum argenteus ordo,
argutumque tuo stridentia limina cornu!
heu, querulae iam sponte fores! uacat ille beatus
15 carcer, et anguisti nusquam conuicia tecti!
huc doctae stipentur aues quis nobile fandi
ius natura dedit: plangat Phoebeius ales,
auditasque memor penitus dimittere uoces
sturnus, et Aonio uersae certamine picae,
20 quique refert iungens iterata uocabula perdix,
et quae Bistonio queritur soror orba cubili.
ferte simul gemitus cognataque ducite flammis
funera, et hoc cunctae miserandum addiscite carmen:
"occidit aeriae celeberrima gloria gentis
25 psittacus, ille plagae uiridis regnator Eoae;
quem non gemmata uolucris Iunonia cauda
uinceret aspectu, gelidi non Phasidis ales,
nec quas humenti Numidae rapuere sub austro."
ille salutator regum nomenque locutus
30 Caesareum et queruli quondam uice functus amici,
nunc conuiua leuis monstrataque reddere uerba
tam facilis! quo tu, Melior dilecte, recluso
numquam solus eras. at non inglorius umbris
mittitur: Assyrio cineres adolentur amomo
et tenues Arabum respirant gramine plumae
Sicaniisque crocis; senio nec fessus inerti
scandet odoratos phoenix felicior ignes.

NOTES

Meter: Dactylic Hexameter.

  6. *toris*—ablative of place where; by metonomy for "couch."

  8. *Lethes*—a Greek genitive.

  9. *Phaethontia*—Phaeton drove his father's horses, and was killed because he could not manage them.

  10. *cygni*—i.e., swans are supposed to sing their own death song in the most beautiful tones.

14. *sponte*—understand "*sua.*"
16. *quis*—for *quibus.*
17. *Phoebeius ales*—i.e., the raven.
19. *Aonio . . . certamine*—maidens who challenged the Muses and were turned to magpies. Aonia is a part of Boeotia in which is Mount Helicon, the home of the Muses.
21. *Bistonio*—i.e., Thracian.
   soror—i.e., Philomela, sister-in-law of Tereus, king of Thrace, turned into a nightingale.
26. *uolucris Iunonia cauda*—i.e., the peacock.
27. *Phasidis ales*—i.e., pheasants.
32. *Melior*—patron and friend of Statius.

QUESTIONS

1. Referring to the Thracians as Bistonians or mentioning Philomela by speaking of her sister or calling a pheasant *Phasidis Ales* are all illustrations of "learned references." Such references tend to show off the author's information and can be used for comic effect as Catullus often uses them. But when the poet employs learned references, the effect is frequently unintentionally funny, because the reader laughs at the author for his pedantry. What is the purpose of the learned allusions in this poem? What evidence can you find to support your contention? Is there any connection between the learned references and the allusions to Greek mythology?

2. The organization of the poem follows that of a typical lamentation for the dead. What are such lamentations like? Compare the details of actual funeral rites with those used in Catullus' poem CI. How does Catullus' use differ? How does Statius use them?

3. Write an essay on the use in this poem of learned references and of references to Roman obsequies.

⋖§⋗

Quintus Horatius Flaccus (65–8 B.C.)
Ode II.10

Rectius uiues, Licini, neque altum
semper urgendo neque, dum procellas
cautus horrescis, nimium premendo
    litus iniquum.

5 auream quisquis mediocritatem
diligit, tutus caret obsoleti
sordibus tecti, caret inuidenda
    sobrius aula.

saepius uentis agitatur ingens
10 pinus et celsae grauiore casu
decidunt turres feriuntque summos
    fulgura montis.

sperat infestis, metuit secundis
alteram sortem bene praeparatum
15 pectus. informis hiemes reducit
    Iuppiter, idem

summouet. non, si male nunc, et olim
sic erit: quondam cithara tacentem
suscitat Musam neque semper arcum
20   tendit Apollo.

rebus angustis animosus atque
fortis appare; sapienter idem
contrahes uento nimium secundo
    turgida uela.

Notes

Meter: Sapphic Stanza.

1. *Licini*—probably Lucius Licinius Murena, possibly a son of
the Murena defended by Cicero. Lucius Licinius Murena was
adopted by Aulus Terentius Varro and thus became a stepbrother
of Proculeius and of Terentia, the wife of Maecenas, Horace's
patron. In 23 B.C. Licinius engaged in a conspiracy against Augus-
tus for which he was condemned and executed.

    altum—the use of an adjective as a substantive by ellipsis is
common in Greek. The full phrase might be *mare altum.*

7. *inuidenda*—i.e., which arouses envy in others.

13. *infestis* and *secundis*—understand *rebus*. Both are dative.

14. *alteram sortem*—depending on the verb used the phrase means "prosperity" or "adversity."

15. *reducit*—i.e., from year to year.

17. *si male*—understand *est*.

18. *Musam*—metonomy for *carmen*.

23. *nimium secundo*—i.e., following too fast.

QUESTIONS

1. How do the metrics, the imagery, the rhetorical figures of metonomy, personification, and synechdoche, and irony help to organize this poem?

◆§◈◈

Marcus Valerius Martialis (c.40–104 A.D.)

Epigram V.8

Edictum domini deique nostri,
quo subsellia certiora fiunt
et puros eques ordines recepit,
dum laudat modo Phasis in theatro,
5   Phasis purpureis rubens lacernis,
et iactat tumido superbus ore:
"tandem commodius licet sedere,
nunc est reddita dignitas equestris;
turba non premimur, nec inquinamur."
10   haec et talia dum refert supinus,
illas purpureas et adrogantes
iussit surgere Leïtus lacernas.

NOTES

Meter: Phalaecean or Hendecasyllabic.

At Rome spectators at the theater sat in seats assigned to the various social classes: senators in the orchestra, knights in the fourteen rows behind the senators, and behind them the populace. The knights had had this privilege at least since 67 B.C. (*Lex Roscia*), but the law was unpopular, and attempts were made to circumvent it. At times the law was reinforced, e.g., *Lex Julia* of Augustus and an edict of Domitian in A.D. 89 or 88.

1. *domini deique*—appears for the first time here.

4. *Phasis*—fictitious name; describes a freedman who had, as a slave, been brought from Colchis.

5. *lacerna*—worn over the toga.

12. *Leïtus*—an "usher;" the word is a trisyllable.

QUESTIONS

1. In this obviously humorous and satirical poem we can see certain phenomena which make it so. What, for example, is the purpose of the quotation in vv. 7–9? How does it affect the tone of the poem?

2. What does the word *Phasis* (4) mean?

3. What purpose does the first verse serve? What is it reminiscent of? How does it help set the tone of the poem? In the light of the whole poem what is the ironic implication of *puros* (3)?

4. The poem is skillfully arranged so that it ends with *lacernas*, an obvious echo from v. 5, *lacernis*. However, does the word also have any further significance which might serve to underscore the irony of Phasis' pretentiousness?

⟞§⟝

Quintus Horatius Flaccus (65–8 B.C.)
Ode I.22

Integer uitae scelerisque purus
non eget Mauris iaculis neque arcu
nec uenenatis grauida sagittis,
    Fusce, pharetra,

5   siue per Syrtis iter aestuosas
siue facturus per inhospitalem
Caucasum uel quae loca fabulosus
    lambit Hydaspes.

namque me silua lupus in Sabina,
10   dum meam canto Lalagen et ultra

terminum curis uagor expeditis,
  fugit inermem,

quale portentum neque militaris
Daunias latis alit aesculetis
15 nec Iubae tellus generat, leonum
  arida nutrix.

pone me pigris ubi nulla campis
arbor aestiua recreatur aura,
quod latus mundi nebulae malusque
20   Iuppiter urget;

pone sub curru nimium propinqui
solis in terra domibus negata:
dulce ridentem Lalagen amabo,
  dulce loquentem.

NOTES

Meter: Sapphic Stanza.

1. *uitae, scelerisque*—genitives with adjectives; almost a Greek construction. Note substantive use of adjective.

4. *Fusce*—Aristus Fuscus, a poet and grammarian as well as an intimate friend of Horace.

5. *Syrtis*—the connotation is of the sandy wastes and the shifting quicksands off the northern coast of Africa.

7. *fabulosus Hydaspes*—reference to numerous marvelous tales of the region through which the river ran.

10. *Lalagen*—from the Greek λαλαγή-prattle.

14. *Daunias*—i.e., Apulia, the land of Daunus, the mythical king of the country.

15. *Iubae tellus*—i.e., Mauretania and Numidia.

17. *pone*—serves as a protasis.

19. *malus Iuppiter*—explanatory of *nebulae*; a gloomy sky.

23. *dulce ridentem*—the "internal accusative," but can also be construed as simply modifying Lalagen, the Greek accusative; the whole phrase is reminiscent of Greek.

QUESTION
How does Horace employ irony in this poem?

◆◆◆

Marcus Valerius Martialis (c.40–104 A.D.)
Epigram III.46

Exigis a nobis operam sine fine togatam:
    non eo, libertum sed tibi mitto meum.
"non est," inquis, "idem." multo plus esse probabo:
    uix ego lecticam subsequar, ille feret.
5 in turbam incideris, cunctos umbone repellet:
    inualidum est nobis ingenuumque latus.
quidlibet in causa narraueris, ipse tacebo:
    at tibi tergeminum mugiet ille sophos.
lis erit, ingenti faciet conuicia uoce:
10   esse pudor uetuit fortia uerba mihi.
"ergo nihil nobis," inquis, "praestabis amicus?"
    quidquid libertus, Candide, non poterit.

NOTES
Meter: Elegiac Couplet.

  5. *incideris*—i.e., he was not always carried.

  umbone—*umbo* of a shield, used to repel a foe; may also be used of the curb of a street, and thus by metonomy mean the road itself. If the last, it is in this sentence an ablative of separation.

  7. *narraueris*—a slang expression.

QUESTIONS
  1. What is the force of *exegis* in v. 1? What are the ambiguities of *ingenuum* (6)?

  2. Write an analysis showing how irony is used in this poem to force us to make a judgment about the man addressed and about the poem itself.

◆◆◆

Quintus Horatius Flaccus (65–8 B.C.)
Ode I.33

Albi, ne doleas plus nimio memor
immitis Glycerae neu miserabilis
decantes elegos, cur tibi iunior
    laesa praeniteat fide,

5 insignem tenui fronte Lycorida
Cyri torret amor, Cyrus in asperam
declinat Pholoen; sed prius Apulis
    iungentur capreae lupis,

quam turpi Pholoe peccet adultero.
10 sic uisum Veneri, cui placet imparis
formas atque animos sub iuga aenea
    saeuo mittere cum ioco.

ipsum me melior cum peteret Venus,
grata detinuit compede Myrtale
15 libertina, fretis acrior Hadriae
    curuantis Calabros sinus.

NOTES

Meter: Third Asclepiadean.

1. *Albi*—perhaps Albius Tibullus who died in 19 B.C. and who had been a poet and friend of Horace. Glycerae does not, however, appear in any of Tibullus' poems.

    plus nimio—"very much more," i.e., too much; *nimium* is colloquial.

2. *miserabilis*—active sense.

3. *elegos*—i.e., love poetry.

4. *praeniteat*—indirect question depends on *decantes*.

5. *tenui fronte*—low forehead because of abundant hair, hence a mark of beauty.

6. *Cyri*—objective genitive.

8. *iungetur*—reflexive, or like the Greek middle voice, "shall join (themselves)."

    lupis—ablative of accompaniment with *iungo* without *cum*; possibly a dative of association.

14. *grata . . . compede*—oxymoron.

15. *Hadriae*—frequently used by Horace to indicate roughness.

QUESTION

Write an essay on the use of irony in this poem.

❧

Gaius Valerius Catullus (c.84–54 B.C.)

XXXII

Amabo, mea dulcis Ipsilla,
meae deliciae, mei lepores,
iube ad te ueniam meridiatum.
et si iusseris illud, adiuuato,
5 ne quis liminis obseret tabellam,
neu tibi lubeat foras abire,
sed domi maneas paresque nobis
nouem continuas fututiones.
uerum, si quid ages, statim iubeto:
10 nam pransus iaceo et satur supinus
pertundo tunicamque palliumque.

Meter: Phalaecean or Hendecasyllabic.

EXERCISE

The poem depends on "double meaning" which is a form of irony. Examine how such irony works in this poem.

❧

Marcus Valerius Martialis (c.40–104 A.D.)

Epigram XI.93

Pierios uatis Theodori flamma penates
    abstulit. hoc Musis et tibi, Phoebe, placet?
o scelus, o magnum facinus crimenque deorum,
    non arsit pariter quod domus et dominus!

Meter: Elegiac Couplet.

QUESTIONS

1. What figures of speech are involved in these four lines? How do the figures affect the poem?

2. What is the significance of the call to the gods?

◈

Marcus Valerius Martialis (c.40–104 A.D.)

Epigram VII.39

Discursus uarios uagumque mane
et fastus et haue potentiorum
cum perferre patique iam negaret,
coepit fingere Caelius podagram.
5 quam dum uolt nimis adprobare ueram
et sanas linit obligatque plantas
inceditque gradu laborioso,
—quantum cura potest et ars doloris!—
desit fingere Caelius podagram.

NOTES

Meter: Phalaecean or Hendecasyllabic.
2. *haue*—i.e., salutation.

QUESTIONS

1. What function does repetition serve in this poem?

2. Where is there a change of emphasis in the poem? Why does it occur?

3. What role does meter play in the poem?

◈

Gaius Valerius Catullus (c.84–54 B.C.)

III

Lugete, o Veneres Cupidinesque,
et quantum est hominum uenustiorum!
passer mortuus est meae puellae,
passer, deliciae meae puellae,

5   quem plus illa oculis suis amabat.
nam mellitus erat suamque norat
ipsam tam bene quam puella matrem,
nec sese a gremio illius mouebat,
sed circumsiliens modo huc modo illuc
10 ad solam dominam usque pipiabat;
qui nunc it per iter tenebricosum
illud, unde negant redire quemquam.
at uobis male sit, malae tenebrae
Orci, quae omnia bella deuoratis:
15 tam bellum mihi passerem abstulistis.
o factum male! io miselle passer!
tua nunc opera meae puellae
flendo turgiduli rubent ocelli.

Notes

Meter: Phalaecean or Hendecasyllabic.

1. *Veneres Cupidinesque*—basically a grecism, for the notion of more than one Eros was common to Greek poetry. *Veneres* also suggests the conceit which sums up all the graces of mind and body.

8. *illius*—short penult.

11. *tenebricosum*—unusual, but found also in Cicero for the more usual *tenebrosum*.

12. The notion is Greek, but from the time of this poem it becomes common in Latin.

16. *miselle*—a colloquial term, used especially of the dead.

Questions

1. Observe the use of *male, malae, bella, bellum* in vv. 13–16. What meaning do they possess? What connotations do they acquire by their placement in these verses?

2. Why should *oculis* (5) be used symbolically for life itself? What are the implications of such a metaphor?

3. Hyperbole and personification are used throughout this poem. How do they prepare the way for the last two verses?

4. Compare this poem with Statius' poem on the death of the

parrot (*Siluae* II.4) and with Catullus' poem on the death of his brother (CI). Write an essay comparing all three.

❦

Gaius Valerius Catullus (c.84–54 B.C.)

XIII

Cenabis bene, mi Fabulle, apud me
paucis, si tibi di fauent, diebus,
si tecum attuleris bonam atque magnam
cenam, non sine candida puella
5   et uino et sale et omnibus cachinnis.
haec si, inquam, attuleris, uenuste noster,
cenabis bene; nam tui Catulli
plenus sacculus est aranearum.
sed contra accipies meros amores
10 seu quid suauius elegantiusue est:
nam unguentum dabo, quod meae puellae
donarunt Veneres Cupidinesque,
quod tu cum olfacies, deos rogabis,
totum ut te faciant, Fabulle, nasum.

Notes

Meter: Phalaecean or Hendecasyllabic.

9. *contra*—"in return."
10. *seu quid*—for *uel si quid.*
12. *Veneres Cupidinesque*—see note on Catullus III.1.

Questions

1. What are the meanings of *sale* (5)?
2. Analyze the imagery of the poem.
3. Analyze the tone of the poem. How is it achieved and what effect does it have?

❦

Marcus Valerius Martialis (c.40–104 A.D.)

Epigram I.27

Hesterna tibi nocte dixeramus,

quincunces puto post decem peractos,
cenares hodie, Procille, mecum.
tu factam tibi rem statim putasti
5 et non sobria uerba subnotasti
exemplo nimium periculoso:
μισῶ μνάμονα συμπόταν, Procille.

NOTES

Meter: Phalaecean or Hendecasyllabic.

2. *quincunces*—a *quincunx* was 5/12 of any whole. Here it is 5/12 of the *sextarius* which is 1/6 of a *congius* or 3.283 liters. A *sextarius vini* was a more than adequate amount to take at a meal (Horace, *S.* I.1.74).

7. μισῶ etc.—"I hate a table companion who remembers." *Procille*—a grecism, probably, for πρo + κίλλος—*asinus*.

QUESTIONS

1. Explain the use of the Greek in v. 7. What relationship does it have to the proper name? What purpose, then, does the whole line have in the light of the poem?

2. Compare the tone, imagery, and effectiveness of this poem with those same qualities in Catullus XIII.

◄§§►

Claudius Claudianus (c.395–404 A.D.)
Epigram XX
Felix, qui patriis aeuum transegit in agris,
    ipsa domus puerum quem uidet, ipsa senem:
qui baculo nitens, in qua reptauit harena,
    unius numerat saecula longa casae.
5 illum non uario traxit fortuna tumultu,
    nec bibit ignotas mobilis hospes aquas.
non freta mercator tremuit, non classica miles:
    non rauci lites pertulit ille fori.
indocilis rerum, uicinae nescius urbis,
10   adspectu fruitur liberiore poli.

frugibus alternis, non consule, computat annum:
    autumnum pomis, uer sibi flore notat.
idem condit ager soles idemque reducit,
    metiturque suo rusticus orbe diem;
15 ingentem meminit paruo qui germine quercum,
    aequaeuumque uidet consenuisse nemus:
proxima cui nigris uerona remotior Indis,
    Benacumque putat litora rubra lacum;
sed tamen indomitae uires, firmisque lacertis
20   aetas robustum tertia cernit auum.
erret, ex extremos alter scrutetur Hiberos;
    plus habet hic uitae, plus habet ille uiae.

NOTES

Meter: Elegiac Couplet.

8. *fori*—because it was the center of banking, business, and law courts.

15. *germine*—ablative of origin.

18. *Benacum*—i.e., Lago di Garda.

21. *erret*—subject is *alter* to be understood from the *alter* in the verse.

QUESTIONS

1. Examine the position and usage of the relative pronouns in this poem. What effect does the poet achieve by them?

2. What is the meaning of *classica* (7) and what are its connotations?

3. How is the poem divided and how are the parts arranged?

4. Examine the use of the rhetorical figure of chiasmus. Is its repetition justified? How does the poet vary the effect? What other devices does he use in the poem?

5. Does the poem justify the assertion of the opening line? Explain.

      ⋞§⋟

Gaius Valerius Catullus (c.84–54 B.C.)

VII

Quaeris quot mihi basiationes

tuae, Lesbia, sint satis superque.
quam magnus numerus Libyssae harenae
lasarpiciferis iacet Cyrenis,
5 oraclum Iouis inter aestuosi
et Batti ueteris sacrum sepulcrum;
aut quam sidera multa, cum tacet nox,
furtiuos hominum uident amores,
tam te basia multa basiare
10 uesano satis et super Catullo est,
quae nec pernumerare curiosi
possint nec mala fascinare lingua.

NOTES

Meter: Phalaecean or Hendecasyllabic.

1. *basiationes*—colloquial.

2. *tuae*—subjective.

4. *Cyrenis*—Cyrene, capital of Cyrenaica, a district of Libya, was founded in the seventh century B.C. by the Greek Battus (his real name was Aristotles) from Thera. It was a center of trade, birthplace of Eratosthenes, Aristippus, and Callimachus.

5. *oraclum Iouis*—the Egyptian Ammon had a famous temple and oracle in the oasis of Siwah in the Libyan desert 400 miles from Cyrene; he is identified with Zeus and Jupiter.

6. *sacrum sepulcrum*—the tomb of the founder, who was revered as a god, stood in the city of Cyrene.

9. *te*—subject of *basiare*.
basia—cognate accusative.

QUESTIONS

1. Explain how the final two verses (11–12) depend upon and expand the imagery of the earlier lines of the poem. What is the distinction between the two comparisons, the sands and the stars, and what unites them?

2. What relation do the first two lines have to the rest of the poem?

3. What irony is there in this poem? How are learned references used in the poem?

Marcus Valerius Martialis (c.40–104 A.D.)

Epigram I.68

Quidquid agit Rufus, nihil est nisi Naeuia Rufo.
    si gaudet, si flet, si tacet, hanc loquitur.
cenat, propinat, poscit, negat, innuit: una est
    Naeuia; si non sit Naeuia, mutus erit.
5 scriberet hesterna patri cum luce salutem,
    "Naeuia lux," inquit, "Naeuia lumen, haue."
haec legit et ridet demisso Naeuia voltu.
    Naeuia non una est: quid, uir inepte, furis?

Meter: Elegiac Couplet.

QUESTIONS

1. In this poem vv. 1–6 describe an infatuated lover. What happens in vv. 7–8? What are the possible ambiguities of *haec* in v. 7? How does this word serve as the pivot on which the following verse turns?

2. What are the implications of the last verse?

❧

Gaius Valerius Catullus (c.84–54 B.C.)

XLIX

Disertissime Romuli nepotum,
quot sunt quotque fuere, Marce Tulli,
quotque post aliis erunt in annis,
gratias tibi maximas Catullus
5 agit pessimus omnium poeta,
tanto pessimus omnium poeta,
quanto tu optimus omnium patronus.

NOTES

Meter: Phalaecean or Hendecasyllabic.

4–5. *gratias . . . agit*—a common formula in Cicero's letters.

7. *optimus omnium patronus*—Cicero was a patron of many Italian towns. The position of the words suggests one of the titles actually given to Cicero (*Ad Fam.* VI.7.4): *ubi hoc omnium*

patronus facis quid me ueterem tuum nunc omnium clientem
sentire oportet.

QUESTIONS

1. The epithet *disertissime* (1) is frequently used by Cicero
with the connotation of high praise. What is the point of its use
here? How does it function in relation to the rest of v. 1? What
purpose does the formal address, *Marci Tulli*, serve in connection
with v. 1?

2. What purpose do the superlatives have in this poem?

3. Carefully examine the use of *omnium* in vv. 5–7.

4. If irony appears in this poem, explain how it is used.

5. How does the meter aid in the understanding of this poem?
Scan the poem and note the metrics.

❧

Petronius Arbiter (d. 66 A.D.)

    Foeda est in coitu et breuis uoluptas,
    et taedet Veneris statim peractae.
    non ergo ut pecudes libidinosae
    caeci protinus irruamus illuc,
5 nam languescit amor peritque flamma.
    sed sic sic sine fine feriati
    et tecum iaceamus osculantes.
    hic nullus labor est ruborque nullus:
    hoc iuuit, iuuat et diu iuuabit;
10 hoc non deficit incipitque semper.

Meter: Phalaecean or Hendecasyllabic.

QUESTION

Examine the tone of this poem and how it is achieved. What
part do rhetorical figures play in the poem?

❧

Quintus Horatius Flaccus (65–8 B.C.)
Ode I.38

Persicos odi, puer, apparatus,
displicent nexae philyra coronae;
mitte sectari, rosa quo locorum
    sera moretur.
5 simplici myrto nihil allabores
sedulus curo: neque te ministrum
dedecet myrtus neque me sub arta
    uite bibentem.

Notes

Meter: Sapphic Stanza.

  1. *apparatus*—the *ad* as in *allabores* (5) suggests excess.
    puer—i.e., a slave.

  2. *nexae philyra coronae*—i.e., garlands made by sewing flowers
on a strip of the inner bark or bast of the linden tree. Such garlands
were often of great elegance when professionally made.

  3. *mitte sectari*—periphrasis for prohibition; *mitte* for *omitte.*
    locorum—partitive genitive.

  5. *simplici myrto*—dative with *allabores*, which is a verb of a
substantive clause dependent on *curo.*

  6. *sedulus*—goes with both verbs.
    ministrum—the opposite of *magister.*

Questions

  1. Explain the rhetorical figures used in the first stanza.

  2. What purpose do they serve?

  3. Explain *nihil* in v. 5. Why is it chosen? What effect does it
have?

  4. Write an analysis of the poem.

❦§❧

Publius Ovidius Naso (43 B.C.–18 A.D.)
Heroides I
Penelope Vlixi

Hanc tua Penelope lento tibi mittit, Vlixe;
nil mihi rescribas at tamen ipse ueni!

Troia iacet certe Danais inuisa puellis:
uix Priamus tanti totaque Troia fuit.
5 o utinam tum, cum Lacedaemona classe petebat,
    obrutus insanis esset adulter aquis!
non ego deserto iacuissem frigida lecto;
    non quererer tardos ire relicta dies
nec mihi quaerenti spatiosam fallere noctem
10   lassasset uiduas pendula tela manus.
quando ego non timui grauiora pericula ueris?
    res est solliciti plena timoris amor.
in te fingebam uiolentos troas ituros,
    nomine in Hectoreo pallida semper eram;
15 siue quis Antilochum narrabat ab Hectore uictum,
    Antilochus nostri causa timoris erat;
siue Menoetiaden falsis cecidisse sub armis,
    flebam successu posse carere dolos;
sanguine Tlepolemus Lyciam tepefecerat hastam:
20   Tlepolemi leto cura nouata mea est;
denique, quisquis erat castris iugulatus Achiuis,
    frigidius glacie pectus amantis erat.
sed bene consuluit casto deus aequus amori:
    uersa est in cineres sospite Troia uiro.
25 Argolici rediere duces: altaria fumant;
    ponitur ad patrios barbara praeda deos;
grata ferunt nymphae pro saluis dona maritis,
    illi uicta suis Troica fata canunt;
mirantur iustique senes trepidaeque puellae,
30   narrantis coniunx pendet ab ore uiri.
atque aliquis posita monstrat fera proelia mensa,
    pingit et exiguo Pergama tota mero:
"hac ibat Simois, haec est Sigeia tellus,
    hic steterat Priami regia celsa senis;
35 illic Aeacides, illic tendebat Vlixes,
    hic lacer admissos terruit Hector equos."
omnia namque tuo senior te quaerere misso
    rettulerat nato Nestor, at ille mihi.

rettulit et ferro Rhesumque Dolonaque caesos,
40   utque sit hic somno proditus, ille dolo.
ausus es, o nimium nimiumque oblite tuorum,
      Thracia nocturno tangere castra dolo
totque simul mactare uiros, adiutus ab uno!
      at bene cautus eras et memor ante mei!
45 usque metu micuere sinus, dum uictor amicum
      dictus es Ismariis isse per agmen equis.
sed mihi quid prodest uestris disiecta lacertis
      Ilios et, murus quod fuit, esse solum,
si maneo, qualis Troia durante manebam,
50   uirque mihi dempto fine carendus abest?
diruta sunt aliis, uni mihi Pergama restant,
      incola captiuo quae boue uictor arat.
iam seges est, ubi Troia fuit, resecandaque falce
      luxuriat Phrygio sanguine pinguis humus;
55 semisepulta uirum curuis feriuntur aratris
      ossa; ruinosas occulit herba domos.
uictor abes nec scire mihi, quae causa morandi
      aut in quo lateas ferreus orbe, licet!
quisquis ad haec uertit peregrinam litora puppim,
60   ille mihi de te multa rogatus abit,
quamque tibi reddat, si te modo uiderit usquam,
      traditur huic digitis charta notata meis.
nos Pylon, antiqui Neleia Nestoris arua,
      misimus: incerta est fama remissa Pylo;
65 misimus et Sparten: Sparte quoque nescia ueri.
      quas habitas terras aut ubi lentus abes?
utilius starent etiamnunc moenia Phoebi:
      (irascor uotis heu! leuis ipsa meis)
scirem, ubi pugnares, et tantum bella timerem,
70   et mea cum multis iuncta querela foret.
quid timeam, ignoro; timeo tamen omnia demens
      et patet in curas area lata meas;
quaecumque aequor habet, quaecumque pericula tellus,
      tam longae causas suspicor esse morae.

75 haec ego dum stulte metuo, quae uestra libido est,
   esse peregrino captus amore potes.
forsitan et narres, quam sit tibi rustica coniunx,
   quae tantum lanas non sinat esse rudes.
fallar, et hoc crimen tenues uanescat in auras,
80   neue, reuertendi liber, abesse uelis!
me pater Icarius uiduo discedere lecto
   cogit et inmensas increpat usque moras.
increpet usque licet: tua sum, tua dicar oportet:
   Penelope coniunx semper Vlixis ero.
85 ille tamen pietate mea precibusque pudicis
   frangitur et uires temperat ipse suas.
Dulichii Samiique et quos tulit alta Zacynthos,
   turba ruunt in me luxuriosa proci
inque tua regnant nullis prohibentibus aula;
90   uiscera nostra, tuae dilacerantur opes.
quid tibi Pisandrum Polybumque Medontaque dirum
   Eurymachique auidas Antinoique manus
atque alios referam, quos omnis turpiter absens
   ipse tuo partis sanguine rebus alis?
95 Irus egens pecorisque Melanthius actor edendi
   ultimus accedunt in tua damna pudor.
tres sumus inbelles numero, sine uiribus uxor
   Laertesque senex Telemachusque puer.
ille per insidias paene est mihi nuper ademptus,
100   dum parat inuitis omnibus ire Pylon;
di, precor, hoc iubeant, ut euntibus ordine fatis
   ille meos oculos comprimat, ille tuos.
hic faciunt custosque boum longaeuaque nutrix,
   tertius inmundae cura fidelis harae!
105 sed neque Laertes, ut qui sit inutilis armis,
   hostibus in mediis regna tenere potest.
Telemacho ueniet, uiuat modo, fortior aetas:
   nunc erat auxiliis illa tuenda patris;
nec mihi sunt uires inimicos pellere tectis:
110   tu citius uenias, portuas et ara tuis!

est tibi sitque, precor, natus, qui mollibus annis
　　in patrias artes erudiendus erat;
respice Laerten: ut iam sua lumina condas,
　　extremum fati sustinet ille diem;
115　certe ego, quae fueram te discedente puella,
　　protinus ut uenias, facta uidebor anus.

NOTES

Meter: Elegiac Couplet.

　1. *Vlixe*—vocative, like the Greek.

　2. *ueni*—the penult is short.

　4. *tanti*—genitive of value.

　7. the protasis is implied from the preceding verses.

　15. *Antilochum*—son of Nestor; Greek warrior at Troy; slain by Memnon.

　17. *Menoetiaden*—Patroclus, son of Menoetius, friend of Achilles. While wearing Achilles' armor, he was killed by Hector.

　19. *Tlepolemus*—son of Hercules and Astyoche; led Rhodians against Troy and was slain by Sarpedon, king of Lycia.

　28. *illi*—i.e., *mariti* who fought at Troy.

　35. *Aeacides*—both Peleus, father of Achilles, and Telamon, father of Ajax, were sons of Aeacus. Achilles is meant.

　36. *admissos*—i.e., at full speed; lit. "given the rein."

　37. *quaerere*—infinitive of purpose.

　39. *Rhesum*—Thracian king who came to aid the Trojans, but Ulysses and Diomed entered his camp and killed him on the night of his arrival in order to capture his horses.

　　Dolon—Trojan scout killed by a trick on the same expedition.

　40. *ut*—"how."

　46. *Ismariis*—of Ismarus, a mountain in Thrace.

　48. *Ilios*—a Greek nominative.

　60. *mihi*—dative of person interested, "from me."

　63. *Pylon*—Nestor, son of Neleus and ruler of Pylos.

　64. *missimus*—used absolutely of messenger.

　75. *uestra*—the "generalizing plural."

　79. *fallar*—subjunctive of wish.

80. *reuertendi liber*—"free to return," i.e., free (for the purpose) of returning; a grecism.

87. *Dulichum*—island at the mouth of the Achilous.

Samos—island off the coast of Asia Minor.

Zacynthos—now Zante, one of a group of islands near Ithaca.

90. *uiscera*—used of children; syllepsis occurs with *dilacerantur*.

91. names of suitors.

94. *tuo sanguine*—qualifies *partis*.

99. *ademptus*—the suitors tried to kill Telemachus when he went to Pylos to seek news of his father, but Minerva (Athena) saved him.

104. *cura*—i.e., Eumaeus, the swineherd.

105. *ut qui sit*—clause of characteristic.

108. *erat*—the "imperfect of neglected duty."

109. *pellere*—infinitive of purpose.

116. *ut*—adversative.

QUESTIONS

1. The poem is one of a group Ovid wrote using the fictional device of a woman writing to a man who has for some reason left her. In this instance it is Penelope writing to Ulysses. The tale comes, of course, in general from the *Odyssey*. Nevertheless the poem stands on its own and can be evaluated without reference to that source. What effect does the epistolary device achieve? In this instance what tone does the poem have?

2. Quite clearly the device of the letter forces one particular viewpoint, that of the writer, which may not be that of the author. How does Ovid solve the problem of letting us know what he thinks about the matter? How are we informed about the Trojan War and its effects not only on Penelope but on Ulysses as well?

3. Carefully examine vv. 1–4. What subjects are suggested there? Is there any evidence from the rest of the poem that they are developed? What judgment does the poem make on war? How is this judgment heightened or reinforced by the device of the epistle? What values seem especially regarded by the poet as worthy of man's attention? What do all these have in common; that is, how are they related?

4. This poem is a plea of a wife for the return of her husband who has gone to war and who has been delayed in returning home. But threaded throughout the poem is an equally serious concern for the possibility that Ulysses may have found another love. The notion is expressed most clearly in vv. 75–76. What other passages suggest or hint at this same concern? Though the war might be any war, in actuality it is not, it is the Trojan War. Why is this fact important, and how does the poet make us aware of it?

5. Rhetorical figures abound in the poem. Besides those already discussed in this chapter, another occurs in v. 90, that of syllepsis. This figure is often confused with zeugma, but a distinction should be observed between the two. Both figures arise when the relationship of a single word to two other words seems to be but is not the same. For example, he lost his hat and his temper. The distinction between zeugma and syllepsis is that syllepsis is grammatically correct, but requires the single word to be understood in a different sense with each member of the pair. In zeugma the single word is grammatically correct with only one of the other two, e.g., with *weeping* eyes and hearts. Weeping goes only with *eyes*, for hearts do not weep. In v. 90 of this poem the figure is syllepsis, for *uiscera* and *opes* are both correct with *dilacerantur*; only a shift in the meaning in that word is required. What is the purpose of the syllepsis here? Is it effective? Observe and comment on the other rhetorical figures in the poem, indicating their effectiveness or lack of it.

6. Carefully examine the organization of topics in the poem. What pattern becomes clear? How does this reinforce the subject and themes of the poem? What is the effect of the last two lines?

7. Explain the imagery of the poem.

☙§❧

Sextus Propertius (c.50–c.16 B.C.)

Elegy I.3

Qualis Thesea iacuit cedente carina
languida desertis Cnosia litoribus;

qualis et accubuit primo Cepheia somno
  libera iam duris cotibus Andromede;
5 nec minus assiduis Edonis fessa choreis
  qualis in herboso concidit Apidano:
talis uisa mihi mollem spirare quietem
  Cynthia non certis nixa caput manibus,
ebria cum multo traherem uestigia Baccho,
10 et quaterent sera nocte facem pueri.
hanc ego, nondum etiam sensus deperditus omnis,
  molliter impresso conor adire toro;
et quamuis duplici correptum ardore iuberent
  hac Amor hac Liber, durus uterque deus,
15 subiecto leuiter positam temptare lacerto
  osculaque admota sumere †et arma† manu,
non tamen ausus eram dominae turbare quietem,
  expertae metuens iurgia saeuitiae;
sed sic intentis haerebam fixus ocellis,
20 Argus ut ignotis cornibus Inachidos.
et modo soluebam nostra de fronte corollas
  ponebamque tuis, Cynthia, temporibus;
et modo gaudebam lapsos formare capillos;
  nunc furtiua cauis poma dabam manibus;
25 omniaque ingrato largibar munera somno,
  munera de prono saepe uoluta sinu;
et quotiens raro duxti suspiria motu,
  obstupui uano credulus auspicio,
ne qua tibi insolitos portarent uisa timores,
30 neue quis inuitam cogeret esse suam:
donec diuersas praecurrens luna fenestras,
  luna moraturis sedula luminibus,
compositos leuibus radiis patefecit ocellos.
  sic ait in molli fixa toro cubitum:
35 "tandem te nostro referens iniuria lecto
  alterius clausis expulit e foribus?
namque ubi longa meae consumpsti tempora noctis,
  languidus exactis, ei mihi, sideribus?

o utinam talis perducas, improbe, noctes,
40   me miseram qualis semper habere iubes!
nam modo purpureo fallebam stamine somnum,
      rursus et Orpheae carmine, fessa, lyrae;
interdum leuiter mecum deserta querebar
      externo longas saepe in amore moras:
45 dum me iucundis lapsam sopor impulit alis.
      illa fuit lacrimis ultima cura meis."

NOTES

Meter: Elegiac Couplet.

1. *carina*—by synecdoche for ships.

2. *Cnosia*—i.e., Crete; Cnossos is the home of Minos, father of Ariadne.

3. *Cepheia*—daughter of Cepheus, king of Ethiopia.

5. *Edonis*—the Edoni lived in Thrace and were associated with the worship of Bacchus.

16. *et arma*—felt to be "an almost impossibly harsh zeugma with *oscula*," but suggested emendations are not satisfactory. The text might well be left alone. A passage with daggers indicates a difficulty in the text which seems incapable of solution.

20. *ignotis cornibus*—dative with *haerebam*.

44. *saepe*—understand an *esse*.

QUESTIONS

1. What is the occasion of the poem?

2. What function do the three metaphors from mythology serve?

3. Examine the connotations of the following words: *iuberent* (13), *durus* (14), *arma* (16), *metuens urgia saeuitiae* (18), and compare them with *obstupui* (28), *insolitos timores* (29), *cogeret, inuitam* (30). What do these clusters of words reveal about love or the lover's attitude and the context in which they appear? What figures of speech, if any, are involved with these words?

4. Explain the shift in point of view in v. 35. Why does the point of view not return to that of the opening passage? What relationship does Cynthia's speech have to the rest of the poem? How does

the speech fit in with the mythological references found earlier in the poem? Explain v. 46 with regard to the whole poem.

※§※

Quintus Horatius Flaccus (65–8 B.C.)
Ode III.7

Quid fles, Asterie, quem tibi candidi
primo restituent uere Fauonii
    Thyna merce beatum,
        constantis iuuenem fide

5 Gygen? ille Notis actus ad Oricum
post insana Caprae sidera frigidas
    noctes non sine multis
        insomnis lacrimis agit.

atqui sollicitae nuntius hospitae,
10 suspirare Chloen et miseram tuis
    dicens ignibus uri,
        temptat mille uafer modis.

ut Proetum mulier perfida credulum
falsis impulerit criminibus nimis
15   casto Bellerophontae
        maturare necem refert:

narrat paene datum Pelea Tartaro,
Magnessam Hippolyten dum fugit abstinens;
    et peccare docentis
20   fallax historias monet.

frustra: nam scopulis surdior Icari
uoces audit adhuc integer. at tibi
    ne uicinus Enipeus
        plus iusto placeat caue;

25 quamuis non alius flectere equum sciens
aeque conspicitur gramine Martio,
    nec quisquam citus aeque
        Tusco denatat alueo.

prima nocte domum claude neque in uias
30   sub cantu querulae despice tibiae,
et te saepe uocanti
duram difficilis mane.

NOTES

Meter: Fourth Asclepiadean.

1. *fles*—the object grammatically is an understood *eum* as antecedent of *quem* and with which *iuuenem* and *Gygen* are in apposition.

Asterie—"star bright," "radiant as the stars."

candidi—i.e., bringing fair weather.

3. *Thyna*—i.e., Bithynia.

4. *fide*—an early form of the genitive.

6. *insana Caprae sidera*—"the mad constellation of the Goat," i.e., referring to stormy weather at its rising. Its evening rising occurred about 1 October; hence the time is autumn.

9. *sollicitae*—understand *amore.*

12. *uafer*—the adjective has adverbial force, or it is to be construed with *mille modis*, as "artful" or "crafty."

13. *Proetum mulier perfida*—the *mulier perfida* was Antea or Sthenoboea. Proetus, king of Tiryns, was her husband. She had fallen in love with Bellerophon who rejected her. Angered, she went to her husband, accused Bellerophon of having made improper proposals. Proetus, unwilling to kill Bellerophon, dispatched him to Iobates, king of Lycia, with instructions to put Bellerophon to death, whereupon Iobates sent Bellerophon to fight the chimera.

15. *Bellerophontae*—a Greek genitive.

16. *maturare*—infinitive with *impello* is poetic.

17. *Pelea*—Hippolyte, wife of king Acastus, the Thessalian, had fallen in love with Peleus. The same general story is alluded to as in the earlier reference to the wife of Proteus. *Magnessam* indicates who the lady was and distinguished her from the Amazon, *Hippolyte.*

21. *surdior*—with *audit* the word forms an oxymoron.

26. *aeque*—with *sciens* and *conspicitur*.

28. *denatat*—"swims down." The word is found only here.

31. *uocanti*—adversative; the case depends on *difficilis*.

EXERCISE

Write an essay in which you explain the use of the rhetorical figures and the imagery.

&§&

Quintus Horatius Flaccus (65–8 B.C.)

Epode III

Parentis olim si quis impia manu
    senile guttur fregerit,
edit cicutis alium nocentius.
    o dura messorum ilia!
5 quid hoc ueneni saeuit in praecordiis?
    num uiperinus his cruor
incoctus herbis me fefellit, an malas
    Canidia tractauit dapes?
ut Argonautas praeter omnis candidum
10   Medea mirata est ducem,
ignota tauris illigaturum iuga
    perunxit hoc Iasonem;
hoc delibutis ulta donis paelicem
    serpente fugit alite.
15 nec tantus umquam siderum insedit uapor
    siticulosae Apuliae,
nec munus umeris efficiacis Herculis
    inarsit aestuosius.
at si quid umquam tale concupiueris,
20   iocose Maecenas, precor
manum puella sauio opponat tuo,
    extrema et in sponda cubet.

NOTES

Meter: Iambic Stanza.

2. *fregerit*—future perfect.

3. *edit*—archaic subjunctive form of *edat*.

7. *incoctus me fefellit*—i.e., it has been brewed without my knowing it.

8. *Canidia*—name of a sorceress.

9. *ut*—temporal, "when."

10. *Medea*—the prototype of the poisoner.
    ducem—i.e., Jason.

11. *ignota . . . iuga*—one of Jason's tasks imposed by Aeetes when Jason sought the golden fleece was the yoking of the fire-breathing bulls. Medea's magic helped him accomplish the task.

12. *hoc*—i.e., garlic.

13. *hoc*—the reference is to the cloak and diadem presented by Medea to Creusa, the daughter of Creon, whereby that young princess was destroyed, for as soon as Creusa put them on they burst into flame. The cause for such revenge was Jason's abandonment of Medea for Creusa.

14. *serpente alite*—singular for plural.

17. *nec munus*, etc.—allusion to the cloak Nessus gave Deineira. Nessus, the Centaur, as he was dying from a wound inflicted by Hercules, had dipped the cloak into his poisonous blood. Deineira, unaware of this fact, sent the cloak to Hercules when he fell in love with Iole to try to prevent that alliance by reminding him of her love. The poisoned cloak killed Hercules.

18. *aestuosius*—predicate.

20. *Maecenas*—Augustus' intimate and Horace's patron.

21. *sauio*—dative with *opponat*.
    opponat, cubet—subjunctive of wish possible of realization. Very possibly the verbs depend on *precor* with a suppressed *ut*. But, if *precor* is parenthetical, then the verbs are independent subjunctives.

EXERCISE

Examine and explain the tone of the poem.

◈

Sextus Propertius (c.50–c.16 B.C.)
Elegy I.16

"Quae fueram magnis olim patefacta triumphis,
    ianua Tarpeiae nota pudicitiae;
cuius inaurati celebrarunt limina currus,
    captorum lacrimis umida supplicibus;
5 nunc ego, nocturnis potorum saucia rixis,
    pulsata indignis saepe queror manibus,
et mihi non desunt turpes pendere corollae
    semper ex exclusis signa iacere faces.
nec possum infamis dominae defendere noctes,
10   nobilis obscenis tradita carminibus;
(nec tamen illa suae reuocatur parcere famae,
    purior et saecli uiuere luxuria.)
has inter grauibus cogor deflere querelis,
    supplicis a longis tristior excubiis.
15 ille meos numquam patitur requiescere postis,
    arguta referens carmina blanditia:
'Ianua uel domina penitus crudelior ipsa,
    quid mihi tam duris clausa taces foribus?
cur numquam reserata meos admittis amores,
20   nescia furtiuas reddere mota preces?
nullane finis erit nostro concessa dolori,
    turpis et in tepido limine somnus erit?
me mediae noctes, me sidera plena iacentem,
    frigidaque Eoo me dolet aura gelu:
25 tu sola humanos numquam miserata dolores
    respondes tacitis mutua cardinibus.
O utinam traiecta caua mea uocula rima
    percussas dominae uertat in auriculas!
sit licet et saxo patientior illa Sicano,
30   sit licet et ferro durior et chalybe,
non tamen illa suos poterit compescere ocellos,
    surget et inuitis spiritus in lacrimis.
nunc iacet alterius felici nixa lacerto,
    at mea nocturno uerba cadunt Zephyro.
35 sed tu sola mei tu maxima causa doloris,
    uicta meis numquam, ianua, muneribus.

te non ulla meae laesit petulantia linguae,
  quae solet †irato dicere tota loco†,
ut me tam longa raucum patiare querela
40   sollicitas triuio peruigilare moras.
at tibi saepe nouo deduxi carmina uersu,
  osculaque impressis nixa dedi gradibus.
ante tuos quotiens uerti me, perfida, postis,
  debitaque occultis uota tuli manibus!'
45 haec ille et si quae miseri nouistis amantes,
  et matutinis obstrepit alitibus.
sic ego nunc dominae uitiis et semper amantis
  fletibus aeterna differor inuidia."

NOTES

Meter: Elegiac Couplet.

2. *pudicitae*—descriptive genitive with either *ianua* or *nota*; probably both.

9–10. *infamis*—may be accusative plural with *noctes* or genitive singular with *dominae*; but the latter is suspect, for *dominae* is probably a dative with *defendere*.

12. *purior*—so difficult is this passage of interpretation if *turpior*, which appears in mss., is retained that I, following Enk and Fonteine, prefer *purior*.

13. *haec inter*—*inter* is post positive, "anastrophe."

14. *a*—the preposition used to express cause or instrument; not the *a* of exclamation.

38. *irato . . . loco*—an extremely vexed passage; *tota* may be a colloquialism for *omnia*, but if so the usage is unusual.

47. *semper*—probably with *amantis*.

QUESTIONS

1. In the light of the entire poem, explain the significance of *Tarpeiae*.

2. Contrast vv. 1 to 4 and 5 to 8. What do the triumphs become?

3. The poem employs the literary conceit known as the "paraclausitheron," the song at the door sung usually by a lover. But in this poem the door itself does the talking. It describes clearly the

shame it feels for what is going on inside the house. Carefully observe how the door describes itself in the first eight verses. What is the function of the proper name in v. 2? How does it add an ironic effect to the opening of the poem? Does this suggest that there may be more irony in the first eight verses than first appears? How does the arrangement of the verses suggest this? Verse 8 contains *et exclusis signa iacere faces*. What ironic notion is there in these words? What does *faces* mean and what does it connote?

4. Verses 9–14 describe the current state of the door. Comment on how the lines are connected to the preceding passage. Is there any ambiguity in the use of *defendere* in v. 9? How does this ambiguity affect vv. 10–14? What does this suggest then about the door and the mistress of the house? Is there an ironic suggestion in the use of *carminibus* in v. 10? What does the word connote? What does *supplicis* in v. 14 suggest? How has this same word been employed earlier in the poem? What is the effect of this repetition?

5. The scene shifts to the excluded lover who begins a long lament to the door. What is the purpose of this change? Why is the door made to report what the shutout lover says? Examine the use of *carmina* in v. 16.

6. The suitor's lament begins with a series of questions. What effect is achieved by them? What is the arrangement of the questions? How do they in any way justify *arguta . . . blanditia* (16)? In the address to the door what becomes clear about the nature of the door? How is it too a symbol? How does v. 22 reflect this suggestion?

7. Examine the contrast between vv. 23 and 24 and vv. 25 and 26. What effect is achieved by this contrast? In the light of what has been suggested earlier, how do these verses achieve an even further ironic effect?

8. The passage from v. 27 to v. 32 is connected with the previous one in what way? What point is made by the description of the girl? Why should she weep? What does this suggest about the particular sense involved? What comment is implied in sight? How does this form a contrast with the time of the whole drama of the poem?

9. The time of day when all the action is taking place continues to be stated in the following passage. How does it reinforce what has been suggested before?

10. Verse 36 refers again to the door, and the address continues in verse 37. Carefully examine these verses in the light of the organization of the suitor's song. What has definitely happened now to the suggested symbolism of the door? What does the suitor do? Why?

11. The poem moves rapidly to its conclusion in the last four verses. Carefully examine these verses to discover whether there is any indication that the character of the door is changed from the earlier speech of the door itself. What is the final effect of the poem?

12. This poem has been called an *apologia* for the door. In what way is such an epithet justified? Does the door succeed in achieving its aim?

13. As we examine the poem, the irony and the paradox become clear. But is there not a further irony implicit in the whole poem? The poem is, after all, about the door which excludes the would-be suitor or lover. What sort of man is he? In the light of your familiarity with the Roman character and the emphasis placed on what are called the "Roman virtues," how does the character of such a man as this poem implies compare with those qualities? Is the man a slave or a free man? What does this suggest about the lover? Has some change come over the Roman man? How would the Roman as he is pictured in most handbooks like this kind of poem? What might be the implications of our assumptions based on the handbooks?

14. Write an essay discussing the "modern" sensibility of this poem.

ADDITIONAL EXERCISES

Not all the rhetorical figures used in poetry are cited in this section. Return to Horace's *Ode* I.30, lines 5–6. The arrangement of the phrase *puer et salutis/ Gratiae zonis properentque* shows an interlocked word order: the nominatives alternate with the ablatives. What effect does such an arrangement have here? This figure, called synchysis, is common in Latin poetry, and one should especially observe how effective its usage is. Examine Horace's *Ode* II.16 for the use of this figure, and comment on its effectiveness.

Another device found primarily in poetry and sometimes in prose is the use of constructions which derive from Greek. The notes have called attention to grecisms so that the reader should be familiar with some of them. On the one hand they betray the indebtedness of Latin poetry to ancient Greek poetry, but they also serve as a kind of rhetorical figure. Review how they are used in Catullus IV, XXXI, LI, Horace's *Ode* I.4. Do they contribute to the purpose of these poems? Would it be easier or better to have used Latin rather than Greek constructions? Is there a gain or a loss? In what way do they affect the tone? Observe also the other indications of grecisms in other poems. Can one generalize to any purpose about the use of grecisms?

The discussion of rhetorical figures presented in this chapter is not meant to be exhaustive. Poems appearing later in this book will employ other figures which will be noted. Nor are the names for the figures of primary importance. The figures serve a useful function in that they eliminate the need for elaborate periphrasis. The important point, however, is to become aware of the placement of words and to understand how a particular collocation is effective in a poem. The more we observe these phenomena, the more familiar they become, the more the reading of poetry becomes a meaningful experience for us. Like other parts of a poem, they encourage us to read sensitively in order to appreciate what the poem is saying.

A final set of questions might be asked on the use of rhetorical figures. What effect does Latin as an inflected language have on the employment of these figures? Is there any connection between the use of rhetorical figures and the fact that endings for different cases in Latin are the same? Do the Roman poets exploit, for example, the fact that the ablative and dative cases of the various declensions show frequently the same endings in the singular and always the same endings in the plural? Often one finds the form *deum* for *deorum* or *tuum* for *tuorum*. Might this similarity be used deliberately by a poet to create certain effects? Are rhetorical figures easier or more difficult to employ in Latin than in English? Does their use permit us to generalize about the mental habits of Roman authors? About their way of expressing ideas and emotions? What relationship might there be between Latin as a language and the attitudes of Roman poets?

THEME AND STATEMENT
6

Poets make statements about experiences. In doing so they must use words which are concepts. Though words may indicate some feeling and summon up remembrances of sensual impressions, they do so by reason of their conceptual identity. Hence in any poem ideas such as *deus*, *tempus*, and *omnia* necessarily play a large part. In the earlier sections of this book themes and statements have been mentioned, for no matter how much we talk about metrics or imagery or rhetorical figures or ideas, we are nonetheless talking in some sense about the theme or meaning of the poem, in short, about what the poem signifies. To take the parts of the poem as the entire poem is a mistake. To discuss them as we have done here is relevant to the criticism and understanding of a poem, but we must be aware at all times that these are parts of an organic whole and have been isolated for purposes of discussion.

The word "idea" is ambiguous in English. Often we find the word "idea" used in criticism, in such phrases as: the idea of Catullus' poem XXXI is that of the emotional response to returning home, when what is meant is the theme of the poem. To avoid the ambiguity of the word "idea" in literary criticism it would be well to restrict its use to mental representations such as *tempus*, *omnia*, etc., which may appear in a poem.

The theme of a poem is the attitude growing out of the drama of the poem. Poems, then, are not only statements about experience, they are also interpretations and evaluations of experience.

For example, Catullus attempts to evaluate the experience of his grief in his poem about the death of his brother; it is a presentation of a mood in an attempt to understand an experience. All the details so far discussed in this book are the means at a poet's disposal to order and evaluate his experience, to state his theme.

In examining this matter further, let us consider the implications of point of view, imagery, figures of speech, and of changes of tone. These changes imply shifts in feeling and indicate different ways of looking at reality. Conversely a shift in feeling and attitude is expressed by the shifts of tone, point of view, etc. Each poem then offers a unique theme, a unique way of looking at reality. Consider for example the idea of death as it was treated in three poems already read: Catullus' poem on the death of his brother, his poem on the death of his mistress' sparrow, and Statius' on the death of a parrot. The first has a melancholy tone of grief; the next has the ironic tone of the mock tragic; the third has a pathetic quality. All three are different evaluations of experience although all three are concerned in one way with the same idea. Each one shifts its tone in keeping with its theme, and thus the feeling communicated in each is proper to the understanding of the experience.

This discussion brings us to the problem of sincerity in poetry. Sincerity is an often misused word in literary criticism. Put as simply as possible, a poem is sincere if it holds together as an organic whole. Is the poet's evaluation of the experience valid to the statement of that experience? If the poem asks us to believe or to accept an evaluation when inadequate or even "improper" evidence has been presented for that evaluation, then the poem is insincere. Carefully observe Statius' poem on the death of the parrot and see how close to being insincere it is. The sincerity of the poet as a human being is not really the issue here. Quite "sincere," that is, good, kind, upright men who would no more think of telling a falsehood than of committing a crime might write bad, insincere poetry. The converse also follows: men whom one would seriously hesitate about inviting into one's home might write excellent poetry. Sincerity in poetry concerns the valid presentation and evaluation of experience, in which the feeling communicated is proper to the rational understanding of the experience.

A poem then necessarily develops consistently its theme and does so through the means we have discussed earlier. Poems may express beliefs and values which we do not accept. Are we then to reject a poem because it fails to conform to our individual standards? Hardly, if we wish to be sympathetic readers of poetry. Few people today accept the Roman notions of religion. Yet, when we meet them in a poem such as Catullus' lament for his brother, we accept them through a sympathetic act of the imagination. None of us believes in the same way as the ancients believed in Venus or Mars or time, yet nevertheless we recognize the worth of various poets' ideas about them. As readers we are obliged to try to see the poem as it is and to recognize that it is a serious and intelligent attempt to bring order out of chaos, to make sense out of experience. When we grasp that the poem does this, we then, usually, accept the poem as successful. We make that sympathetic leap of the imagination to an attitude which is different in some way from our own. If we thus accept the poem, we then in some way, even though it be to a slight degree, modify our own beliefs. This is the great worth to us in reading poetry, for it affects like life itself our beliefs, our attitudes, and our understanding of the world.

In analyzing the poems of this section, as well as in the other sections, it is necessary to be able to state the theme as clearly as possible. But we must do more than simply look for the theme of the poem. Too often looking for the theme of a poem degenerates into message-hunting, as though the poem could be reduced to a simple prose statement. We must understand the extensions, the changes, the subtleties of the theme which the poem embodies in order "to respond fully, delicately, and with discriminating accuracy to the subtle and precise use of words."[1]

[1] F. R. Leavis, *Education and the University* (Chatto & Windus, London, 1943), 268.

Marcus Valerius Martialis (c.40–104 A.D.)
Epigram V.58

Cras te uicturum, cras dicis, Postume, semper.
　　dic mihi, cras istud, Postume, quando uenit?
quam longe cras istud, ubi est? aut unde petendum?
　　numquid apud Parthos Armeniosque latet?
5　iam cras istud habet Priami uel Nestoris annos.
　　cras istud quanti, dic mihi, posset emi?
cras uiues? hodie iam uiuere, Postume, serum est:
　　ille sapit quisquis, Postume, uixit heri.

NOTES

Meter: Elegiac Couplet.

1. *Postume*—may be an allusion to Horace's Postumus in *Odes* II.14.1 ff.
4. *Parthos Armeniosque*—i.e., the ends of the earth.

This poem embraces a theme which is common enough to Latin poetry, that of *Carpe diem*, the notion of living in the present not in the future. Put so baldly, though, the paraphrase does not admit of the subtlety in handling we sense in our reading of the poem. After an opening generalization, several verses which illuminate the initial statement appear. An examination of these verses reveals how the generalization is made particular, and thus how it is changed from the bald statement of the paraphrase.

Verse 2 is a straightforward one expressing a notion we are familiar with. When will your tomorrow come? What is suggested by the phrase is that "your tomorrow" is somehow different from the one we all know. The use of *istud* emphasizes the particularization of *cras*. We all know that *cras* never comes, yet Postumus apparently believes that he owns his own tomorrow, for *cras* is treated as a personal possession of Postumus. Ironically the poet suggests that Postumus can seek and find it among the Parthians and Armenians (vv. 3–4). But the irony turns back on Postumus, for these very references to the persistent enemies of ancient Rome suggest the inaccessibility of *cras* hidden in a far distant land whose inhabitants are deadly enemies. The task of seeking *cras*, the verse implies, is at best foolhardy and at worst fatal.

The next verse changes the image from one based on distance to one based on time. Priam and Nestor are symbols of old age. *Cras* is as many years away as the lifetime of a Nestor or a Priam. Furthermore, the evocation of these two legendary characters, wealthy and powerful kings in their time, prepares for the next verse and its question: for how much can you buy tomorrow? The implication is that not all the riches in the world can buy it. Finally, the names of Nestor and Priam inevitably conjure up images of violence, death, and total destruction; and it is the thought of death and of its ever-present threat which underlies the final verses of the poem.

The paradox played upon in this poem is that tomorrow is always there but never comes. It is predicated on our awareness that "tomorrow" is not a material thing, but an abstraction, a concept devised by men to express a relationship, that of time. Time and its divisions are ideas agreed to by men. As v. 7 indicates we do not live tomorrow but today. But it is too late even to plan to live today, for the present is lived willy-nilly. The wise man recognizes the fact, as v. 8 recapitulates, for he asserts only that he lived yesterday. The future is always provisional; the past alone is knowable; the present is what we are going through, what we must live, but what we can only know when it is past.

The implications of the presentation of the theme of the poem do not differ greatly from the Biblical notion of "Live today as though it were your last." Further ramifications of the concept become apparent when we realize that the attitude Martial advocates is characteristic of the adult, mature person. The mature person accepts the present as the only actuality and understands the past only as knowable, who, although he may plan for the future, nonetheless regards it as conditional. To be mature is thus to be capable of accepting death as the appointed completion of life, and because of that acceptance, to be capable of living as fully as possible in the present. Who, after all, lives in the future?

Children. Postumus is being childish in his belief that tomorrow always comes. Ultimately he is being irresponsible, for presumably he is a grown man capable of mature thought.

Some commentators may consider it necessary to discover the "historical event" which gave rise to Martial's poem, the "why" of Postumus' refusal of the invitation. There might be any number of reasons for it, and the occasion of the poem may well be a very minor one. In fact the occasion is irrelevant. What is important is that Martial has drawn a philosophic lesson from experience: he has evaluated it.

QUESTIONS

1. Carefully explain the grammatical function of every use of *cras* as well as of *hodie* and *heri*.

2. Assuming that the Postumus is a reference to Horace's Postumus in *Eheu fugaces* (*Ode* II.14), write an essay comparing the themes of the two poems.

❦

Lucius Annaeus Seneca (4 B.C.–65 A.D.)

Omnia Tempus

Omnia tempus edax depascitur, omnia carpit,
    omnia sede mouet, nil sinit esse diu.
flumina deficiunt, profugum mare litora siccant,
    subsidunt montes et iuga celsa ruunt.
5 quid tam parua loquor? moles pulcherrima caeli
    ardebit flammis tota repente suis.
omnia mors poscit. lex est, non poena, perire:
    hic aliquo mundus tempore nullus erit.

NOTES

Meter: Elegiac Couplet.

Stoics, of whom Seneca is a leading example, regarded fire as the original element from which emerged air, water, and earth. They thought that the universe moved in a succession of giant cycles and that at some time a conflagration would return all to fire, and then that the whole process would be repeated.

QUESTIONS

1. What images are involved in this poem? Carefully trace all of them and their relationships.

2. Explain the figure of speech in v. 8. Is it effective? Does it help to illuminate the theme? How?

3. Carefully explain the first clause of v. 5. *Parua* has what effect?

4. What is the theme of the poem, and how does v. 7 form a part of it?

⋯⋯

Marcus Valerius Martialis (c.40–104 A.D.)
Epigram III.29

Has cum gemina compede dedicat catenas,
Saturne, tibi Zoilus, anulos priores.

NOTES

Meter: Ionic a maiore.

2. *Saturnus*—on gaining their freedom slaves commonly dedicated their fetters to this god on whose festival, the Saturnalia, they had enjoyed some freedom.

Zoilus—the name of a censorious critic.

QUESTIONS

1. Comment on the metrics of this poem.

2. Explain how the past of Zoilus is conveyed to us. What is his current status? How does Martial judge it? What kind of man is Zoilus?

3. What assumptions underlie Martial's attitude? Are the assumptions justified in the poem?

⋯⋯

Gaius Valerius Catullus (c.84–54 B.C.)
LXXII

{156}

Dicebas quondam solum te nosse Catullum,
    Lesbia, nec prae me uelle tenere Iouem.
dilexi tum te non tantum ut uulgus amicam,
    sed pater ut gnatos diligit et generos.
5   nunc te cognoui: quare etsi impensius uror,
    multo mi tamen es uilior et leuior.
qui potis est, inquis? quod amantem iniuria talis
    cogit amare magis, sed bene uelle minus.

Notes

Meter: Elegiac Couplet.

   7. *potis est . . .*—understand *fieri.* Before a vowel *potis* stands for *pote.*

Questions

  1. What is the distinction between *dilexi* and *amaui* (3)?

  2. What is the significance of *nosse* (1) and *cognoui* (5)?

  3. The verse "*sed pater ut gnatos diligit et generos*" (4) appears strange in a poem addressed to a woman. Has the poet fallen into a lapse of taste, or does he have some reason for such a comparison?

  4. What is the effect of the meter of this poem?

  5. How do all the details discussed in the previous questions affect the theme of the poem?

❧

Marcus Valerius Martialis (c.40–104 A.D.)

Epigram III.20

Dic, Musa, quid agat Canius meus Rufus:
utrumne chartis tradit ille uicturis
legenda temporum acta Claudianorum?
an quae Neroni falsus adstruit scriptor,
5 an aemulatur improbi iocos Phaedri?
lasciuus elegis an seuerus herois?
an in cothurnis horridus Sophocleis?
an otiosus in schola poetarum
lepore tinctos Attico sales narrat?
10 hinc si recessit, porticum terit templi

an spatia carpit lentus Argonautarum?
an delicatae sole rursus Europae
inter tepentes post meridie buxos
sedet ambulatue liber acribus curis?
15 Titine thermis an lauatur Agrippae
an inpudici balneo Tigillini?
an rure Tulli fruitur atque Lucani?
an Pollionis dulce currit ad quartum?
an aestuantis iam profectus ad Baias
20 piger Lucrino nauculatur in stagno?
"uis scire quid agat Canius tuus? ridet."

Notes

Meter: Choliambic.

1. *Canius Rufus*—a contemporary of Martial, a poet and an orator.

4. *falsus*—some verb such as *recenset* is to be understood.

5. *Phaedri*—a freedman of Augustus and a poet and translator of Aesop's fables into Latin.

6. understand *gaudet.*

7. understand *uersatur.*

11. *spatia*—properly the courses of a stadium or circus.
    Argonautarum—i.e., the companions of Jason who went on the search for the golden fleece.

12. *Europae*—i.e., the *Porticus Europae* on the *Campus Agrippae.*

15. *Agrippae*—on the *Campus Martius* west of the Temple of Isis.

17. *Tulli . . . Lucani*—Domitius Tellus and Domitius Lucanus were brothers who were devoted to each other.

18. *Pollionis*—unknown.

Questions

1. Carefully examine the organization of the poem, and indicate the logical divisions and their connections.

2. In the light of Question 1, what significance does *ridet* (21) have? What are the implications of the word?

3. What role does meter play in this poem?
4. Write an analysis of the theme of this poem.

❧

Quintus Horatius Flaccus (65–8 B.C.)
Ode I.5

Quis multa gracilis te puer in rosa
perfusus liquidis urget odoribus
     grato, Pyrrha, sub antro?
        cui flauam religas comam,

5 simplex munditiis? heu quotiens fidem
mutatosque deos flebit et aspera
     nigris aequora uentis
        emirabitur insolens,

qui nunc te fruitur credulus aurea,
10 qui semper uacuam, semper amabilem
     sperat, nescius aurae
        fallacis! miseri, quibus

intemptata nites. me tabula sacer
uotiua paries indicat uuida
15   suspendisse potenti
        uestimenta maris deo.

NOTES

Meter: Fourth Asclepiadean.

   5. *fidem*—understand *mutatam* from *mutatos* in v. 6.

   8. *emirabitur*—the word is found only here; it is an intensification of *mirabitur*.

     insolens—almost *insuetus*.

   9. *aurea*—predicate to *te*.

 10. *uacuam*—understand *te fore*.

 16. *maris*—dependent upon *potenti*.

     deo—i.e., Neptune.

Horace explores in this poem the ambiguities of love. He begins with a scene of dalliance and ends with a description of himself making a votive offering to the god of the sea. The implication throughout the poem is that the youth will eventually make a similar offering. The images and the point of view of the poem are complex, for they involve a movement from credulity perceived with ironic detachment to awareness understood through experience.

In his description of the *gracilis puer* the poet employs a reminiscence of the ritual of the Greek symposium (*multa . . . in rosa, perfusus liquidis . . . odoribus*, and even *urget*) which suggests that love-making is a game. The point of view suggests sympathy for the obvious delight of the *gracilis puer*; the tone is one of urbane amusement. But even in this stanza an undertone of seriousness appears in *urget*. Although the obvious meaning is "urge on," "encourage," another more fundamental notion lies in this word: the urge of "press upon," a physical act as distinct from the urging of the will and emotions.

The notion that there is something more important than play afoot receives confirmation in the opening phrase of the second stanza. *Simplex munditiis*, joined to the first stanza by enjambment, is itself an oxymoron. The simplicity of Pyrrha is complex and is achieved with deceptive artistry. The phrase hints that the appearance and the reality of the girl are distinct. The hint becomes a statement in the very next phrase, in which the speaker of the poem asserts that, when the boy realizes this disparity in the girl, he will weep for the changed gods and marvel at the sea of passion which affords a rougher crossing than he originally expected. That this is so is emphasized by vv. 8–13. The interlocked word order of *aspera/ nigris aequora uentis*, and the ambiguities of *uacuam, aurae fallacis*, and *nites*, as well as the repeated use of *semper*, underline the youth's earlier credulity and bitter realization.

What had begun as a game has now turned into a serious and painful reality. The metaphor of the sea in vv. 8–13 is clearly the sea of passion, of love, which is deceptively mutable. The implication is that nothing can be safe and securely fixed in love, even as nothing is sure on the sea.

Combined with the sea-of-passion metaphor is another, closely related set of images which refer to Pyrrha. Her name refers to her flaming hair. Verse 4 furthers this notion with *flauam . . . comam* as does the *aurea* of v. 9. The girl is the beacon of the love-tossed mariner, an idea seen in the first phrase of the last stanza, *intemptata nites*. However, by the juxtaposition of the other metaphors of sea and breeze this beacon, which should be a source of safety, is also deceptive, for it leads not only to bliss but also to shipwreck and misery. There is no guarantee that Pyrrha, the seemingly safe beacon of security, will guide the voyager safely.

Another pattern of images demands comment. These images too are related to the sea of passion and also culminate in the last stanza. At the beginning of the poem the youth is described as dallying with Pyrrha in a cave. At the end of the poem the poet speaks of his own safe return from the sea of passion and of his offering to the god of the sea. Both the cave and the temple are regarded as sources of safety and security. But each has a slightly different connotation, for the cave represents the safe trysting spot for the trusting but inexperienced lover, and the temple represents the safe spot for the experienced lover. The two places are the beginning and the end of the tempestuous voyage of love.

What Horace is saying is that one may begin love as a game whose pleasure lies simply in its momentary enjoyment, but that love itself is not a simple matter. We are led onward through passion to acknowledge the power of love. The *potenti . . . maris deo* commands. The commands are ultimately holy. We see the girl, Pyrrha, change before our eyes from a simple strawberry blonde to the goddess of love herself. Passion is a changing emotion which will dominate us no matter how trusting we be in its security, but it is also capable of giving us an experience of the holy.

QUESTIONS

1. Explain the use of assonance in the poem.
2. What are the ambiguities of the words in vv. 8–13?

3. Comment on how the tenses of the verbs aid the point of view and the tone of the poem.

⤜§⤛

Quintus Horatius Flaccus (65–8 B.C.)
Ode III.30

Exegi monumentum aere perennius
regalique situ pyramidum altius,
quod non imber edax, non Aquilo impotens
possit diruere aut innumerabilis
5   annorum series et fuga temporum.
non omnis moriar, multaque pars mei
uitabit Libitinam: usque ego postera
crescam laude recens, dum Capitolium
scandet cum tacita uirgine pontifex.
10   dicar, qua uiolens obstrepit Aufidus
et qua pauper aquae Daunus agrestium
regnauit populorum, ex humili potens
princeps Aeolium carmen ad Italos
deduxisse modos. sume superbiam
15   quaesitam meritis et mihi Delphica
lauro cinge uolens, Melpomene, comam.

NOTES

Meter: First Asclepiadean.

7. *Libitinam*—the death goddess, *Venus Libitina*, at whose temple materials for funerals were stored and rented, and where a registry of deaths was preserved.

   usque—modifies *crescam*.

10. *Aufidus*—a river of Apulia.

11. *aquae*—genitive with adjectives.

   agrestium populorum—a grecism.

12. *ex humili*—i.e., Daunus was a refugee from Illyricum. Horace also rose from humble origins.

13. *deduxisse*—governed by *dicar*.

   Aeolium—i.e., Aeolic poetry of Sappho and Alcaeus.

15. *mihi*—dative of possession or reference.

Delphica lauro—i.e., because sacred to Apollo.

QUESTIONS

1. Observe the scansion of the poem and indicate how diaeresis is used.

2. After examining closely the details of the organization of this poem, write an essay showing the relevance to the theme of the poem of vv. 14 to 16 (*sume . . . to end*).

◆§§◆

Quintus Horatius Flaccus (65–8 B.C.)

Epode II

"Beatus ille, qui procul negotiis,
　　ut prisca gens mortalium,
paterna rura bubus exercet suis,
　　solutus omni faenore,
5　neque excitatur classico miles truci,
　　neque horret iratum mare,
forumque uitat et superba ciuium
　　potentiorum limina.
ergo aut adulta uitium propagine
10　　altas maritat populos,
aut in reducta ualle mugientium
　　prospectat errantis greges,
inutilisque falce ramos amputans
　　feliciores inserit,
15　aut pressa puris mella condit amphoris,
　　aut tondet infirmas ouis;
uel cum decorum mitibus pomis caput
　　Autumnus agris extulit,
ut gaudet insitiua decerpens pira
20　　certantem et uuam purpurae,
qua muneretur te, Priape, et te, pater
　　Siluane, tutor finium!
libet iacere modo sub antiqua ilice,

       modo in tenaci gramine:
25 labuntur altis interim riuis aquae,
       quereuntur in siluis aues,
fontesque lymphis obstrepunt manantibus,
       somnos quod inuitet leuis.
at cum tonantis annus hibernus Iouis
30   imbris niuesque comparat,
aut trudit acris hinc et hinc multa cane
      apros in obstantis plagas,
aut amite leui rara tendit retia,
      turdis edacibus dolos,
35 pauidumque leporem et aduenam laqueo gruem
      iucunda captat praemia.
quis non malarum, quas amor curas habet,
      haec inter obliuiscitur?
quodsi pudica mulier in partem iuuet
40   domum atque dulcis liberos,
Sabina qualis aut perusta solibus
      pernicis uxor Apuli,
sacrum uetusti exstruat lignis focum
      lassi sub aduentum uiri,
45 claudensque textis cratibus laetum pecus
      distenta siccet ubera,
et horna dulci uina promens dolio
      dapes inemptas apparet;
non me Lucrina iuuerint conchylia
50   magisue rhombus aut scari,
si quos Eois intonata fluctibus
      hiems ad hoc uertat mare,
non Afra auis descendat in uentrem meum,
      non attagen Ionicus
55 incundior, quam lecta de pinguissimis
      oliua ramis arborum
aut herba lapathi prata amantis et graui
      maluae salubres corpori,
uel agna festis caesa Terminalibus

60   uel haedus ereptus lupo.
      has inter epulas ut iuuat pastas ouis
          uidere properantis domum,
      uidere fessos uomerem inuersum boues
          collo trahentis languido,
65 positosque uernas, ditis examen domus,
          circum renidentis Lares!"
      haec ubi locutus faenerator Alfius,
          iam iam futurus rusticus,
      omnem redegit Idibus pecuniam,
70   quaerit Kalendis ponere.

NOTES

Meter: Iambic Stanza.

  1. *procul*—preposition with the ablative.
  2. *ut prisca gens*—reference to the "golden age."
  4. *solutus omni faenore*—i.e., he is out of debt.
  6. *horret*—transitive.
  7. *forum; limina*—the allusions are to law and politics and to the custom of clients' making their morning calls on patrons.
  11. *mugientum*—a participle used as a substantive; *boum* is to be understood.
  14. *feliciores*—uses the radical sense of the word.
  18. *agris*—ablative of place; the preposition is often omitted in poetry.
  19. *ut*—exclamatory.
      gaudet decerpens—a grecism; "delights to pluck," "delights in plucking."
  20. *certantem purpurae*—a grecism; the dative used after verbs of contending, struggling, differing.
  21. *Priape*—the god of gardens, vineyards, who served as a scarecrow.
  22. *Siluane*—an old Italian god of woods and fields, who was protector of flocks and guardian of boundaries.
  28. *quod inuitet*—antecedent of *quod* is implied in *obstrepunt*.
  29. *annus hibernus*—partitive use of the adjective. The phrase equals *hiems*.

34. *dolos*—in apposition with *retia*.

37. *curas*—antecedent to *quas* but put in the relative clause and in the case of the pronoun; it should, logically, be *curarum*. This usage derives from Greek.

38. *haec inter*—anastrophe.

39. *in partem*—adverbial; equals *partim*.

44. *sub aduentum*—i.e., against his return; in anticipation of it.

47. *dulci*—transferred epithet. Keep it transferred.

49. *iuuerint*—understand *magis*; similarly in 50 understand *iuuerint*. This kind of figure is called brachyology where expressions common to two phrases are inferred from each other.

51. *intonata*—with active force.

53. *Afra auis*—i.e., guinea hen.

55. *iucundior*—adverbial, as often.

59. *Terminalibus*—"festival of the boundaries" fell on 23 February. Neighbors decorated the respective sides of the boundary stones with garlands and offered sacrifices in common.

60. *ereptus lupo*—meat was a rarity for the peasant.

61. *ut*—exclamatory.

67. *Alfius*—a *faenerator*; used as a type.

69. *Idibus, Kalendis*—along with the *Nones* these were the regular points of the month for financial settlements.

70. *ponere*—i.e., to put out at interest; to invest.

QUESTIONS

1. Carefully scan the whole poem, observing how the metrical variants permissible in this pattern of verse affect the poem.

2. Comment on the effectiveness of asyndeton and brachyology in this poem, especially vv. 49–50 and 70.

3. Write an essay examining the effect of vv. 67 to 70 on the whole poem. How does "sincerity" operate in this poem?

❧

Quintus Horatius Flaccus (65–8 B.C.)

Ode III.11

Mercuri—nam te docilis magistro

mouit Amphion lapides canendo—
tuque testudo resonare septem
  callida neruis,

5 nec loquax olim neque grata, nunc et
diuitum mensis et amica templis,
dic modos, Lyde quibus obstinatas
  applicet auris,

quae uelut latis equa trima campis
10 ludit exsultim metuitque tangi,
nuptiarum expers et adhuc proteruo
  cruda marito.

tu potes tigris comitesque siluas
ducere et riuos celeris morari;
15 cessit immanis tibi blandienti
  ianitor aulae,

Cerberus, quamuis furiale centum
muniant angues caput eius atque
spiritus taeter saniesque manet
20 ore trilingui.

quin et Ixion Tityosque uultu
risit inuito, stetit urna paulum
sicca, dum grato Danai puellas
  carmine mulces.

25 audiat Lyde scelus atque notas
uirginum poenas et inane lymphae
dolium fundo pereuntis imo,
  seraque fata,

quae manent culpas etiam sub Orco.
30 impiae—nam quid potuere maius?—
impiae sponsos potuere duro
  perdere ferro.

una de multis face nuptiali
digna periurum fuit in parentem

35 splendide mendax et in omne uirgo
    nobilis aeuum,

"surge," quae dixit iuueni marito,
"surge, ne longus tibi somnus, unde
non times, detur; socerum et scelestas
40   falle sorores,

quae uelut nactae uitulos leaenae
singulos eheu lacerant: ego illis
mollior nec te feriam neque intra
    claustra tenebo.

45 me pater saeuis oneret catenis,
quod uiro clemens misero peperci:
me uel extremos Numidarum in agros
    classe releget.

i pedes quo te rapiunt et aurae,
50 dum fauet nox et Venus, i secundo
omine et nostri memorem sepulcro
    scalpe querelam."

Notes

Meter: Sapphic Stanza.

  1. *te magistro*—ablative absolute.

  2. *mouit Amphion lapides*—the walls of Thebes were said to have risen to the music from the lyre of Amphion, king of Thebes and husband of Niobe.

  3. *testudo*—metonomy; the lyre was supposedly made from strings stretched on a tortoise shell.

  4. *neruis*—ablative; for *fidibus*.

  9. *trima*—i.e., unbroken; in their fourth year colts were broken in.

  10. *exsultim*—found only here.

  11. *cruda*—opposite of *matura*.

  13. *tu*—i.e., the lyre.

    comites—predicate to *tigris* and *siluas*.

20. *ore trilingui*—synecdoche.

25. *audiat*—i.e., and take warning.

26. *lymphae*—genitive with *inane* on the analogy of its opposite *plenus*.

27. *pereuntis*—also with the connotation of "going to war to."

34. *periurum*—Danaus had offered his daughters in good faith.

46. *clemens*—with adverbial force.

47. *uel*—intensive, "even."

52. *querelam*—i.e., an epitaph.

QUESTIONS

1. Explain how the ideas expressed in this poem are connected.

2. Explain the imagery involved in vv. 1–12. In what ways are these verses connected with vv. 33–52?

3. What purpose do the mythical allusions serve in vv. 13–32?

⋖§§⋗

Quintus Horatius Flaccus (65–8 B.C.)
Ode I.15

Pastor cum traheret per freta nauibus
Idaeis Helenen perfidus hospitam,
ingrato celeris obruit otio
    uentos, ut caneret fera

5   Nereus fata: mala ducis aui domum,
quam multo repetet Graecia milite,
coniurata tuas rumpere nuptias
    et regnum Priami uetus.

heu heu, quantus equis, quantus adest uiris
10 sudor! quanta moues funera Dardanae
genti! iam galeam Pallas et aegida
    currusque et rabiem parat.

nequiquam Veneris praesidio ferox
pectes caesariem grataque feminis
15 imbelli cithara carmina diuides,
    nequiquam thalamo grauis

hastas et calami spicula Gnosii
uitabis strepitumque et celerem sequi
Aiacem; tamen heu serus adulteros
20   crines puluere collines.

non Laertiaden, exitium tuae
gentis, non Pylium Nestora respicis?
urgent impauidi te Salaminius
     Teucer, te Sthenelus sciens

25 pugnae, siue opus est imperitare equis,
non auriga piger. Merionen quoque
nosces. ecce furit te reperire atrox
     Tydides melior patre,

quem tu, ceruus uti uallis in altera
30 uisum parte lupum graminis immemor,
sublimi fugies mollis anhelitu,
     non hoc pollicitus tuae.

iracunda diem proferet Ilio
matronisque Phrygum classis Achillei;
35 post certas hiemes uret Achaicus
     ignis Iliacas domos.

NOTES

Meter: Third Asclepiadean.

  1. *Pastor*—i.e., Paris.

  5. *Nereus*—subject also of *obruit.* It is drawn into the dependent *ut* clause. He is a sea god who was son of Pontus and Tellus and possessed of prophetic powers.

  6. *quam*—antecedent is understood.

    multo milite—person is treated as the means of the action, hence the ablative of means.

  7. *rumpere*—infinitive of purpose.

  14. *caesariem*—essentially poetic, denoting beautiful hair.

  17. *Gnosii*—ancient capital of Crete; Cretans were famous archers.

  18. *sequi*—depends on *celerem*; epexegetic infinitive; a grecism.

21. *Laertiaden*—i.e., Ulysses.
26. *non piger*—litotes.
    Merionem—Cretan warrior, follower of Idomeneus.
27. *reperire*—depends on *furit*, by analogy with *cupio*.
32. *non hoc*—litotes.
    tuae—used as substantive.

QUESTIONS

1. What is the dramatic story of the poem? What are we obliged to know about the background? What aspects of the background does Horace emphasize in the poem?

2. Explain the effect of the position of *perfidus* (2) and of *fata* (5).

3. Verses 7–8 have the rhetorical figure of zeugma. Here *nuptias* and *regnum* are both objects of *rumpere*. What purpose does this figure serve?

4. Carefully observe the tenses in the first three stanzas. How do they relate to vv. 4–5, *ut caneret fera/ Nereus fata*? What is the relationship of *ingrato . . . uentos* (3–4) to the whole poem?

5. In the third stanza examine the effect of the repeated use of enjambment, the repetition of *quantus* and the nouns *galeam, Aegida currusque et rabum*. What function do all these rhetorical figures and words serve?

6. What does the juxtaposition of Venus and Athena imply?

7. Does Paris in any way form a parallel to Nereus? How? Why?

8. Verse 20 shows in our text *crines*. Another possible reading based on the mss. is *cultus*. Which is better? Why is *crines* chosen here? What is the difference in the poem if *cultus* is used?

9. From vv. 9 to 20 carefully examine the sound pattern. Does it play any part in the organization of the poem? What effect do repetition and alliteration have in the passage?

10. Carefully observe and comment on how the motives and effects of the passage from vv. 21–32 relate to the previous sections of the poem. What ironic parallels which were implicit earlier are used here?

11. Examine the imagery of the stag and wolf in the poem. How useful are these images in the poem?

12. How does the final stanza effectively conclude the poem? What relationship does it have with earlier parts of the poem? What effect does *hiemes* have? Is *domos* a particularly telling word for ending the poem?

13. State as accurately as you can the theme of the poem.

❧

Gaius Valerius Catullus (c.84–54 B.C.)

LXXVI

Si qua recordanti benefacta priora uoluptas
    est homini, cum se cogitat esse pium,
nec sanctam uiolasse fidem, nec foedere in ullo
    diuum ad fallendos numine abusum homines,
5 multa parata manent in longa aetate, Catulle,
    ex hoc ingrato gaudia amore tibi.
nam quaecumque homines bene cuiquam aut dicere possunt
    aut facere, haec a te dictaque factaque sunt.
omnia quae ingratae perierunt credita menti.
10   quare iam te cur amplius excrucies?
quin tu animo offirmas atque istinc teque reducis,
    et dis inuitis desinis esse miser?
difficile est longum subito deponere amorem,
    difficile est, uerum hoc qua lubet efficias:
15 una salus haec est, hoc est tibi peruincendum,
    hoc facias, siue id non pote siue pote.
o di, si uestrum est misereri, aut si quibus umquam
    extremam iam ipsa in morte tulistis opem,
me miserum aspicite et, si uitam puriter egi,
20   eripite hanc pestem perniciemque mihi,
quae mihi subrepens imos ut torpor in artus
    expulit ex omni pectore laetitias.
non iam illud quaero, contra me ut diligat illa,
    aut, quod non potis est, esse pudica uelit:

25 ipse ualere opto et taetrum hunc deponere morbum.
    o di, reddite mi hoc pro pietate mea.

NOTES

Meter: Elegiac Couplet.

6. *ingrato*—the passive notion dominates, i.e., unrewarded, as distinct from *ingratae* in v. 9 where the meaning is active.

14. *qua lubet*—"no matter how."

16. *pote*—understand *est fieri.*

17. *si*—perhaps like *si umquam.*

23. *contra*—"in return."

24. *potis*—since it appears before a vowel it is used for *pote.*

QUESTIONS

1. In the poem Catullus addresses himself, that is, he looks upon himself as though he were distinct from the speaker of the poem. How does such usage differ from addressing someone else, say a Postumus? What effect does it have on the theme of the poem?

2. Examine the imagery of the poem. What is the underlying metaphor of the poem? How does the metaphor affect the details of the poem, and how is it related to the theme?

3. Catullus is often said by critics to have written his poems in the first flush of emotional enthusiasm. Is this a particularly important or valid notion? What critics really mean is that Catullus communicates an intensity of feeling in his poems, so that the poems give the illusion of spontaneity which is one of the hallmarks of Catullus' style. Whether lines or whole poems sprang into his mind we do not know. What we do know, for we can observe it, is the way in which his poems are organized and his effects are worked out. Carefully examine this poem for its illusion of spontaneity. What resources does the poet call on? How does he employ them?

◈

Gaius Valerius Catullus (c.84–54 B.C.)

LXXV

Huc est mens deducta tua, mea Lesbia, culpa

atque ita se officio perdidit ipsa suo,
ut iam nec bene uelle queat tibi, si optima fias,
nec desistere amare, omnia si facias.

NOTES

Meter: Elegiac Couplet.

   2. *officio suo*—ablative of either means or cause.

   4. *omnia*—for *quidlibet.*

QUESTIONS

   1. Compare this short epigram with Catullus LXXVI. Note that the attitude is simple but has the formal complexity of the elegiac epigram. How do antithesis and juxtaposition operate in LXXV and LXXVI? What does Catullus achieve by them?

   2. Compare the treatment of the theme in LXXVI with that in LXXV.

Sextus Propertius (c.50–c.16 B.C.)

Elegy III.2

Carminis interea nostri redeamus in orbem,
   gaudeat in solito tacta puella sono.
Orphea detinuisse feras et concita dicunt
   flumina Threicia sustinuisse lyra;
5 saxa Cithaeronis Thebas agitata per artem
   sponte sua in muri membra coisse ferunt;
quin etiam, Polypheme, fera Galatea sub Aetna
   ad tua rorantis carmina flexit equos:
miremur, nobis et Baccho et Apolline dextro,
10 turba puellarum si mea uerba colit?
quod non Taenariis domus est mihi fulta columnis,
   nec camera auratas inter eburna trabes,
nec mea Phaeacas aequant pomaria siluas,
   non operosa rigat Marcius antra liquor;
15 at Musae comites et carmina cara legenti,
   et defessa choris Calliopea meis.
fortunata, meo si qua es celebrata libello!

carmina erunt formae tot monumenta tuae.
nam neque Pyramidum sumptus ad sidera ducti,
20   nec Iouis Elei caelum imitata domus,
nec Mausolei diues fortuna sepulcri
mortis ab extrema condicione uacant.
aut illis flamma aut imber subducet honores,
annorum aut ictu, pondere uicta, ruent.
25   at non ingenio quaesitum nomen ab aeuo
excidet: ingenio stat sine morte decus.

NOTES

Meter: Elegiac Couplet.

5. *Thebas*—Amphion by the music of his lyre caused stones to gather and form the walls of Thebes.

7. *Galatea*—sea nymph loved in vain by Polyphemus whose music drew her from the sea. She, however, loved Acis, the shepherd.

13. *Phaeacas*—reference is to the gardens of Alcinous (*Odys.* VII 12); the adjective is not found elsewhere.

20. The temple of Zeus at Olympia is compared to heaven because of its beauty, and because of Phidias' chryselephantine statue of Zeus.

21. The Mausoleum of Halicarnassus, tomb of Mausolus, king of Caria (died 353 B.C.).

24. *ruent*—transitive.

25. *ab*—probably ablative of source.

QUESTIONS

1. Explain how time and the image of time are used in this poem.

2. What is the subject of the poem? What is the stated purpose of the poem? How does the poet make his art serve this purpose?

3. Explain the effect the mythological references have in the poem.

❧

Quintus Horatius Flaccus (65–8 B.C.)
Ode I.8

> Lydia, dic, per omnis
> hoc deos uere, Sybarin cur properes amando
>   perdere, cur apricum
> oderit campum, patiens pulueris atque solis,
> 5   cur neque militaris
> inter aequalis equitet, Gallica nec lupatis
>   temperet ora frenis?
> cur timet flauum Tiberim tangere? cur oliuum
>   sanguine uiperino
> 10 cautius uitat neque iam liuida gestat armis
>   bracchia, saepe disco,
> saepe trans finem iaculo nobilis expedito?
>   quid latet, ut marinae
> filium dicunt Thetidis sub lacrimosa Troiae
> 15   funera, ne uirilis
> cultus in caedem et Lycias proriperet cateruas?

Notes

Meter: Second or Greater Sapphic Stanza.

   1. *Lydia*—a common name for a coquette.

   4. *campum*—i.e., *Campus Martius*, used for exercise, especially by soldiers.

   6. *equitet*—encouraged by Augustus.

   7. *Gallica*—excellent horses came from Gaul.

   8. *tangere*—during the Augustan age the infinitive after *timere* is confined to poetry.

      oliuum—used to anoint the body before wrestling.

  13. *marinae*—Thetis was a Nereid.

  14. *filium Thetidis*—i.e., Achilles.

      dicunt—understand *latuisse.*

      sub—temporal, "just before."

  16. *Lycias*—Lycians were allies of Trojans; hence by metonomy this word stands for the Trojans.

    This brief poem conveys the poet's scorn for lascivious infatuation. But it does so not by addressing the young man who has fallen so short of the Roman ideal of manliness but by addressing his mistress. Yet, although the poet addresses Lydia, she is not the center of attention. Here we have a first example of the device of indirection which lies at the heart of the poem and is the means whereby Horace unfolds and illuminates his theme.

Although the poem apostrophizes Lydia, Horace does not put all the blame on the girl for leading the young man astray. Sybaris, as his name implies, is predisposed to luxury, ruinous infatuation. He rejects the things proper to a Roman youth because of his sentimental regard for the girl. But such a sentimental attachment reduces the man to effeminacy, just as Achilles was reduced to denying his *arete* by hiding in woman's clothes lest he die at Troy. The woman who would save the man for love succeeds only in emasculating him, after which presumably she would despise him for having become her creature.

Horace apportions responsibility and implies his judgment by making use of several of the phenomena of the Latin language, its structure and syntax. Through a series of questions which begin indirectly in the subjunctive and then move directly into the indicative, which conveys the actuality of events, he involves both Lydia and Sybaris, and adumbrates the role each plays in relation to the other. The same questions directed only to Sybaris would lessen the effect, for the responsibility of the woman would not be so immediately present, and the poem would run the risk of failing to make the point of the last quatrain. By questioning Lydia about Sybaris, the poet allows us to see both at once.

Lydia's share of responsibility, although Lydia is mentioned but once, is underlined by the fact that the poem begins with a direct address to her. Furthermore, no other woman is mentioned until v. 14 when Thetis is alluded to. The allusion is in fact to Achilles, but he is referred to not by his name but by his relationship to Thetis. He hides here under his mother's name, as he hid among women and in women's clothes to escape his destiny. Sybaris also, with Lydia's complicity, would escape his fate, i.e., that of a soldier trained to meet death. In these final verses, indirectly, Horace reminds the reader of the proximate cause of man's downfall.

Nevertheless, these same verses also emphasize that fault lies as well with Sybaris himself. Throughout the first twelve lines of the poem each of the questions, whether direct or indirect, has been introduced by *cur*. The last question which bears the point of the poem asks "what" (*quid*) he hides. To construe this word as "why" is to miss the point. It is not "why does he hide?" but rather "what does he hide?" The answer, of course, is that, first, he hides himself, for he is not going out to exercise; next, he hides his strength by his absence from the field; finally, he hides his virtue, his manhood, because, like Achilles, he seeks irresponsibility in feminine garb.

The ultimate consequences are to be drawn also by inference, by motivation; for the indirect technique lies not only on the surface of the poem but also within its organization. Sybaris is portrayed as abandoning the pursuits which made him an outstanding athlete, and a rising young warrior. Presumably it was his attainment in these manly pursuits as well as his physical attributes which made him attractive to Lydia. In the poetry of the ancient world prowess in military matters is traditionally equated with prowess in love. Note how often from Homer's time onward Venus and Mars are coupled. Consequently, if the young man fails in one, he suffers as well in the other. Horace does not explicitly say that such is the case; rather we are led to that inference because we have been made aware in other matters of how the poem proceeds. The conclusion, although only implied, is nevertheless that Sybaris, in failing to honor the practices of manliness, will be reduced not only to the shame of wearing woman's clothes as Achilles once did, but that, more importantly for him, he will forfeit the devotion (however dubious it may appear to us) of Lydia herself.

By a series of indirections involving the nature of the Latin language, literary allusion, and logical inference, Horace subtly and gracefully demonstrates that we foolishly destroy what we would love. By shunning the olive Sybaris in reality embraces the *sanguine uiperino*.

QUESTIONS

1. How do the metrics of this poem support the theme?
2. What appropriateness is there in the allusion to Achilles?
3. Why is the method of indirection preferred by the poet to that of direct statement?

☙§❧

Gaius Valerius Catullus (c.84–c.54 B.C.)

VIII

<pre>
    Miser Catulle, desinas ineptire,
    et quod uides perisse perditum ducas.
    fulsere quondam candidi tibi soles,
    cum uentitabas quo puella ducebat
 5 amata nobis quantum amabitur nulla.
    ibi illa multa tum iocosa fiebant,
    quae tu uolebas nec puella nolebat,
    fulsere uere candidi tibi soles.
    nunc iam illa non uult: tu quoque, impotens, noli,
10 nec quae fugit sectare, nec miser uiue,
    sed obstinata mente perfer, obdura.
    uale, puella! iam Catullus obdurat,
    nec te requiret nec rogabit inuitam.
    at tu dolebis, cum rogaberis nulla.
15 scelesta, uae te! quae tibi manet uita?
    quis nunc te adibit? cui uideberis bella?
    quem nunc amabis? cuius esse diceris?
    quem basiabis? cui labella mordebis?
    at tu, Catulle, destinatus obdura.
</pre>

NOTES

Meter: Choliambic.

1. *ineptire*—a colloquial word occurring only in Terence and Catullus.

6. *ibi tum*—temporal, in contrast to *nunc iam* in v. 9.

9. *impotens*—i.e., powerless to help itself because in subjection to its own passion.

{179}

14. *nulla*—colloquial for "*non.*"

15. *uae te*—accusative of exclamation, though the dative with *uae* is more common.

17. *cuius esse diceris*—"who will call you his own"; more literally "whose will you be said to be." The literal translation suggests a formality lacking in the Latin.

19. *destinatus*—this is the first occurrence of the word in the sense of *obstinatus* (11) and shows the search for variety of expression, which is characteristic of Catullus' poetry. We see the same thing in the shift from *quondam* (3) to *uere* (8).

QUESTIONS

1. Carefully examine the dramatic event in this poem. How does that little drama help to form the basic image which appears in the poem? Explain how the theme of the poem is thus illuminated.

ক§ৡৈ

Quintus Horatius Flaccus (65–8 B.C.)

Ode II.13

Ille et nefasto te posuit die
quicumque primum, et sacrilega manu
    produxit, arbos, in nepotum
        pernicem opprobriumque pagi;

5 illum et parentis crediderim sui
fregisse ceruicem et penetralia
    sparsisse nocturno cruore
        hospitis; ille uenena Colcha

et quidquid usquam concipitur nefas
10 tractauit, agro qui statuit meo
    te triste lignum, te caducum
        in domini caput immerentis.

quid quisque uitet numquam homini satis
cautum est in horas: nauita Bosphorum

15   Poenus perhorrescit neque ultra
       caeca timet aliunde fata;

    miles sagittas et celerem fugam
    Parthi, catenas Parthus et Italum
       robur; sed improuisa leti
20   uis rapuit rapietque gentis.

    quam paene furuae regna Proserpinae
    et iudicantem uidimus Aeacum
       sedesque discriptas piorum et
         Aeoliis fidibus querentem

25   Sappho puellis de popularibus,
    et te sonantem plenius aureo,
       Alcaee, plectro dura nauis,
         dura fugae mala, dura belli!

    utrumque sacro digna silentio
30   mirantur umbrae dicere; sed magis
       pugnas et exactos tyrannos
         densum umeris bibit aure uulgus.

    quid mirum, ubi illis carminibus stupens
    demittit atras belua centiceps
35   auris et intorti capillis
         Eumenidum recreantur angues?

    quin et Prometheus et Pelopis parens
    dulci laborem decipitur sono,
       nec curat Orion leones
40   aut timidos agitare lyncas.

Notes

Meter: Alcaic Stanza.

  2. *quicumque*—understand *te posuit.*
  3. *nepotum*—i.e., posterity.
  6. *penetralia*—used as a substantive.
  8. *Colcha*—home of Medea.

9. *quidquid*—adjectival.

11. *caducum*—i.e., *casurum*.

13. *homini*—dative of agent with impersonal *cautum est*, a gnomic perfect.

15. *perhorrescit*—transitive.

   ultra . . . fata—i.e., after passing the known dangers of the Bosphorus.

16. *caeca*—passive.

   timet—ultima is long; an archaizing lengthening.

18. *catenas*—by metonomy for captivity.

20. *rapuit*—gnomic perfect.

21. *Proserpina*—o is short.

22. *Aeacum*—a judge of the lower world.

24. *Sappho*—a Greek accusative.

29. *sacro . . . silentio*—i.e., such as at a religious ceremony.

30. *dicere*—used where a participle would be more common.

32. *umeris*—ablative of specification.

   uulgus—understand *umbrarum*.

34. *belua centiceps*—Cerberus is meant, though he usually is said to have three heads.

37. *et*—intensive, like Greek καί, "even."

   Prometheus—only here is he punished in Hades; usually he undergoes his punishment on Mount Caucasus.

38. *laborem*—object of *decipitur* which has a middle force, similar to the Greek middle voice.

40. *timidos*—lynx, usually feminine, but here masculine; *lyncas* is a Greek accusative.

This poem offers an excellent opportunity for examining a work which most commentators regard as a unity but which appears to be held together by a tenuous connection. An easily recognizable division occurs at v. 20. The poem which has started out exaggeratedly cursing a man who might have caused the poet's death moves to a generalized reflection on unforeseen death (1–20). From the notion of death, the poem then expatiates on how Hades would appear to the poet (21–40). The question is what is the theme of the poem. Why should Horace have decided to write a single poem on matters which seem more suitable for two poems? Is the poem a failure despite the critics' assertions to the contrary? In other words, how and why is this poem a unity?

Long ago a Frenchman commented that the subject of the poem was the power of art, specifically the power of poetry. Clearly this theme is evident in the second half of the poem where the poet, after briefly locating the scene, describes how the shades and monsters of Hades respond to the singing of Sappho and especially Alcaeus. We understand that their power is so great that all toil ceases and even joy seems to come upon that region which is reputedly joyless. In this light vv. 21 and 22, *quam paene . . . uidimus*, seem to express a regret that the accident was not fatal, so that the poet, too, could be part of the *densum . . . uulgus*. This tone is quite different from that of vv. 1–20. From anger, because he might have been killed, the poet has moved to regret that he was not. One of the triumphs of the poem is this shift in tone, which repays study. But even so, that does not completely illuminate the success of the poem. Twenty lines still remain which seem to have no connection with the notion of the power of art.

One might reasonably expect that the exact division of the poem would imply parallelism or chiastic arrangement of thoughts between the two parts. Such exactness, however, does not occur here, possibly because it would be too mechanical. Nevertheless, there does exist a certain correspondence between the parts. For example, vv. 27–28 reflect vv. 14–19, and the penultimate quatrain reflects the second quatrain. By these echoes between the first and second parts the poet clearly wishes to mark a connection between them.

By intermediate steps a further link is forged between the two parts. The first twenty lines concern the tree which almost fell on Horace, and the last twenty lines concern the power of poetry which beguiles all Hades. These two things are closely connected through an intermediary. The tree starts out as an *arbos* (3) which is cursed for having been planted. Further, the man who planted it is also cursed. The next time the tree is referred to, it becomes a *triste lignum* (11) and finally a *caducum* (11). These phrases signify a change in attitude and foreshadow the change which will occur in the whole poem. At the beginning of the poem the tree is cursed for falling, and in the third reference the tree becomes a thing destined to fall. The attitude which prompted the cursing changes to the realization that the tree was destined by its very nature to fall; hence the dissipation of the tone which began the poem.

As attendant to the change in attitude toward the tree some subordinate notions reinforce the central idea. The tree is spoken of as *triste lignum* and as *caducum*. The tree is *triste lignum* not only because it may fall on an unsuspecting head but also because it suggests by metonomy the coffin housing the dead. The idea of death is also hinted at in the word *caducum* which in this particular context implies the *caduceus* of Mercury who marshals the dead to Hades.

The notion of death from an unexpected source dominates the first half of the poem. In each instance the appearance of death is accountable even if unsuspected. The obvious implication of this idea is that it is the nature of things to die. Opposed to this idea is that found in the second half of the poem. There death is the given situation, the scene, as it were. In that scene the power of poetry dominates even death. Again the poet uses direct address, *te* (26), in referring to Alcaeus who along with Sappho becomes a symbol for the transcending of death. Note that Alcaeus' *plectrum* is spoken of as golden, the metal which age cannot tarnish or corrupt.

From the juxtaposition of these two basic ideas of the poem, from the arrangement of the two parts, and from their connections we can see Horace's point and how he chose to express it: *uita breuis ars longa*. We can see further how inevitably right the poem is, for its organization permits us to witness the transformation of attitude about one specific fact, the accidental falling of a tree, into an awareness about the distinction between life and art and into the perception that art transcends both life and death. By its ordering of experience art shows the pattern in the nature of things.

QUESTIONS

1. Explain the use of verb tenses and moods in the poem.
2. What part does meter play in this poem?

◅§⧽▻

Publius Vergilius Maro (70–19 B.C.)

Eclogue V

Menalcas   *Mopsus*

Me. Cur non, Mopse, boni quoniam conuenimus ambo,
    tu calamos inflare leuis, ego dicere uersus,
    hic corylis mixtas inter consedimus ulmos?

Mo. Tu maior; tibi me est aequum parere, Menalca,
5   siue sub incertas Zephyris motantibus umbras,
    siue antro potius succedimus. aspice, ut antrum
    siluestris raris sparsit labrusca racemis.

Me. Montibus in nostris solus tibi certat Amyntas.

Mo. Quid, si idem certet Phoebum superare canendo?

10 Me. Incipe, Mopse, prior, si quos aut Phyllidis ignis
    aut Alconis habes laudes aut iurgia Codri.
    incipe: pascentis seruabit Tityrus haedos.

Mo. Immo haec, in uiridi nuper quae cortice fagi
    carmina descripsi et modulans alterna notaui,
15   experiar: tu deinde iubeto ut certet Amyntas.

Me. Lenta salix quantum pallenti cedit oliuae,
    puniceis humilis quantum saliunca rosetis,
    iudicio nostro tantum tibi cedit Amyntas.
    sed tu desine plura, puer: successimus antro.

20 Mo. Exstinctum Nymphae crudeli funere Daphnim
    flebant (uos coryli testes et flumina Nymphis),
    cum complexa sui corpus miserabile nati,
    atque deos atque astra uocat crudelia mater.
    non ulli pastos illis egere diebus
25   frigida, Daphni, boues ad flumina; nulla neque amnem
    libauit quadripes nec graminis attigit herbam.

Daphni, tuum Poenos etiam gemuisse leones
interitum montesque feri siluaeque loquuntur.
Daphnis et Armenias curru subiungere tigris
30   instituit, Daphnis thiasos inducere Bacchi
et foliis lentas intexere mollibus hastas.
uitis ut arboribus decori est, ut uitibus uuae,
ut gregibus tauri, segetes ut pinguibus aruis,
tu decus omne tuis. postquam te fata tulerunt
35   ipsa Pales agros atque ipse reliquit Apollo.
grandia saepe quibus mandauimus hordea sulcis,
infelix lolium et steriles nascuntur auenae;
pro molli uiola, pro purpureo narcisso
carduus et spinis surgit paliurus acutis.
40   spargite humum foliis, inducite fontibus umbras,
pastores (mandat fieri sibi talia Daphnis),
et tumulum facite, et tumulo superaddite carmen:
"Daphnis ego in siluis, hinc usque ad sidera notus,
formosi pecoris custos, formosior ipse."
45 Me. Tale tuum carmen nobis, diuine poeta,
quale sopor fessis in gramine, quale per aestum
dulcis aquae saliente sitim restinguere riuo.
nec calamis solum aequiperas, sed uoce magistrum:
fortunate puer, tu nunc eris alter ab illo.
50   nos tamen haec quocumque modo tibi nostra uicissim
dicemus, Daphnimque tuum tollemus ad astra;
Daphnim ad astra feremus: amauit nos quoque Daphnis.
Mo. An quicquam nobis tali sit munere maius?
et puer ipse fuit cantari dignus, et ista
55   iam pridem Stimichon laudauit carmina nobis.
Me. Candidus insuetum miratur limen Olympi
sub pedibusque uidet nubes et sidera Daphnis.
ergo alacris siluas et cetera rura uoluptas
Panaque pastoresque tenet Dryadasque puellas.
60   nec lupus insidias pecori, nec retia ceruis
ulla dolum meditantur: amat bonus otia Daphnis.
ipsi laetitia uoces ad sidera iactant

intonsi montes; ipsae iam carmina rupes,
ipsa sonant arbusta: "deus, deus ille, Menalca!"
65   sis bonus o felixque tuis! en quattuor aras:
ecce duas tibi, Daphni, duas altaria Phoebo.
pocula bina nouo spumantia lacta quotannis
craterasque duo statuam tibi pinguis oliui,
et multo in primis hilarans conuiuia Baccho,
70   ante focum, si frigus erit, si messis, in umbra
uina nouum fundam calathis Ariusia nectar.
cantabunt mihi Damoetas et Lyctius Aegon;
saltantis Satyros imitabitur Alphesiboeus.
haec tibi semper erunt, et cum sollemnia uota
75   reddemus Nymphis, et cum lustrabimus agros.
   dum iuga montis aper, fluuios dum piscis amabit,
dumque thymo pascentur apes, dum rore cicadae,
semper honos nomenque tuum laudesque manebunt.
ut Baccho Cererique, tibi sic uota quotannis
80   agricolae facient: damnabis tu quoque uotis.
Mo. Quae tibi, quae tali reddam pro carmine dona?
nam neque me tantum uenientis sibilus Austri
nec percussa iuuant fluctu tam litora, nec quae
saxosas inter decurrunt flumina uallis.
85 Me. Hac te nos fragili donabimus ante cicuta.
haec nos "formosum Corydon ardebat Alexim,"
haec eadem docuit "cuium pecus? an Meliboei?"
Mo. At tu sume pedum, quod, me cum saepe rogaret,
non tulit Antigenes (et erat tum dignus amari),
90   formosum paribus nodis atque aere, Menalca.

Notes

Meter: Dactylic Hexameter.

   2. *inflare* and *dicere*—dependent on *boni*; a grecism.

   3. *corylis*—ablative of accompaniment without *cum*, or ablative of association.

      consedimus—perfect used like a Greek aorist.

   6. *ut . . . sparsit*—after *aspice, uide, dic, quaeso*, the subordinate

verb is treated as the principal one and put in the indicative. The main verb, *aspice*, etc., is simply an interjection.

8. *tibi*—dative with verbs of contending, etc.

10–11. *Phyllidis, Alconis*—objective genitives.

13–15. *quae . . . carmina . . . experiar*—antecedent attracted into relative clause.

15. *iubeto*—a legal form, rather than *iube*.

16–17. Willow and olive leaves are alike in shape and color, but the latter are more valuable; the wild nard as fragrant as the rose was useless for making garlands because of its brittleness.

18. *iudicio nostro*—ablative of manner or specification.

20. Daphnis, son of Hermes by a nymph. He was reared on the slopes of Mount Aetna in Sicily and taught to play the flute by Pan. Daphnis preferred music to love. This attitude angered Venus who inspired in him an unrequited passion for Xenia, a nymph. Daphnis in despair drowned himself. Mourned by all nature, he became the ideal shepherd of pastoral poetry and supposedly invented the form.

21. *Nymphis*—dative of reference.

23. *atque . . . atque*—probably emphatic for *et . . . et*.

astra—i.e., astrology. Stars supposedly influenced a man's life.

28. *loquuntur*—with indirect discourse the verb is unusual.

29–31. Daphnis introduced worship of Bacchus, a beneficent agricultural deity whose car was drawn by tigers and whose worshipers bore the *thyrsus* (spears wreathed with ivy and tipped with pine cones); an eastern worship in origin, hence *Armenias*.

curru—nouns in -*us* sometimes show this contracted form of the dative.

35. *Pales*—Italian deity of flocks and herds, joined with Apollo.

40. *fontibus*—dative with compounds, as is *tumulo* in 42.

41. *mandat fieri*—the infinitive, though rare, does occur for *ut* and the subjunctive after verbs of commanding, e.g., *iubeo*.

49. *alter ab illo*—remember that in counting in Latin one includes both beginning and end.

53. *sit*—although deliberative subjunctive, the verse is almost an exclamation.

54. *cantari*—epexegetic infinitive.

64. *Menalca*—Greek vocative.

65. *aras*—exclamatory accusative as is *altaria* in 66.

77. *rore*—the drink usually attributed to crickets in antiquity.

80. *damnabis . . . votis*—note the contractual idea in Roman religious language.

85. *donabimus*—ablative of gift and accusative of person, as here, appears with this verb as well as dative of person and accusative of gift.

QUESTIONS

1. This poem clearly represents certain conventions common to the writing of ancient pastoral. It involves a dramatic scene between two shepherds who are piping and singing about the figure of Daphnis, the prototype of all such pastoral shepherds. The real or actual world is not described in traditional pastoral poetry, except by inference. Nevertheless that inference is the justification for such poetry. As we carefully read this poem, we discover it is about the power of art, that is, what poetry can achieve within the world. Examine the organization of the poem. The main body of the poem is concerned with the death of Daphnis and his translation to Olympus and subsequent deification. But what then is the purpose of the opening verses, from 1 to 19? What function do they serve in relation to the songs the two men sing? Why is such stress laid on finding a cave? Why do they go into the cave rather than remain outside? What symbolic value does the cave have for the poem? What, furthermore, does the final exchange of gifts, vv. 81–90, serve in the poem? What are we obliged to consider is the purpose of this exchange? How does Vergil deliberately employ the artificiality of the "bucolic tradition," the shepherds, the references to animals and flocks, the story of Daphnis, etc., to further his ends?

2. Verses 85–87 clearly refer to other eclogues of Vergil, specifically II and III, which fact suggests that they were written before this one. Further it may not unreasonably be inferred from these verses that Vergil is identifying himself as Menalcas. Such an inference has led scholars and critics from ancient times to modern

days to hunt out the identity of other references in this poem as well as in other *Eclogues*. Every shepherd is supposed to be some historical figure; the eclogue is supposed to be an allegory. However, it is not necessary to read it as such, nor to take so simple a view of Vergil's poetry. Such a reading reduces poetry to the level of a puzzle which, if one is clever enough, one can easily solve and thus feel he has exhausted the poem. But a careful reading of the poem suggests that the introduction of references to Vergil's own works is a way of indicating that this poem is also a bucolic poem with the same unreality of the setting and governed by the same conventions. The reminder of these conventions warns us that the idyllic world of the pastoral is not taken as either a reflection of the real world or as an allegory of the real world. He has created in effect the world of poetry and set up a perspective by which he can judge the actual world. The conventions of bucolic poetry emphasize what is inherent in all poetry, that is the transfiguration of reality the better to judge it. Carefully consider how the particular details in this poem create a perspective in order to illuminate the theme of the poem.

3. The first poem in this book, Vergil, *Eclogue* I, has repeatedly been subjected to historical interpretation. The "god" is supposedly Augustus who returned Vergil's homestead to him after the confiscations arising from the settlement of the soldiers following cessation of war. Tityrus, then, is often said to be Vergil, and the poem is reputedly Vergil's way of thanking the Emperor. (Almost any commentary on Vergil will discuss this thesis.) Reread the poem and comment on what validity there is in this criticism.

4. Write an essay on *Eclogue* V in which you discuss the use of metrics in relation to the theme of the poem and its organization.

⤶⧨⤷

Publius Papinius Statius (c.40–c.45–96 A.D.)
Siluae II.5
Leo Mansuetus
Quid tibi monstrata mansuescere profuit ira?

quid scelus humanasque animo dediscere caedis
imperiumque pati et domino parere minori?
quid, quod abire domo rursusque in claustra reuerti
5   suetis et a capta iam sponte recedere praeda
insertasque manus laxo dimittere morsu?
occidis, altarum uastator docte ferarum,
non grege Massylo curuaque indagine clausus,
non formidato supra uenabula saltu
10 incitus aut caeco foueae deceptus hiatu,
sed uictus fugiente fera. stat cardine aperto
infelix cauea, et clausas circum undique portas
hoc licuisse nefas placidi intumuere leones.
tum cunctis cecidere iubae, puduitque relatum
15 aspicere, et torvas duxere in lumina frontes.
at non te primo fusum nouus obruit ictu
ille pudor: mansere animi, uirtusque cadenti
a media iam morte redit, nec protinus omnes
terga dedere minae. sicut sibi conscius alti
20 uulneris aduersum moriens it miles in hostem
attollitque manum et ferro labente minatur:
sic piger ille gradu solitoque exutus honore
firmat hians oculos animamque hostemque requirit.
magna tamen subiti tecum solatia leti,
25 uicte, feres, quod te maesti populusque patresque,
ceu notus caderes tristi gladiator harena,
ingemuere mori; magni quod Caesaris ora
inter tot Sythicas Libycasque, et litore Rheni
et Pharia de gente feras, quas perdere uile est,
30 unius amissi tetigit iactura leonis.

NOTES

Meter: Dactylic Hexameter.

2. *animo*—ablative of separation.

8. *Massylo*—an African tribe.

15. *frontes*—i.e., their brows.

18. *a media . . . morte*—ablative of separation as though place from which.

19. *terga dedere*—i.e., defeat, grant defeat.
29. *uile est*—i.e., cheap.

QUESTIONS

1. This poem is about an animal, but is it like the previous poems which also had animals in them? What differences are there? Is there anything pastoral about this poem?
2. What imagery does the poem use?
3. How are rhetorical figures used?
4. What is the theme of the poem?

❧

Quintus Horatius Flaccus (65–8 B.C.)
Ode II.3

Aequam memento rebus in arduis
seruare mentem, non secus in bonis
    ab insolenti temperatam
      laetitia, moriture Delli,

5 seu maestus omni tempore uixeris,
seu te in remoto gramine per dies
    festos reclinatum bearis
      interiore nota Falerni.

quo pinus ingens albaque populus
10 umbram hospitalem consociare amant
    ramis? quid obliquo laborat
      lympha fugax trepidare riuo?

huc uina et unguenta et nimium breuis
flores amoenae ferre iube rosae,
15   dum res et aetas et sororum
      fila trium patiuntur atra.

cedes coemptis saltibus et domo
uillaque flauus quam Tiberis lauit;
    cedes, et exstructis in altum
20   diuitiis potietur heres.

diuesne prisco natus ab Inacho
nil interest an pauper et infima
   de gente sub diuo moreris,
      uictima nil miserantis Orci.

25 omnes eodem cogimur, omnium
    uersatur urna serius ocius
      sors exitura et nos in aeternum
        exsilium impositura cumbae.

NOTES

Meter: Alcaic Stanza.

  2. *in bonis*—understand *rebus.*

  4. *Dellius*—probably Quintus Dellius, called *desultor bellorum ciuilium* because of his frequent changes of allegiance. A *desultor* was a circus rider who leaped from one horse to another while both horses were going full speed. Dellius became a friend of Octavian in 31 B.C. and wrote an account of Antony's Parthian campaign.

     moriture—used as the apodosis of the two subsequent conditions.

  5. *omni tempore*—ablative of extent of time.

  6. *te*—with *bearis.*

  7. *reclinatum*—verb is used in a reflexive sense.

  8. *interiore nota Falerni*—*nota* is the mark or label attached to a wine jar giving the date of vintage. *Interiore* refers to the inner part of the store room. Hence this is the best wine.

  10. *umbram*—accusative of "result"; object of infinitive.
      amant—personification.

  11. *quid*—an accusative of respect; usage derives from Greek.

  12. *lympha*—metonomy for "clear water."

  15. *sororum triuum*—i.e., the three Fates.

  16. *atra*—because cutting the *fila* brings death.

  21f. the adjectives are predicate to the subject contained in the verb *moreris.*

  23. *sub diuo moreris*—equals *uiuis*; suggests a brief span of life.

24. *uictima*—understand *es*, the apodosis of the previous protasis in vv. 21–23.

25. *omnium*—used for sake of anaphora; *cuiusque* is the proper word.

26. *serius ocius*—"sooner or later"; asyndeton.

27. The verse is hypermetric.

28. *cumbae*—i.e., *Charonis*.

QUESTIONS

1. What is the purpose of the vocative, *moriture Delli*, in v. 4?
2. Explain how the theme of the poem is worked out.

Publius Vergilius Maro (70–19 B.C.)
Eclogue IV

> Sicelides Musae, paulo maiora canamus!
> non omnis arbusta iuuant humilesque myricae
> si canimus siluas, siluae sint consule dignae.
>   Ultima Cumaei uenit iam carminis aetas;
> 5 magnus ab integro saeclorum nascitur ordo.
> iam redit et uirgo, redeunt Saturnia regna,
> iam noua progenies caelo demittitur alto.
> tu modo nascenti puero, quo ferrea primum
> desinet ac toto surget gens aurea mundo,
> 10 casta faue Lucina: tuus iam regnat Apollo.
> teque adeo decus hoc aeui, te consule, inibit,
> Pollio, et incipient magni procedere menses;
> te duce, si qua manent sceleris uestigia nostri,
> inrita perpetua soluent formidine terras.
> 15 ille deum uitam accipiet diuisque uidebit
> permixtos heroas et ipse uidebitur illis,
> pacatumque reget patriis uirtutibus orbem.
>   At tibi prima, puer, nullo munuscula cultu
> errantis hederas passim cum baccare tellus
> 20 mixtaque ridenti colocasia fundet acantho;
> 23 ipsa tibi blandos fundet cunabula flores.

21 ipsae lacte domum referent distenta capellae
    ubera, nec magnos metuent armenta leones;
    occidet et serpens, et fallax herba ueneni
25 occidet; Assyrium uulgo nascetur amomum.
    at simul heroum laudes et facta parentis
    iam legere et quae sit poteris cognoscere uirtus,
    molli paulatim flauescet campus arista,
    incultisque rubens pendebit sentibus uua,
30 et durae quercus sudabunt roscida mella.
    pauca tamen suberunt priscae uestigia fraudis,
    quae temptare Thetim ratibus, quae cingere muris
    oppida, quae iubeant telluri infindere sulcos.
    alter erit tum Tiphys, et altera quae uehat Argo
35 delectos heroas; erunt etiam altera bella
    atque iterum ad Troiam magnus mittetur Achilles.
    hinc, ubi iam firmata uirum te fecerit aetas,
    cedet et ipse mari uector, nec nautica pinus
    mutabit merces: omnis feret omnia tellus.
40 non rastros patietur humus, non uinea falcem;
    robustus quoque iam tauris iuga soluet arator;
    nec uarios discet mentiri lana colores,
    ipse sed in pratis aries iam suaue rubenti
    murice, iam croceo mutabit uellera luto;
45 sponte sua sandyx pascentis uestiet agnos.
        "Talia saecla" suis dixerunt "currite" fusis
    concordes stabili fatorum numine Parcae.
    adgredere o magnos (aderit iam tempus) honores,
    cara deum suboles, magnum Iouis incrementum!
50 aspice conuexo nutantem pondere mundum,
    terrasque tractusque maris caelumque profundum:
    aspice uenturo laetentur ut omnia saeclo!
    o mihi tum longae maneat pars ultima uitae,
    spiritus et quantum sat erit tua dicere facta:
55 non me carminibus uincet nec Thracius Orpheus,
    nec Linus, huic mater quamuis atque huic pater adsit,
    Orphei Calliopea, Lino formosus Apollo.

Pan etiam, Arcadia mecum si iudice certet,
Pan etiam Arcadia dicat se iudice uictum.
60 incipe, parue puer, risu cognoscere matrem
    (matri longe decem tulerunt fastidia menses)
    incipe, parue puer: qui non risere parenti,
    nec deus hunc mensa, dea nec dignata cubili est.

NOTES

Meter: Dactylic Hexameter.

1. *Sicelides*—traditional home of Vergil's muses.

3. *consule*—Pollio is apparently meant. He was consul in 40 B.C. and helped negotiate the treaty of Brundisium between Antony and Octavian, under which the Second Triumvirate was defined.

4. *Cumaei carminis*—reference is to Sibyl of Cumae.

6. *Saturnia regia*—Saturnus, Italian god of agriculture, was regarded as a beneficent ruler of earth; he later became confused with Greek Cronus who, according to the story, was driven from Greece by Zeus, and came to Italy, bringing the Golden Age.

8. *quo*—"under whom."

10. *Lucina*—i.e., Diana, protectress of childbearing women. The name implies "bringing to light." Although the title is also given to Juno, Diana may be meant here, for the following phrase is *tuus Apollo.*

12. *magni menses*—the periods which go to make up the *magnus annus.*

15. *deum*—genitive plural.

diuis—ablative of accompaniment without *cum,* or ablative of association.

16. *illis*—dative of agent.

18. *nullo cultu*—ablative of manner.

21. For this arrangement see G. Duckworth, *TAPA* 89, pp. 1–8.

24. *fallax*—i.e., treacherous because of its concealed poison.

30. According to ancient legend honey fell like dew and was so collected by the bees.

34. Reference is to Jason and the voyage of the Argonauts, a type of journey for wealth; Tiphys was pilot.

38. *mari*—ablative of separation.

41. *tauris*—dative of reference or ablative of separation.

43. *suaue*—cognate accusative.

47. *Parcae*—Clotho, Lachesis, Atropos; one spun, one measured, and one cut the thread of human life.

49. *deum*—genitive plural.

50. *pondere*—ablative of means or manner.

52. *ut*—technically introduces a dependent interrogative, but, in such phrases as *aspice ut*, the phrase itself is an interjection and is regularly followed by the indicative.

54. *dicere*—infinitive of purpose.

55. *non . . . nec . . . nec*—breaking up of the negative is common in Greek and Latin.

56. *Linus*—originally a hero whose early death was lamented in a dirge called "Song of Linus." He came to be regarded as the off-spring of Apollo and Calliope and half brother of Orpheus. Linus in ancient myth assumed the role then of singer and of performer on the lyre.

57. *Orphei*—disyllabic; Greek dative.

61. *tulerunt*—tulĕrunt.

QUESTIONS

1. In this poem about the birth of a child, perhaps the most famous of the *Eclogues*, how does the organization of the material reflect the prophesied life of the child?

2. Of what does the child become a symbol as the poem progresses? What is meant, then, by the notion of the Golden Age?

3. Carefully examine how the opening three verses of the poem set the pattern for what is to follow. Explain.

4. What does the poem reveal about the aspirations of Vergil?

Sextus Propertius (c.50–c.16 B.C.)

Elegy IV.11

Desine, Paulle, meum lacrimis urgere sepulcrum:
panditur ad nullas ianua nigra preces;

    cum semel infernas intrarunt funera leges,
      non exorato stant adamante uiae.
5 te licet orantem fuscae deus audiat aulae:
      nempe tuas lacrimas litora surda bibent.
    uota mouent superos: ubi portitor aera recepit,
      obserat herbosos lurida porta rogos.
    sic maestae cecinere tubae, cum subdita nostrum
10   detraheret lecto fax inimica caput.
    quid mihi coniugium Paulli, quid currus auorum
      profuit aut famae pignora tanta meae?
    non minus immitis habuit Cornelia Parcas:
      et sum, quod digitis quinque legatur, onus.
15 damnatae noctes et uos, uada lenta, paludes,
      et quaecumque meos implicat unda pedes,
    immatura licet, tamen huc non noxia ueni:
      det Pater hic umbrae mollia iura meae.
    aut si quis posita iudex sedet Aeacus urna,
20   in mea sortita uindicet ossa pila:
    assideant fratres, iuxta et Minoida sellam
      Eumenidum intento turba seuera foro.
    Sisyphe, mole uaces; taceant Ixionis orbes;
      fallax Tantaleus corripiare liquor;
25 Cerberus et nullas hodie petat improbus umbras;
      et iaceat tacita laxa catena sera.
    ipsa loquor pro me: si fallo, poena sororum
      infelix umeros urgeat urna meos.
    si cui fama fuit per auita tropaea decori,
30   Afra Numantinos regna loquuntur auos:
    altera maternos exaequat turba Libones,
      et domus est titulis utraque fulta suis.
    mox, ubi iam facibus cessit praetexta maritis,
      uinxit et acceptas altera uitta comas,
35 iungor, Paulle, tuo sic discessura cubili:
      in lapide hoc uni nupta fuisse legar.
    testor maiorum cineres tibi, Roma, colendos,
      sub quorum titulis, Africa, tunsa iaces,

†et Persen proauo stimulantem pectus Achille,
40   quique tuas proauo fregit Achille domos,†
me neque censurae legem mollisse neque ulla
     labe mea uestros erubuisse focos.
non fuit exuuiis tantis Cornelia damnum:
     quin et erat magnae pars imitanda domus.
45   nec mea mutata est aetas, sine crimine tota est:
     uiximus insignes inter utramque facem.
mi natura dedit leges a sanguine ductas,
     nec possis melior iudicis esse metu.
quaelibet austeras de me ferat urna tabellas:
50   turpior assessu non erit ulla meo,
uel tu, quae tardam mouisti fune Cybeben,
     Claudia, turritae rara ministra deae,
uel† cuius rasos† cum Vesta reposceret ignis,
     exhibuit uiuos carbasus alba focos.
55   nec te, dulce caput, mater Scribonia, laesi:
     in me mutatum quid nisi fata uelis?
maternis laudor lacrimis urbisque querelis,
     defensa et gemitu Caesaris ossa mea.
ille sua nata dignam uixisse sororem
60   increpat, et lacrimas uidimus ire deo.
et tamen emerui generosos uestis honores,
     nec mea de sterili facta rapina domo.
tu, Lepide, et tu, Paulle, meum post fata leuamen,
     condita sunt uestro lumina nostra sinu.
65   uidimus et fratrem sellam geminasse curulem;
     consule quo, festo tempore, rapta soror.
filia, tu specimen censurae nata paternae,
     fac teneas unum nos imitata uirum.
et serie fulcite genus: mihi cumba uolenti
70   soluitur auctoris tot mea facta meis.
haec est feminei merces extrema triumphi,
     laudat ubi emeritum libera fama rogum.
nunc tibi commendo communia pignora natos:
     haec cura et cineri spirat inusta meo.

75 fungere maternis uicibus pater: illa meorum
     omnis erit collo turba ferenda tuo.
oscula cum dederis tua flentibus, adice matris:
     tota domus coepit nunc onus esse tuum.
et si quid doliturus eris, sine testibus illis!
80   cum uenient, siccis oscula falle genis!
sat tibi sint noctes, quas de me, Paulle, fatiges,
     somniaque in faciem credita saepe meam:
atque ubi secreto nostra ad simulacra loqueris,
     ut responsurae singula uerba iace.
85 seu tamen aduersum mutarit ianua lectum,
     sederit et nostro cauta nouerca toro,
coniugium, pueri, laudate et ferte paternum:
     capta dabit uestris moribus illa manus;
nec matrem laudate nimis: collata priori
90   uertet in offensas libera uerba suas.
seu memor ille mea contentus manserit umbra
     et tanti cineres duxerit esse meos,
discite uenturam iam nunc sentire senectam,
     caelibis ad curas nec uacet ulla uia.
95 quod mihi detractum est, uestros accedat ad annos:
     prole mea Paullum sic iuuet esse senem.
et bene habet: numquam mater lugubria sumpsi;
     uenit in exsequias tota caterua meas.
causa perorata est. flentes me surgite, testes,
100   dum pretium uitae grata rependit humus.
moribus et caelum patuit: sim digna merendo,
     cuius honoratis ossa uehantur auis.

Notes

Meter: Elegiac Couplet.

   5. *fuscae*—i.e., the absence of light.

  10. *caput*—synecdoche for the whole body.

  11. *currus auorum*—the triumphal chariot; reference is to triumphs of Scipio and Aemilius Paullus.

18. *Pater*—probably Pluto, who was supreme in the underworld.

20. *uindicet in*—used personally here; a rare usage in Latin.
    sortita—transitive.

21. *fratres*—Minos and Rhadamanthus.

23. *orbes*—may be a genuine plural, i.e., revolutions; or the plural for the singular, i.e., wheel.

27. *sororum*—i.e., the Danaids; an objective genitive.

31. *exaequat*—transitive.

41. allusion to her husband's censorship in 22 B.C.

52. *turritae*—alludes to turreted crown worn by Cybele.

59. *sua ... sororem*—Cornelia was half sister to Julia, daughter of Augustus.

63. *Lepide*—M. Aemilius Lepidus, consul in A.D. 6, served in Pannonia under Tiberius and was awarded *ornamenta triumphalia*.

   Paulle—Lucius Aemilius Paullus, consul in A.D. 1 with Gaius Caesar; married Julia, granddaughter of Augustus. He later conspired against Augustus and was put to death.

69. *serie*—i.e., by carrying on the family line without interruption.

79. *sine testibus*—understand *a doleto*.

85. *aduersum*—colloquial for the *lectus genialis*, a symbolic marriage bed which stood in the *atrium* opposite the *ianua*.

96. *prole*—causal ablative or ablative of attendant circumstances.

99. *causa perorata est*—technical phrase for the conclusion of a speech.

Questions

1. What effect does the point of view, which is that of the first person, have in this poem? How does it solve problems of the poem that the third-person point of view would not?

2. What is the scene of Cornelia's speech, and how does this conceit operate in the poem?

3. Examine the poem for the rhetorical device of personification. Epithets are often transferred in Latin poetry from the words they ordinarily go with. What effect does such transference have in this poem? What purpose do they serve, and how do they relate

to the central conceit of this poem? Compare the use of transferred epithets with that use in Catullus LI.

4. In view of the organization of the poem, as it so far has been examined, what is the purpose of the references to Cornelia's ancestors and descendants as well as to the famous women of Rome?

5. By the end of the poem we are aware that this is not simply a poem about a particular dead woman but a poem discussing the highest virtues of Roman womanhood. It is the *matrona* who is praised here. Write an essay indicating what values were especially regarded as becoming to a Roman woman. Does Propertius in this poem believe in those same virtues? Comment.

EVALUATION

7

THE FINAL ACT of criticizing a poem is that of judgment. Implicit throughout this book has been the notion of judgment. Insofar as each poem is an attempt to order an experience and thus to interpret it, the poet himself is making a judgment about that experience. The task of the reader is to decide whether that judgment is a valid one from all the "testimony" given, i.e., from the way the experience has been presented. In our ordinary lives we judge constantly, frequently automatically, and so we appear to act spontaneously. But in other matters we are obliged to speculate long before reaching a decision; thus it is in literary criticism. Nevertheless, the more we question critically, the easier it becomes, and the more immediate becomes our response. The accumulation of decisions makes each new one easier. So, in reading poetry, we can develop an ease in distinguishing between what is worth attention and what is not and why. The task of judging and demonstrating the validity of our judgments nevertheless is constantly with us. In a classroom one can be told by an instructor that such and such is a good poem, and as a student one tends naturally enough to accept such *dicta* as final. But we do not become serious readers of poetry unless we ourselves are capable of deciding independently and with reasonable arguments why we favor one poem and condemn another. The following poems have been variously judged by critics: some have been praised, and some severely condemned. With the help of the questions and essays, come to your own decisions, bearing in mind all the suggestions made earlier in this book.

Marcus Valerius Martialis (c.40–104 A.D.)

Epigram VI.28

Libertus Melioris ille notus,
tota qui cecidit dolente Roma,
cari deliciae breues patroni,
hoc sub marmore Glaucias humatus
5   iuncto Flaminiae iacet sepulchro:
castus moribus, integer pudore,
uelox ingenio, decore felix.
bis senis modo messibus peractis
uix unum puer adplicabat annum.
10 qui fles talia, nil fleas, uiator.

NOTES

Meter: Phalaecean or Hendecasyllabic.

3. *breues*—i.e., like the rose.

4. *Glaucias*—a freedman of Atedius Melior, a dandy, and a dilettante of letters.

    humatus—i.e., *sepultus.*

5. *Flaminiae*—understand *uiae*; dative with *iungo.*

10. *fles*—transitive.

QUESTIONS

1. How does the last verse affect the entire poem? What is the subject of the verbs *fles* and *fleas*? What does this suggest about the previous verses? Who utters those verses?

2. What role does meter play in the poem?

3. Evaluate the poem.

Appendix Vergiliana
Copa Surisca
Copa Surisca caput Graeca redimita mitella,

crispum sub crotalo docta mouere latus,
ebria fumosa saltat lasciua taberna
    ad cubitum raucos excutiens calamos.
5 "quid iuuat aestiuo defessum puluere abesse,
    quam potius bibulo decubuisse toro?
sunt topia et kelebes, cyathi, rosa, tibia, chordae,
    et triclia umbrosis frigida harundinibus.
en et, Maenalio quae garrit dulce sub antro,
10   rustica pastoris fistula more sonat.
est et uappa cado nuper defusa picato
    et strepitans rauco murmure riuus aquae.
sunt etiam croceo violae de flore corollae,
    sertaque purpurea lutea mixta rosa,
15 et quae uirgineo libata Achelois ab amne
    lilia uimineis attulit in calathis.
sunt et caseoli quos iuncea fiscina siccat.
    sunt autumnali cerea pruna die.
castaneaeque nuces et suaue rubentia mala,
20   est hic munda Ceres, est Amor, est Bromius.
sunt et mora cruenta et lentis uua racemis,
    et pendet iunco caeruleus cucumis.
est tuguri custos armatus falce saligna,
    sed non et uasto est inguine terribilis.
25 huc Calybita ueni, lassus iam sudat asellus.
    parce illi, Vestae delicium est asinus.
nunc cantu crebro rumpunt arbusta cicadae,
    nunc uepris in gelida sede lacerta latet.
si sapis, aestiuo recubans te prolue uitro,
30   seu uis crystalli ferre nouos calices.
heia, age, pampinea fessus requiesce sub umbra
    et grauidum roseo necte caput strophio,
†formosum† tenerae decerpens ora puellae.
    a pereat cui sunt prisca supercilia!
35 quid cineri ingrato seruas bene olentia serta?
    anne coronato uis lapide ista tegi?

pone merum et talos. pereat qui crastina curat.
　　Mors aurem uellens, 'uiuite,' ait, 'uenio.' "

NOTES

Meter: Elegiac Couplet.
　1. *caput*—accusative of specification.
　2. *mouere*—epexegetic infinitive dependent on *docta*.
　6. *quam potius*—anastrophe.
　15. *Achelois*—daughter of Achelous, the river god.
　24. *et*—"also," "even."

QUESTIONS

　1. Describe the scene of the poem. How does the scene affect the poem?

　2. What sorts of pleasures are described in this poem? In what order are they mentioned?

　3. What effect, if any, does the meter have in the organization of the poem?

　4. Explain what purpose the last verse of the poem serves. How does the verse relate to all that has gone before? What is the kind of death described or rather suggested? What does this suggest about the attitude of the poet? What attitude are we to take towards the poem?

　5. Write an essay evaluating the poem.

�''⋅❧

Quintus Horatius Flaccus (65–8 B.C.)
Epode XVI

Altera iam teritur bellis ciuilibus aetas,
　　suis et ipsa Roma uiribus ruit:
quam neque finitimi ualuerunt perdere Marsi
　　minacis aut Etrusca Porsenae manus,
5　aemula nec uirtus Capuae nec Spartacus acer
　　nouisque rebus infidelis Allobrox,
nec fera caerulea domuit Germania pube
　　parentibusque abominatus Hannibal,

impia perdemus deuoti sanguinis aetas,
10   ferisque rursus occupabitur solum.
barbarus heu cineres insistet uictor et Vrbem
        eques sonante uerberabit ungula,
quaeque carent uentis et solibus ossa Quirini,
        nefas uidere! dissipabit insolens.
15 forte quid expediat communiter aut melior pars
        malis carere quaeritis laboribus.
nulla sit hac potior sententia, Phocaeorum
        uelut profugit exsecrata ciuitas
agros atque Lares patrios, habitandaque fana
20   apris reliquit et rapacibus lupis,
ire pedes quocumque ferent, quocumque per undas
        Notus uocabit aut proteruus Africus.
sic placet? an melius quis habet suadere? secunda
        ratem occupare quid moramur alite?
25 sed iuremus in haec: simul imis saxa renarint
        uadis leuata, ne redire sit nefas;
neu conuersa domum pigeat dare lintea, quando
        Padus Matina lauerit cacumina,
in mare seu celsus procurrerit Appenninus,
30   nouaque monstra iunxerit libidine
mirus amor, iuuet ut tigris subsidere ceruis,
        adulteretur et columba miluo,
credula nec rauos timeant armenta leones,
        ametque salsa leuis hircus aequora.
35 haec et quae poterunt reditus abscindere dulcis
        eamus omnis exsecrata ciuitas,
aut pars indocili melior grege; mollis et exspes
        inominata perprimat cubilia!
uos quibus est uirtus, muliebrem tollite luctum,
40   Etrusca praeter et uolate litora.
nos manet Oceanus circumuagus: arua, beata
        petamus arua, diuites et insulas,
reddit ubi Cererem tellus inarata quotannis
        et imputata floret usque uinea,

45 germinat et numquam fallentis termes oliuae,
    suamque pulla ficus ornat arborem,
mella caua manant ex ilice, montibus altis
    leuis crepante lympha desilit pede.
illic iniussae ueniunt ad mulctra capellae,
50   refertque tenta grex amicus ubera;
nec uespertinus circumgemit ursus ouile,
    neque intumescit alta uiperis humus:
pluraque felices mirabimur; ut neque largis
    aquosus Eurus arua radat imbribus,
55 pinguia nec siccis urantur semina glaebis,
    utrumque rege temperante caelitum.
non huc Argoo contendit remige pinus,
    neque impudica Colchis intulit pedem;
non huc Sidonii torserunt cornua nautae
60   laboriosa nec cohors Vlixei:
nulla nocent pecori contagia, nullius astri
    gregem aestuosa torret impotentia.
Iuppiter illa piae secreuit litora genti,
    ut inquinauit aere tempus aureum;
65 aere, dehinc ferro durauit saecula, quorum
    piis secunda uate me datur fuga.

NOTES

Meter: Second Pythiambic.

    1. *altera aetas*—i.e., the first began about 88 B.C., the time of Marius and Sulla. This is the second generation.

    3. *quam*—antecedent is an understood *eam.*

    Marsi—leaders in Social War of 91–88 B.C. They intended to destroy Rome and make Corfinium the capital of Italy.

    5. *Capuae*—after Cannae, the citizens of Capua went over to Hannibal, aspired to the leadership of Italy, but were put down by the Romans who never forgave the Capuans.

    Spartacus—leader of the slave revolt of 73–71 B.C.

    6. *Allobrox*—alludes to the conspiracy of Catiline. The *Allo-*

broges, who betrayed the conspirators, afterwards revolted against Rome.

7. Alludes to the invasion of Roman territory by the Cimbrians and Teutons who were defeated by Marius and Catulus (102–101 B.C.).

8. *parentibus abominatus—parentibus* is dative of agent; *abominatus* is passive.

13. *quae . . . ossa*—the antecedent is placed in the relative clause.

carent . . . solibus—i.e., are in the tomb and so sheltered. The tomb of Romulus was said to be behind the *rostra*. According to legend, however, Romulus was translated in the chariot of Mars to heaven.

14. *insolens*—adverbial force.

15. *quid*—antecedent is an understood *id*. The clause is in apposition to *carere laboribus. Carere* is an infinitive of purpose.

17. *hac*—explained by *ire* (21).

sententia—technical term for a proposal passed by a vote.

Phocaeorum—the inhabitants of Phocaea on the west coast of Asia Minor abandoned their city in 534 B.C. rather than submit to Harpagus, the general of Cyrus. They sank a piece of iron into the sea and swore never to return until the iron rose.

18. *exsecrata*—"having bound themselves by a curse."

23. *sic placet, suadere*—technical terms in legislative procedure.

25. *in haec*—understand *uerba*. Note that the Roman has four impossibilities.

28. *Matina*—Mount Matinus, a spur of Mount Garganus on the eastern coast of Apulia.

30. *monstra*—proleptic, as is *credula* in 33 and *leuis* in 34.

36. *ciuitas*—appositive with subject of *eamus*.

37. *mollis et exspes*—adjectives used as substantives.

38. *inominata*—word found only here: "ill-fated," "ill-omened."

43. *Cererem*—by metonomy for grain.

46. *suam . . . arborem*—i.e., not grafted as good varieties of figs had to be to insure a proper harvest.

53. *ut*—"how."

58. *neque impudica Colchis*—i.e., no Medea.

59. *Sidonii*—Phoenicians of Tyre and Sidon were the great seamen of antiquity.

torserunt cornua—i.e., and so directed their ships.

60. *Vlixei*—a genitive form. Such nouns are treated as though they had endings of *-e-us*.

64. *ut*—"ever since."

65. *dehinc ferro*—Hesiod's five ages were the age of gold, of silver, of bronze, of Trojan heroes, and of iron.

quorum—objective genitive with *fuga*; or may be construed with *piis*, i.e., the better part.

EXERCISE

Write a detailed analysis of this poem.

ఆర్ట్

Quintus Horatius Flaccus (65–8 B.C.)
Ode III.29

Tyrrhena regum progenies, tibi
non ante uerso lene merum cado
    cum flore, Maecenas, rosarum et
      pressa tuis balanus capillis

5 iamdudum apud me est. eripe te morae,
nec semper udum Tibur et Aefulae
    decliue contempleris aruum et
      Telegoni iuga parricidae.

fastidiosam desere copiam et
10 molem propinquam nubibus arduis;
    omitte mirari beatae
      fumum et opes strepitumque Romae.

plerumque gratae diuitibus uices
mundaeque paruo sub lare pauperum
15   cenae sine aulaeis et ostro
      sollicitam explicuere frontem.

iam clarus occultum Andromedae pater
ostendit ignem, iam Procyon furit
    et stella uesani Leonis,
20   sole dies referente siccos:

iam pastor umbras cum grege languido
riuumque fessus quaerit et horridi
    dumeta Siluani, caretque
        ripa uagis taciturna uentis.

25 tu ciuitatem quis deceat status
curas et Vrbi sollicitus times
    quid Seres et regnata Cyro
        Bactra parent Tanaisque discors.

prudens futuri temporis exitum
30 caliginosa nocte premit deus,
    ridetque si mortalis ultra
        fas trepidat. quod adest memento

componere aequus; cetera fluminis
ritu feruntur, nunc medio alueo
35   cum pace delabentis Etruscum
        in mare, nunc lapides adesos

stirpesque raptas et pecus et domos
uoluentis una non sine montium
    clamore uicinaeque siluae,
40   cum fera diluuies quietos

irritat amnis. ille potens sui
laetusque deget, cui licet in diem
    dixisse "uixi: cras uel atra
        nube polum Pater occupato

45 uel sole puro; non tamen irritum,
quodcumque retro est, efficiet neque
    diffinget infectumque reddet,
        quod fugiens semel hora uexit.

Fortuna saeuo laeta negotio et
50 ludum insolentem ludere pertinax
transmutat incertos honores,
nunc mihi, nunc alii benigna.

laudo manentem; si celeris quatit
pennas, resigno quae dedit et mea
55 uirtute me inuoluo probamque
pauperiem sine dote quaero.

non est meum, si mugiat Africis
malus procellis, ad miseras preces
decurrere et uotis pacisci
60 ne Cypriae Tyriaeque merces

addant auaro diuitias mari.
tunc me biremis praesidio scaphae
tutum per Aegaeos tumultus
aura feret geminusque Pollux."

Notes

Meter: Alcaic Stanza.

1. *tibi*—depends on *est* (5).

2. *cado*—ablative of place.

5. *morae*—dative of separation.

7. *nec contempleris*—a jussive clause introduced by *nec*.

8. *Telegoni iuga parricidae*—i.e., Tusculum, supposed to have been founded by Telegonus, the son of Ulysses and Circe, who came to Ithaca and unwittingly slew Ulysses.

9. *fastidiosam*—i.e., boredom from satiety and weariness.

11. *omitte*—ŏmitte.

14. *lare*—metonomy for *tecto*.

16. *explicuere*—gnomic perfect; used of a general truth.

17. *pater*—i.e., Cepheus, king of Aethiopia, husband of Cassiopeia, and father of Andromeda. Husband, wife, and daughter are well-known constellations.

18. *ostendit ignem*—used of a rising constellation.

Procyon—the lesser dog star; forms an apparent equilateral triangle with the greater dog star, Sirius, and with Betelgeuse which is in the shoulder of the constellation of Orion.

19. *stella*—Regulus, rises on 30 July.

uesani—because of the intense heat accompanying its rising.

27. *Seres*—Serĕs; Greek inflection.

regnata—transitive.

Cyro—dative of agent; Cyrus the Elder is meant.

28. *Tanais*—the river Don.

35. The verse is hypermetric. Elision occurs with the *m*.

48. *uexit*—*aduexit*.

54. *resigno*—a commercial term; "enter on the opposite side," "cancel a debt."

56. *paueriem*—almost personification.

quaero—i.e., as one seeks a wife.

58. *mālus*.

60. *ne addant*—a substantive clause used as the object of *pacisci*.

64. *geminus Pollux*—i.e., Castor and Pollux, patron deities of mariners.

Horace in *Tyrrhena regum progenies* examines three ways of viewing reality. He suggests in the poem that two of them do not afford a perception of reality which can sustain men in their daily lives, whereas the third, because of its greater depth, gives to men the means of coping with the problems of this world.

The poem begins with an invitation to Maecenas, addressed as *Tyrrhena regum progenies*, to come to the country. Horace promises wine, flowers, and scent (1–5). Deceptively simple in appearance, these five lines comprise so many rhetorical figures that they almost drown the thought. Hypallage, or transferred epithet, occurs in v. 1, chiasmus in v. 2, a grammatically subordinate *cum* phrase for what is logically one of the three subjects in v. 3, and interlocked word order in v. 4. But Horace, who is generally admired as a master craftsman, does not, as we have seen in others of his poems, vainly decorate a simple thought. By such an exploitation of rhetoric, he forces our attention to a scrutiny of what he is saying in this invitation to Maecenas. He compels us to re-examine that opening line, *Tyrrhena regum progenies*, which sounds like hyperbole. If he were simply employing hyperbole in addressing Maecenas, the flattery would be a trifle blatant. However, because the poem at the beginning proposes to a son of kings a stay in the country, a proposition in itself somewhat extraordinary, we might further suspect that an ironic intention lies behind both the invitation to the bucolic life and the royal allusion to Maecenas.

Throughout the first sixteen verses of the poem, Horace continues the conceit of the poor man asking the royal scion to visit him at his simple home. In his series of imperatives beginning in v. 5 and continuing to v. 12 Horace skillfully reveals the sort of man that the Maecenas of the poem is. He is one who delays, who gazes upon Tibur, Aefula, and Tusculanum (5–8), who lives in cloying luxury in a tower which climbs to the clouds, and who marvels at the smoke, wealth, and noise of Rome (9–12). From this indirect portrayal of the man, we deduce that he is unable to move, isolated from the world, even that world in which he is most involved—Rome and its daily concerns. Viewed in this fashion Maecenas appears enmeshed in the midst of meaningless activity. All these verses are artfully fashioned in a manner suitable for a *regum progenies*. For example, the variety of imperatives is startling: *eripe* (5), *nec . . . contempleris* (6–7), followed by another positive, *desere* (9), followed by another imperative comprising a verb which contains a negative idea followed by an infinitive, *omitte mirari* (11). No less startling is the arrangement of nouns and adjectives in these same verses. After his simple imperative in v. 5, with which he uses the dative where one would ordinarily expect an ablative,[1] Horace proceeds to use a complex system of three items in the accusative, *udum Tibur, Aefulae/ decliue . . . aruum*, and *Telegoni iuga parricidae* (a rather complicated and chiastic way of saying Tusculum, 6–8), *fastidiosam copiam, molem propinquam nubibus arduis*, and *beatae/ fumum et opes strepitumque Romae*, in which again the last involves chiasmus (9–12). In each group, 6–8, 9–12, the first noun has a simple ad-

[1] It is possible that a pun may be intended here.

jective attached to it, the second an adjective and a dative, and the third has dependent genitives in a chiastic arrangement. This kind of tessellated verse would be too contrived were this poem as simple as the motif of the invitation to the country would lead us to believe, and were the opening address merely a decorative hyperbole. Such an organization compels our attention to the manner of speaking and thus to a questioning of what is being said. The verses abound in complex phrases which dazzle and almost paralyze our critical intelligence, even as Maecenas is dazzled and paralyzed at Rome. They suggest the very decor of Maecenas' life: artificial, convoluted, and ultimately vain.

In verses 13–16 Horace somewhat abates his complex technique for the sake of a comparatively straightforward justification of his invitation to Maecenas. Simple fare in a simple house, says Horace, has often been able to smooth the brows of the rich (13–16). The conceit of the invitation ends at this point. What Horace has apparently said so far is, "Maecenas, come to me in the country away from Rome, for even a rich man can be refreshed by a poor one." At the same time he has suggested that Maecenas is unable to move; he is caught in the web of town life, the life of the busy world, to such a degree that he is powerless to act in it. Surely this is a long way from the freedom of action we are accustomed to think of as becoming a royal princeling who for all his state duties ought nevertheless to be able to move without regard for the concerns a poor man has to face. The suspicion begins to grow that perhaps Maecenas in an important sense is not royalty for all his royal descent, for all his troops and towers.

The next three quatrains go far to foster this suspicion. Opposed to the attitude of Maecenas as it was implied in the previous verses is that of the shepherd. Horace counterpoises to Maecenas, who can only view from a distance such pleasures, the shepherd who searches for shady groves and cool water. The transition from the earlier stanzas appears somewhat abrupt, yet in reality it is not, for from v. 17 to the end of the poem Horace explores the significance of the invitation he has given Maecenas. At the same time he begins to anticipate the rest of the poem which in turn reflects upon the first sixteen verses. Although the texture of the language is not so consistently dense as it has been, the argument is considerably more complex.

To examine the argument let us look at the presentation of the two other characters of this poem: the shepherd, and the *Ille potens sui laetusque* of vv. 41 ff.

That Maecenas and the shepherd are to be seen as juxtaposed cannot be doubted when we look at vv. 21–24 and 25–28. The shepherd who looks after his flock is performing a function analogous to that of Maecenas who, as Augustus' agent, looks after the state (25–26); the metaphor is not an uncommon one in poetry, even ancient poetry, but the connections are quite pointedly emphasized. In vv. 17–20 Horace describes the heat of the day. These verses not only continue the reason for the invitation—it is summer; it is hot—which was the ostensible business of vv. 1–16, but also they describe an immediate situation (the verbs are in the present tense, *ostendit*, *furit*, *referente*, and are emphasized by the repeated *iam*). To this situation presented by nature the shepherd responds with an immediate action: *iam* (21) begins the quatrain; the verbs are again present, *quaerit* (22) and *caret* (23). On the other hand, Maecenas in vv. 25–28, although he thinks in the present, *curas* and *times* (26), thinks about what may happen, *deceat* (25) and *parent* (28). Latin syntax, of course, normally requires the subjunctive in indirect questions, but Horace takes advantage of this fact to emphasize his point that Maecenas, unlike the shepherd, is concerned with probability, with what may happen. These lines further strengthen the earlier delineation of Maecenas as a spectator, not an actor.

The concern with the probable, and thus with the future, is at the root of this poem. It is the attitude toward the future which forms the basis for the judgments of the three points of view presented in the ode. Maecenas worries over it; the shepherd does not. The shepherd lives solely in the present. It is this characteristic which connects the shepherd with the third figure of the poem, *ille potens sui/ laetusque*. But, before showing us the third figure, Horace (in vv. 31–41) makes quite clear how he regards the future.

It is unknown, for some farseeing god has clouded it with smoky night and laughs at the attempts of mortals to see beyond that cloud (29–32). Occurring where they do, these verses offer a rebuke to Maecenas' concern for what the Syrians, the Bactrians, and the Tanaians may do (27–28). Horace continues to describe the future in 33–41. In the only simile in the poem he compares the future to a river which now moves serenely and now, stirred by a fierce storm (*fera diluuies*, 40), rages violently, uprooting, destroying all in its path. This river is one which all must travel; it symbolizes the life of the individual which can be either peaceful or stormy, and stormy it may well be. As though to emphasize this point, Horace uses five verses and a half to describe the effect of the violent storm on the river and the surrounding countryside. Earlier in the poem he had presented a picture of the banks of a river as calm, unstirred by even a breeze (23–24). That passage was concerned with the present, while the storm verses, 36–41, deal with the future. Behind this notion of the future shrouded in blackness as a darkling storm lies the fact of death. Death, whose approach cannot be foreseen, is the goal of all men. This undiscernible end is the one sure thing we know about the future. Further, death, which is necessarily synonymous in the Horatian odes with the future, destroys all that men have done or can do; it rages against life, our present life. Therefore, the only time we have is the present which it is best to attend to, as Horace declares in vv. 32–33, *quod adest memento/ componere aequus*. What seems to emerge from the two descriptions of the river which link the present with calm, the future with stress, is the thought that serenity accompanies the acceptance of what is at hand, that anxiety and fear are the lot of the man who looks only to the future.

Before presenting the third figure (v. 41), Horace has discussed in twelve verses the notion of the future in order that he may effectively show the man who is self-controlled and happy. He uses the third figure as a means of illustrating his beliefs and as a way of suggesting the efficacy of those beliefs. The *ille potens sui* is somewhat like the shepherd, yet he differs in that he possesses self-consciousness, the lack of which limits the shepherd's point of view. To help us to understand this notion, Horace makes the third figure speak in the first person.

In choosing the first person as the mode of speaking Horace has created an ambiguity in that portion of the ode from v. 41 to the end. Four possibilities of interpretation occur, depending on how the passage is punctuated: (1) the direct quotation of *Ille potens sui* may run from *uixi* (43) to *uexit* (48); or (2) from *uixi* to the end of the poem; or (3) the quotation may simply be used for the one word *uixi*; or (4) all quotation marks may be omitted. Since neither the manuscripts nor the Roman habits of punctuation help to solve this question, the problem becomes one of interpretation. The third possibility mentioned above can be discarded, for the speaker of *cras . . . uexit* is certainly the same as the speaker of *uixi*. The first possibility arises from the interpretation of vv. 49–51: Are they uttered by the same person as the earlier speaker, or by the "I" of the last three quatrains? If not by the earlier speaker, *ille potens sui*, then we must suppose the "I" of the last three strophes to be the Horace of this poem. If this be so, then the editors, who enclose in quotation marks vv. 43–48, arbitrarily force Horace to increase the "I's" of the poem in the manner of prose, not poetry. But a more satisfactory reading of the text exists if we follow either the second or the fourth alternative, i.e., make the whole passage the quotation of *ille potens sui* or omit quotation marks altogether. Of the two I favor making the whole passage the quotation of *ille potens sui*. But, if that be chosen, what are we to make of the stanza on *Fortuna*? Horace creates an ambiguity here by his use of the first person. When he inserts the *Fortuna* stanza, he partially destroys the illusion of the *ille potens sui* as speaker. But by returning to the first person he suggests the return of *ille potens sui* and at the same time implies an identification of that speaker with himself. Both "I's" have the same philosophy of life which, as we shall see, is at variance with the implied attitudes of Maecenas and the shepherd. Further, the first person echoes the *apud me* of v. 5 and makes a connection with the first portion of the poem. By such an ambiguity Horace delicately suggests that he is opposed to the Maecenean view of reality. Three advantages derive from this reading of the text. It permits the poem to have not four but three distinct yet closely connected parts, a division which is commonly found in the *Odes*, and which is emphasized by verb forms involving first, second, and third persons. Second, the last section of the poem falls into three parts: first, the statement of the "philosophical" attitude (43–48); next, the presentation of the ever-present problem of "fortune" as an external force operating upon life and thus a matter which the attitude must take into account (49–56); and then, the illustration of the value of that attitude in worldly or "practical" terms (57–64). This order is almost the reverse of the sequence of thought found in the first sixteen verses of the poem. There Horace moved from the particular (the vine, the flowers, the scent) to the general (even a poor man's country house can erase a rich man's cares). Finally, the first-person point of view subtly binds the last part of the poem with the earlier part. Although *apud me* occurs in v. 5, and although there must be a speaker of the imperatives (5–12), the greater part of our attention was not focused on him, even though we may have been aware of his existence. Now he declares himself. Through the use of the first person he is, as it were, explaining and justifying his original imperatives; he is taking responsibility for his original invitation.

To turn from these considerations to a scrutiny of the argument of the concluding stanza, which is, of course, what the poet wants us to do, we find Horace describing the man who is poised and therefore happy, with whom Horace indirectly identifies himself and contrasts Maecenas. In this poem he is the paradigm for all men to emulate, for he follows the philosophy outlined in vv. 20–41.

Similar to the shepherd in his ability to live in the present and to Maecenas in his awareness of the future, he is nevertheless unlike both. To the one he opposes his consciousness; to the other his freedom. He can deal with what is at hand without being unduly concerned over the future and the vagaries of fortune. He can move between the city and the country, in effect between the public and private worlds. Hence the man who is *ille potens sui* is able to be termed *laetus*.

To underscore these points Horace does several things. First, in vv. 43–44, he repeats the image of a black cloud, which he had employed in v. 30. For contrast he follows it with *sole puro* (45), thus implying that the future may be like the present which in this poem is surrounded by clarity and calm. However, the following *non*, although grammatically dependent upon *irritum*, nevertheless by its position casts doubt on *sole puro*. The effect emphasizes the dubiety of the future. Next, vv. 45–48, in their insistence on the impossibility of changing the shape of the past, contrast with the impossibility of knowing the shape of the future. This effect in turn underlines the quality of fantasy which is inherent in a concern over the future, and reminds us of the phantoms which Maecenas worries about in Syria, Bactria, and Tanaii (26–28), as well as at Rome (11–12). In the personification of *fugiens hora uexit* (48), he repeats the motif of the river carrying all with it.

Horace next describes that mysterious force in life which puts to the test any philosophy of life, for not all the events in his life are necessarily a man's doing. Here the force is labelled *Fortuna*. Verses 49–52 are a masterpiece of construction reminding us of the complexity of the earlier stanzas. Simply stated the thought is, "Fortune, delighting in her capriciousness, offers ambiguous honors now to one, now to another." The *incertos honores* (51) harks back to the seventh stanza (25–28), which alludes to Maecenas' honors deriving from his services to Augustus. *Fortuna*, herself, is personified, and she partakes of deification. Though she echoes *deus* of v. 30, she is not *prudens*, but rather spontaneous and capricious in her ways, and sometimes she even appears kindly disposed. The context defines the *laeta* of *Fortuna*; it arises from her own abundance; nothing limits her power or her capriciousness. *Fortuna*, as the personification implies, is immortal. Hence she can be irresponsible. When *laetus* is used of man it differs because of the very fact of man's mortality, of his limitation by death. From his awareness of that fact he develops his sense of responsibility. Man must be *laetus* in the face of death. The capriciousness of *Fortuna* Horace underlines by employing interlocking word order in v. 49 so that *saeuo* and *laeta* are juxtaposed, repeating the same idea in both a noun and a verb in v. 50, and by the chiastic arrangement of nouns, adjectives, and verbs in vv. 50–51. But though *Fortuna* may be wanton, she does exercise a power over men's lives. This point the position of the adjectives modifying *Fortuna* reinforces: *laeta* in the middle of v. 49, *pertinax* almost in the middle of the stanza, and *benigna* at the end. Such construction of the verses not only reinforces the ideas but also shows the similarity between the effect of *Fortuna* on life and the changes the river undergoes, now calm, now stirred up (33–41). In the next quatrain the rapidity of *Fortuna*'s change is again stressed in the phrase *celeris quatit/ pinnas* (53–54).

The following quatrain explains how the speaker responds to *Fortuna*: by praising her presence, by accepting her departure. These lines more narrowly define *Fortuna*, for her presence is felt to be good, her absence evil. *Fortuna* is thus limited to good fortune. This limitation permits Horace to make a contrast between fortune as wealth and fortune as poverty (56) and thus to suggest a further contrast in the poem: Maecenas, the rich man (9–16), versus the first person of this section, the poor man. The contrast becomes even more effective because of the description of how the speaker responds to the departure of *Fortuna*: he resigns what *Fortuna* gives, wraps himself in his own strength, and seeks poverty (53–56). How different from Maecenas who is surfeited with wealth, wrapped in his vast pile. Because the one has failed to understand how to regard the future, failed to develop a viable attitude toward life, he is at the mercy of *Fortuna*'s shifts; but because the other more accurately comprehends the significance of the future, he is able to manage manfully in the present.

The motif of poverty versus wealth Horace concludes in the last two quatrains of the poem, which draw their imagery from daily life. At the same time they connote much more. The speaker declares that not for him is prayer to the gods for protection from the African winds lest his freighted ships feed the avaricious sea.

This mercantile metaphor reflects again the business of Rome and the concern with far-off places which occupy Maecenas' thought. Such an image suggests something specific about the merchant life, namely the necessity for bargaining. Bargaining underlies the thought of vv. 57–60. Horace will not court *Fortuna* in exchange for her favors. Not for him is the life of the merchant, the bargainer.

Horace, or more properly, the speaker in the last three lines, sets forth the results of his refusal to bargain with *Fortuna*. The breezes and even the gods will bear him safely through Aegean storms because he is a man, *potens sui*. That he is a man who is self-reliant is stressed by *tunc me biremis praesidio scaphae* (62). This two-oared skiff (the man himself, as *biremis* suggests) is not just the poor man's boat in contrast to the rich merchant's vessel, but is also a boat which a man can manage by himself; the use of *praesidio* suggests the stalwartness of the man who is truly *potens sui*. Thus, Horace concludes the water motif of the poem by joining the images of the sea and the river of life. The breezes—nature— and the gods (*geminusque Pollux*) will aid him, even in the future. Thus does man assume his proper role and because of his self-reliance is he helped by nature and the gods.

One point remains to be commented on. In the last stanzas the contrasts between rich and poor have been noted, and now we see the irony which functioned in the first section of the poem, for Maecenas, the materially rich man, emerges as being a poverty-stricken creature. Horace's offerings, which appeared as simple pleasures in the first few lines of the ode, now are seen as the real riches. The wine, the flowers, and the scent are symbols not only of life and happiness, immediate and actual, but also of the means whereby Maecenas himself can become truly rich, for they stand for peacefulness and contentedness.

This function of irony extends even more pointedly to the opening phrase of the poem, *Tyrrhena regum progenies*. Maecenas has only the outward trappings of a scion of a royal line (cf. 9–15) whereas Horace achieves royalty of a true, because spiritual, kind. Maecenas may be of royal descent but his present attitude does not permit him to live royally; he can only gaze, speculate, and pursue changing phantoms of the future; he cannot act cogently or intelligently in the present. Thus, he loses his claim not only to *laetus* but also to royalty.

The invitation Horace issues to Maecenas is an invitation not only to exchange his anxieties and hesitancies over the future for the sureness, clarity, and immediacy of the present, but also to learn wisdom, that is to have a true perspective about the future. It is also an invitation to a royalty worthy of his descent, the royalty of self-mastery and self-possession. Far from being a trader, Horace has the generosity of the man able to make a gift because he himself is *ille potens sui*.

Horace in this ode has proceeded from the particular to the general to the particular. He has exhibited on a conception of reality which he regarded with profound seriousness some of the best of his technical devices. That he believed what has come to be called the *carpe diem* philosophy to be the best means whereby man can live cannot be doubted when we reflect that this poem, with its elaborate ambiguities and ironies expressed both directly and indirectly yet always graciously, was addressed to his patron, Maecenas, the most important private citizen in Rome. More completely here than anywhere else in the first three books of the *Odes* Horace exhibits his deep awareness of what is a tragic view of man's condition, for man stands alone in the world, able to trust only himself. To know that ultimate fact of existence is for Horace to accept full responsibility for being a man. Once a man achieves this self-awareness, then he can be joyful.

Quintus Horatius Flaccus (65–8 B.C.)

Ode IV. 4

Qualem ministrum fulminis alitem,
cui rex deorum regnum in auis uagas
   permisit expertus fidelem
      Iuppiter in Ganymede flauo,

5 olim iuuentas et patrius uigor
nido laborum protulit inscium,
    uernique iam nimbis remotis
      insolitos docuere nisus

uenti pauentem, mox in ouilia
10 demisit hostem uiuidus impetus,
    nunc in reluctantis dracones
      egit amor dapis atque pugnae,

qualemue laetis caprea pascuis
intenta fuluae matris ab ubere
15   iam lacte depulsum leonem
      dente nouo peritura uidit,

uidere Raeti bella sub Alpibus
Drusum gerentem Vindelici—quibus
    mos unde deductus per omne
20   tempus Amazonia securi

dextras obarmet, quaerere distuli,
nec scire fas est omnia—sed diu
    lateque uictrices cateruae
      consiliis iuuenis reuictae

25 sensere, quid mens rite, quid indoles
nutrita faustis sub penetralibus
    posset, quid Augusti paternus
      in pueros animus Nerones.

fortes creantur fortibus et bonis;
30 est in iuuencis, est in equis patrum
    uirtus, neque imbellem feroces
      progenerant aquilae columbam;

doctrina sed uim promouet insitam,
rectique cultus pectora roborant;
35   utcumque defecere mores,
      indecorant bene nata culpae.

quid debeas, o Roma, Neronibus,

testis Metaurum flumen et Hasdrubal
deuictus et pulcher fugatis
40   ille dies Latio tenebris,

qui primus alma risit adorea,
dirus per urbis Afer ut Italas
      ceu flamma per taedas uel Eurus
         per Siculas equitauit undas.

45 post hoc secundis usque laboribus
Romana pubes creuit, et impio
      uastata Poenorum tumultu
         fana deos habuere rectos,

dixitque tandem perfidus Hannibal
50 "cerui, luporum praeda rapacium,
      sectamur ultro, quos opimus
         fallere et effugere est triumphus.

gens, quae cremato fortis ab Ilio
iactata Tuscus aequoribus sacra
55   natosque maturosque patres
         pertulit Ausonias ad urbis,

duris ut ilex tonsa bipennibus
nigrae feraci frondis in Algido,
      per damna, per caedis, ab ipso
60   ducit opes animumque ferro.

non hydra secto corpore firmior
uinci dolentem creuit in Herculem,
      monstrumue submisere Colchi
         maius Echioniaeue Thebae.

65 merses profundo: pulchrior euenit:
luctere: multa proruet integrum
      cum laude uictorem geretque
         proelia coniugibus loquenda.

Carthagini iam non ego nuntios
70 mittam superbos: occidit, occidit

spes omnis et fortuna nostri
nominis Hasdrubale interempto."

nil Claudiae non perficiunt manus,
quas et benigno nimine Iuppiter
75   defendit et curae sagaces
expediunt per acuta belli.

NOTES

Meter: Alcaic Stanza.

1 ff. *ministrum fulminis* is in apposition with *alitem* which is the object, with a modifying *qualem*, of *propulit, docuere, demisit, egit,* all of which are gnomic perfects. *Qualem* is repeated in 13 and is the object of *uidit* (16). *Talem* is to be understood with *uidere Drusum*.

3. The eagle had carried Ganymede to Olympus to be cup-bearer to Jupiter.

10. *hostem*—used predicatively.

13. *pascuis*—dative dependent on *intenta*.

17. *Raetis*—adjective for *Raeticis;* indicates the Raeti who took part in the battle; Laetia was south of the Vindelici.

21. *obarmet*—a new word of Horace's.

24. *iuuenis*—i.e., Drusus was twenty-three.

28. *pueros Nerones*—i.e., Drusus and Tiberius.

38. *testis*—understand *est.*

Metaurum flumen—the battle of the Metaurus (207 B.C.) was turning point of the second Punic War, for Hasdrubal was slain.

39. *fugatis . . . tenebris*—i.e., the previous defeats, especially Cannae; ablative absolute.

40. *Latio*—ablative of separation.

48. *rectos*—predicate to *deos.*

52. *effugere est triumphus*—oxymoron.

58. *nigrae feraci frondis*—genitive with adjectives.

63. Reference to earthborn heroes who sprang from the dragon's teeth sown by Jason.

64. *Echioniaeue Thebae*—from Echion, survivor of those born from dragon's teeth sown by Cadmus at Thebes. He married

Cadmus' daughter and became ancestor of later kings of Thebes.

68. *coniugibus*—dative of agency.

69. *Carthagini*—dative of the goal.

76. *belli*—genitive of the whole; used with neuter plural adjectives which themselves are substantives.

QUESTIONS

1. Explain the function of vv. 18–22 (*quibus . . . omnia*). Are they an irrelevancy inserted in the poem, or do they indicate something about the character of Drusus' enemies?

2. At v. 36 the first portion of the poem ends. Explain vv. 29–36. Do they show any pattern which has already been established in the poem? What connection is there between the animal imagery as it has occurred in the poem so far and vv. 33–36?

3. What are the purpose and the effect of the long first sentence of the poem (1–28)?

4. In the second portion of the poem what purpose does the dramatic scene achieve? Why is the speech put in the mouth of Hannibal?

5. The poem began with reference to Drusus, the individual. Why does the poet then shift to *Romana pubes* and to *gens*?

6. Carefully examine the imagery of the second portion of the poem. Does it in any way relate to the imagery of vv. 1–36?

7. Though often called a poem celebrating the achievement of Drusus and of the Julio-Claudian house, the poem in actuality is a meditation on victory, what it is, and what it means to be a victor; what, in short, the consequences as well as the causes of victory are. How does Horace indicate to the reader what attitude he is expected to take on these matters? What moral judgment does the poem compel us to make?

8. Write an essay analyzing the poem in which you indicate the success or failure of the poem.

❧

Quintus Horatius Flaccus (65–8 B.C.)
Ode III.1

Odi profanum uulgus et arceo;
fauete linguis: carmina non prius
    audita Musarum sacerdos
        uirginibus puerisque canto.

5 regum timendorum in proprios greges,
reges in ipsos imperium est Iouis,
    clari Giganteo triumpho,
        cuncta supercilio mouentis.

est ut uiro uir latius ordinet
10 arbusta sulcis, hic generosior
    descendat in Campum petitor,
        moribus hic meliorque fama

contendat, illi turba clientium
sit maior: aequa lege Necessitas
15   sortitur insignis et imos;
        omne capax mouet urna nomen.

destrictus ensis cui super impia
ceruice pendet, non Siculae dapes
    dulcem elaborabunt saporem,
20   non auium citharaeque cantus

somnum reducent: somnus agrestium
lenis uirorum non humilis domos
    fastidit umbrosamque ripam,
        non Zephyris agitata Tempe.

25 desiderantem quod satis est neque
tumultuosum sollicitat mare
    nec saeuus Arcturi cadentis
        impetus aut orientis Haedi,

non uerberatae grandine uineae
30 fundusque mendax, arbore nunc aquas
    culpante, nunc torrentia agros
        sidera, nunc hiemes iniquas.

contracta pisces aequora sentiunt
iactis in altum molibus; huc frequens
35 caementa demittit redemptor
    cum famulis dominusque terrae

fastidiosus: sed Timor et Minae
scandunt eodem quo dominus, neque
  decedit aerata triremi et
40   post equitem sedet atra Cura.

quodsi dolentem nec Phrygius lapis
nec purpurarum sidere clarior
  delenit usus nec Falerna
    uitis Achaeminiumque costum,

45 cur inuidendis postibus et nouo
sublime ritu moliar atrium?
  cur ualle permutem Sabina
    diuitias operosiores?

NOTES

Meter: Alcaic Stanza.

1. Note how Horace employs religious phraseology here.

2. *fauete linguis*—i.e., avoid words of ill omen; observe a reverent silence.

9. *est ut*—"it is true that," "it is a fact that."

11. *Campum*—i.e., *Campus Martius* where the *Comitia Centuriata* assembled to elect the chief magistrates of Rome.

17. Alludes to the story of the sword of Damocles.
  cui—antecedent is *illi* which is supplied in thought.

41. *Phrygius lapis*—marble quarried at Synnada in Phrygia.

46. *sublime*—predicate to *atrium* which is an example of synechdoche.

QUESTIONS

1. The poem has several parts. The first is vv. 1–4, second 5–16, third 17–32, and fourth 33–48. What devices does the poet use to relate each part to the next? How does he vary the connections?

2. Verses 1–4 are generally regarded as introducing the first six odes of Book III, the so-called "Roman Odes." Even if this be granted for all six odes, these opening verses nevertheless should also be regarded as a part of this poem. Do they in any way fit into the theme of the poem?

3. Explain the imagery of vv. 8–9? Is it connected with anything else in the poem?

4. The verbs of vv. 9–14 are all subjunctive. Comment on the reason for such usage, and explain why the verbs of vv. 15–16 are indicative. What effect is achieved by such variety?

5. Examine the verbs of vv. 18–24, and show how they affect our understanding of the passage.

6. Explain the source of the imagery of vv. 25–32. How does such imagery as is shown here relate to the imagery of the previous eight verses?

7. The imagery of vv. 33–48 derives from what activity? How does such a notion as expressed here fit in with the rest of the poem? Why in the midst of this passage does the poet use *Timor*, *Minae*, and *Cura*?

8. How are the last two verses of the poem prepared for?

9. In the light of your reading of the poem, write a critical exegesis of it in which you indicate the theme, the techniques involved, and your evaluation of the entire poem.

৵৪৽

Quintus Horatius Flaccus (65–8 B.C.)
Ode III.2
Angustam amice pauperiem pati
robustus acri militia puer
   condiscat et Parthos feroces
    uexet eques metuendus hasta

5 uitamque sub diuo et trepidis agat
in rebus. illum ex moenibus hosticis
   matrona bellantis tyranni
    prospiciens et adulta uirgo

suspiret, eheu, ne rudis agminum
10   sponsus lacessat regius asperum
      tactu leonem, quem cruenta
         per medias rapit ira caedis.

dulce et decorum est pro patria mori:
mors et fugacem persequitur uirum,
15   nec parcit imbellis iuuentae
         poplitibus timidoue tergo.

Virtus repulsae nescia sordidae
intaminatis fulget honoribus,
    nec sumit aut ponit securis
20   arbitrio popularis aurae.

Virtus, recludens immeritis mori
caelum, negata temptat iter uia,
    coetusque uulgaris et udam
        spernit humum fugiente penna.

25   est et fideli tuta silentio
merces: uetabo, qui Cereris sacrum
    uulgarit arcanae, sub isdem
        sit trabibus fragilemque mecum

soluat phaselon: saepe Diespiter
30   neglectus incesto addidit integrum:
    raro antecedentem scelestum
        deseruit pede Poena claudo.

NOTES

Meter: Alcaic Stanza.

1. *amice pati*—ultima is long; infinitive is epexegetic.

4. *eques*—predicate.

9. *suspiret*—singular verb with plural subject.

14. *et*—"also," "not less," a grecism.

17. *repulsae*—technical term for defeat at polls, hence lack of prestige, hence *sordidae*.

18. *intaminatis*—for *non contaminatis*; found only in Horace.
honoribus—technical term referring to high political offices.
23. *udam . . . humum*—used figuratively for groveling pursuits and ambitions.
26. *sit, soluat*—*ueto* usually takes infinitive, but this construction seems modeled on *caue sis*, etc.
Cereris sacrum—Eleusinian mysteries of Demeter (Ceres); supposed to be guarded by initiates.
27. *uulgarit*—subjunctive by attraction.
29. *phaselon*—a Greek accusative.
30. Adjectives used as substantives.
32. *deseruit*—gnomic perfect.
pede—ablative of quality.

Questions

1. The theme of the poem is the exposition of *Virtus*. What is the meaning of that word, and how does the poet explore its significance?

2. What does *robustus* (2) connote both in itself and by its position in the verse?

3. Why should *eques* be employed as an illustrative example in v. 4?

4. The most famous verse of the poem is 13, *dulce et decorum est pro patria mori*. In the light of vv. 6–12, to whom does the verse refer, the *illum* or the *sponsus*? What connection do vv. 14–16 serve in relation to 13? Comment, then, on the placing of v. 13.

5. Examine carefully the moods and the tenses of the finite verbs from v. 3 to v. 24. What purpose does the poet achieve by his arrangement of the verbs?

6. After discussing the military quality of *Virtus*, Horace then says *est et fideli tuta silentia/ merces*: (etc. to end). Are these two stanzas related to *Virtus*? How do they affect the understanding of the theme of the poem? Are they related in any way to the earlier part of the poem?

7. Carefully examine the following words: *fideli* (25), *merces*

(26), *integrum* (30), and *scelestum* (31). How do they function in relation to the poem as a whole?

8. Are we to understand, as is commonly said, that *Virtus* in this poem connotes only military courage?

9. Since the poem is the second in the series of "Roman Odes," how is it connected with the earlier poem?

☞

Quintus Horatius Flaccus (65–8 B.C.)
Ode III.3

Iustum et tenacem propositi uirum
non ciuium ardor praua iubentium,
    non uultus instantis tyranni
        mente quatit solida neque Auster,

5 dux inquieti turbidus Hadriae,
nec fulminantis magna manus Iouis:
    si fractus illabatur orbis,
        impauidum ferient ruinae.

hac arte Pollux et uagus Hercules
10 enisus arces attigit igneas,
    quos inter Augustus recumbens
        purpureo bibit ore nectar.

hac te merentem, Bacche pater, tuae
uexere tigres indocili iugum
15   collo trahentes; hac Quirinus
        Martis equis Acheronta fugit,

gratum elocuta consiliantibus
Iunone diuis: "Ilion, Ilion
    fatalis incestusque iudex
20   et mulier peregrina uertit

in puluerem, ex quo destituit deos
mercede pacta Laomedon, mihi

castaeque damnatum Mineruae
cum populo et duce fraudulento.

25 iam nec Lacaenae splendet adulterae
famosus hospes nec Priami domus
periura pugnaces Achiuos
Hectoreis opibus refringit,

nostrisque ductum seditionibus
30 bellum resedit. protinus et grauis
iras et inuisum nepotem,
Troica quem peperit sacerdos,

Marti redonabo; illum ego lucidas
inire sedes, ducere nectaris
35 sucos et adscribi quietis
ordinibus patiar deorum.

dum longus inter saeuiat Ilion
Romamque pontus, qualibet exsules
in parte regnanto beati;
40 dum Priami Paridisque busto

insultet armentum et catulos ferae
celent inultae, stet Capitolium
fulgens triumphatisque possit
Roma ferox dare iura Medis.

45 horrenda late nomen in ultimas
extendat oras, qua medius liquor
secernit Europen ab Afro,
qua tumidus rigat arua Nilus,

aurum irrepertum et sic melius situm,
50 cum terra celat, spernere fortior
quam cogere humanos in usus
omne sacrum rapiente dextra.

quicumque mundo terminus obstitit,
hunc tanget armis, uisere gestiens,

55 qua parte debacchentur ignes,
qua nebulae pluuiique rores.

sed bellicosis fata Quiritibus
hac lege dico, ne nimium pii
rebusque fidentes auitae
60 tecta uelint reparare Troiae.

Troiae renascens alite lugubri
fortuna tristi clade iterabitur,
ducente uictrices cateruas
coniuge me Iouis et sorore.

65 ter si resurgat murus aeneus
auctore Phoebo, ter pereat meis
excisus Argiuis, ter uxor
capta uirum puerosque ploret."

non hoc iocosae conueniet lyrae:
70 quo, Musa, tendis? desine peruicax
referre sermones deorum et
magna modis tenuare paruis.

Notes

Meter: Alcaic Stanza.

2. *iubentium*—*iubeo* is technical term for passing measures by popular assemblies.

4. *mente*—ablative of separation.

8. *impauidum*—predicate to an understood object of *ferient*.
ferient—indicative for the sake of emphasis.

11. *quos inter*—anastrophe.

14. *tigres*—in Greek legend Bacchus' chariot is drawn by panthers which in Roman literature become tigers; control of such beasts indicates the civilizing influence of Bacchus.

17. *gratum*—Juno alone of the gods hated the Romans.

22. *mercede pacta*—Poseidon and Apollo erected the walls of Troy for King Laomedon, who not only refused to pay them but expelled them from his kingdom.

25. *Lacaenae adulterae*—Helen.

26. *domus periura*—allusion is to Laomedon's treachery, the effect of which clung to his descendants.

31. *nepotem*—Romulus, son of Mars, son of Juno.

32. *Troica sacerdos*—i.e., *Rhea Silvia* also called *Ilia*.

33. *redonabo*—syllepsis: with *uias* it means abandon; with *nepotem*, restore.

35. *adscribi*—technical term for citizens, soldiers, colonists who were enrolled on various lists.

43. *fulgens*—predicate to *Capitolium*, temple on Capitoline hill dedicated to Jupiter, Juno, Minerva.

triumphatis—regularly intransitive, but here it is transitive.

50 *spernere*—epexegetic infinitive, as is *cogere* (51).

55. *debacchentur ignes, nebulae*—syllepsis.

57. *Quiritibus*—i.e., the root meaning, "men of spears."

58. *ne . . . uelint*—"stipulative subjunctive," a development from the jussive.

62. *iterabitur*—subject is *fortuna*, but *fortuna* in different sense from that used with *renascens*.

65. *aeneus*—predicate; i.e., even if it be of bronze.

69. *iocosae lyrae*—i.e., lyric poetry.

70. *peruicax*—adverbial.

72. *modis paruis*—i.e., in lyric not epic poetry.

QUESTIONS

1. Examine the rhetorical figures in this poem, and show how they affect the meaning.

2. Verses 1–16 indicate what the *iustum et tenacem propositi uirum* can achieve. What purpose then does the long speech of Juno serve? By what general means does she make her points quite clear? Troy, the legendary ancestor of Rome, symbolizes what in this poem? Why then does Juno resist any attempt to re-establish that ancient city? Explain the function of vv. 49–52. Why should gold suddenly be introduced in the midst of the description of the extent of Rome's influence? Has this passage been prepared for in any way in the previous portions of the poem?

3. In v. 15 *Quirinus* appears. What does the word mean, and why should Horace have elected to use it in this poem? How do the references to heroes in vv. 1–15 differ from the references Juno makes to her enemies? What effect is achieved by this?

4. The final stanza of the poem reverts to Horace himself and to his address to the Muse. Does this seem out of place in so long a poem as this and on such a theme as this? Why, or if not, why not? What purpose, if any, does the final stanza serve? Is it connected in any way with what has gone before, or is it simply a graceful way of ending the poem?

5. Explain how this poem is related to the previous poems.

⊷§§⊷

Quintus Horatius Flaccus (65–8 B.C.)
Ode III.4
Descende caelo et dic age tibia
regina longum Calliope melos,
    seu uoce nunc mauis acuta,
      seu fidibus citharaue Phoebi.

5 auditis an me ludit amabilis
insania? audire et uideor pios
    errare per lucos, amoenae
      quos et aquae subeunt et aurae.

me fabulosae Vulture in Apulo
10 nutricis extra limen Apuliae
    ludo fatigatumque somno
      fronde noua puerum palumbes

texere, mirum quod foret omnibus,
quicumque celsae nidum Acherontiae
15   saltusque Bantinos et aruum
      pingue tenent humilis Forenti,

ut tuto ab atris corpore uiperis
dormirem et ursis, ut premerer sacra

lauroque collataque myrto,
20   non sine dis animosus infans.

uester, Camenae, uester in arduos
tollor Sabinos, seu mihi frigidum
      Praeneste seu Tibur supinum
            seu liquidae placuere Baiae.

25 uestris amicum fontibus et choris
non me Philippis uersa acies retro,
      deuota non exstinxit arbos,
            nec Sicula Palinurus unda.

utcumque mecum uos eritis, libens
30 insanientem nauita Bosphorum
      temptabo et urentis harenas
            litoris Assyrii uiator,

uisam Britannos hospitibus feros
et laetum equino sanguine Concanum,
35   uisam pharetratos Gelonos
            et Scythicum inuiolatus amnem.

uos Caesarem altum, militia simul
fessas cohortis abdidit oppidis,
      finire quaerentem labores
40   Pierio recreatis antro.

uos lene consilium et datis et dato
gaudetis almae. scimus ut impios
      Titanas immanemque turbam
            fulmine sustulerit caduco,

45 qui terram inertem, qui mare temperat
uentosum, et urbes regnaque tristia
      diuosque mortalisque turmas
            imperio regit unus aequo.

magnum illa terrorem intulerat Ioui
50 fidens iuuentus horrida bracchiis

fratresque tendentes opaco
Pelion imposuisse Olympo.

sed quid Typhoeus et ualidus Mimas,
aut quid minaci Porphyrion statu,
55   quid Rhoetus euulsisque truncis
Enceladus iaculator audax

contra sonantem Palladis aegida
possent ruentes? hinc auidus stetit
60   Vulcanus, hinc matrona Iuno et
numquam umeris positurus arcum,

qui rore puro Castaliae lauit
crinis solutos, qui Lyciae tenet
dumeta natalemque siluam,
Delius et Patareus Apollo.

65 uis consili expers mole ruit sua:
uim temperatam di quoque prouehunt
in maius; idem odere uiris
omne nefas animo mouentis.

testis mearum centimanus Gyas
70 sententiarum, notus et integrae
temptator Orion Dianae,
uirginea domitus sagitta.

iniecta monstris Terra dolet suis
maeretque partus fulmine luridum
75   missos ad Orcum; nec peredit
impositam celer ignis Aetnen,

in continentis nec Tityi iecur
reliquit ales, nequitiae additus
custos; amatorem trecentae
80   Perithoum cohibent catenae.

NOTES

Meter: Alcaic Stanza.

2. *Calliope*—used of the Muses generally.

8. *quos . . . aurae*—connected with *subeunt* by zeugma.

9. *Vulture*—Mount Vultur near Venusia in Apulia, birthplace of Horace.

11. *ludo . . . somno*—syllepsis with *fatigatumque.*

13. *mirum . . . omnibus*—relative clause of purpose.

15. *Bantinos*—Bantia, an old Oscan town in Apulia near Venusia.

16. *Forenti*—Forentum, south of Venusia.

17. *ut, ut*—introduce indirect questions dependent on *mirum.*

22. *tollor*—middle force.

23. *Praeneste*—modern Palestrina, a town in Latium 20 miles east of Rome, 2,500 feet above sea level; a summer resort.

23. *supinum*—i.e., because it lies on the hillside.

34. *Cocanum*—the Cocani, a Spanish tribe said to drink horses' blood mixed with milk.

35. *Gelonosos*—a Scythian tribe.

38. After Actium Augustus gave land allotments to about one hundred twenty thousand veterans; later he gave allotments to others (about three hundred thousand in all).

39. *finire*—infinitive of purpose.

41. *consilium*—trisyllabic.

50. *fidens*—pejorative use.

horrida bracchiis—alludes to the hundred hands of the Uranids; *Aegaeon, Cyas, Cotta.*

53. *Typhoeus*—hundred-headed, fire-breathing monster.

55. *truncis*—ablative of means.

58. *possent*—deliberative subjunctive.

62. *Lyciae*—important seat of Apollo's cult.

73. *Terra*—for the Greek Γῆ or Γῆας, the mother of Giants and Titans.

75. The eruptions, earthquakes, etc., were supposed to be struggles of the monsters to change their positions.

77. *Tityi*—attempted to rape Latona and so was consigned to Tartarus.

80. *Perithoum*—King of the Lapithae, who endeavored to steal Proserpina from Hades and was thus put in chains by Pluto.

This longest and most densely written of the "Roman Odes" repays careful reading. The opening stanza connects this ode with the preceding one (III.3) which concluded with a plea to the Muse that, because of the poet's small ability, she should cease singing of the gods and piping of great matters. *Ode* III.4 begins with another imperative, *Descende*, and an exhortation to Calliope to sing a *longum melos*. (Although Horace does not distinguish between the various Muses, nevertheless the name "Calliope" may be used for its radical meaning, "voice of beauty.") The reversal forces us to appreciate the irony of the last stanza of the earlier poem. But further the opening quatrain introduces emphatically the subject matter of this poem, that is, the power of the Muses. They are heavenly beings quite capable of making themselves felt through the modest lyric as well as through the grander epic.

The power of the Muses becomes apparent, moreover, in the next stanza wherein the poet questions his own senses. The phrase *amabilis insania* emphasizes by its oxymoron that this is not simple madness. Yet the poet not only questions the experience, but wonders if he is being mocked. The notion of mockery reinforces the connection between this ode and the previous one, for the tone of the last stanza of III.3 indicates clearly that the poet thinks he is being made sport of by the Muse, a notion suggested especially by the use of *peruicax* in v. 70. However, we see from III.4 vv. 6ff. that he is not deceived. The lack of mockery in III.4 indicates, too, that in the previous ode the Muse was not simply toying with him. The *amabilis insania* is not mockery.

The conceit of madness as the source of poetic inspiration had a distinguished lineage in ancient literature. Indeed it was not simply a conceit but a theory about the poetic impulse, as Plato's *Phaedrus* shows. But in this poem Horace does not say he has become "mad," for he has not lost consciousness of himself. The passive voice of *uideo* (*uideor* v. 6) indicates that he sees himself wandering in the grove of the Muses. The implication is, first, that he wants us to accept the idea that he is the favorite of the gods. The second is that he is wholly conscious of his role. The employment of such symbolism and the manner of its employment imply a much more sophisticated technique than simply asserting the divine madness. The self-consciousness of the poet forces us to remember that a rational mind is at work although appearing to be seized by madness.

In terms which have the sanction of earlier poetry, the narrator of the poem, Horace, proceeds to justify himself as the divinely inspired poet. Since childhood he has been favored by the gods, for the *fabulosae palumbes* took care that as a child in Apulia on Mount Vultur he was protected from vipers and bears and initiated into sacred matters. The ancient Greek conventions common to such a description of a poet's youth are here transferred to Italy: the mountain becomes Mount Vultur, the region that of Apulia, the *palumbes*, the guardians of *saltus Bantinos* and *aruum humilis Forenti*. The reason for such changes is obvious. Horace is a Roman poet, writing in Latin for the edification and entertainment of his fellow Romans. But more is involved than these aims. The Muses have transferred their interests to Rome. A Roman poet lays claim to the same treatment from the Muses as the ancient Greeks, such as Pindar or Stesichorus, received. The implication is manifest not only in the allusions to Pindar which commentators point out, especially to *Pythian* I, but more importantly in the organization of vv. 9–12 which are complex in the fashion of Pindaric poetry; in the interlocked word order of *Vulture in Apulio*, the ambiguity of *limen* (10), the chiasmus in vv. 10–11, and the wide separation of *fabulosae* and *palumbes* which embrace, as it were, the *puerum*. Although, properly speaking, *me* escapes the enclosure of the two words, nevertheless all the defining terms of the poet depend upon the *puerum*, in apposition to *me*. It is truly a woven piece, as the enjambment of *texere* in v. 13 emphasizes. Devices similar but somewhat less elaborate continue in the next two stanzas. All the elaborate weaving comparable to what "doves" might indeed weave in their flight forces us to consider closely what is going on. The effect of such considerations reinforces in us the idea that such dexterity, common enough in Greek poetry, has found a home in Latin poetry. The child was indeed touched *sacra lauroque collataque myrto*, he is a *non sine dis animosus infans*.

When we regard the elaborateness of the verses, the self-consciousness of the second stanza takes on more significance. It is hardly possible that a poet could be so lost in actual madness, whether divine or not, that he could construct such verses. Horace does not cheat his hearer or reader by asserting that he was actually out of his mind. Instead he employs a convention constantly keeping us aware that it is a convention, one that will, when well handled, permit him to say more than is conventionally said. What that more is will become apparent as we continue to examine the poem.

After the description of the divinely protected boyhood, he then declares in quite straightforward language his adherence to the Muses whether at his Sabine farm, at *Praeneste*, *Tibur*, or *Baiae*. These references to actual places remind us again that the Muses have come to Italy, and no longer reside exclusively in Greece. Furthermore, the very prosaicness of the locations suggests that the Muses are capable of inspiring a poet anywhere. The order of the list is interesting: from a quiet retreat to a fashionable watering place. Further, an ambiguity consciously employed exists in the emphasized verb *tollor*. The word means "carry up" or "lift up." It can mean "I am carried up to my Sabine farm," in a chariot or in a cart, or "I am moved or carried by ship to Baiae." But the word quite commonly means "exalted," "translated to heaven." Here the position of the word following *Camenae, uester in arduos* connotes this latter meaning; when *Sabinos* is combined with *in arduos*, *tollor* clearly means the former. Aware of the deliberate ambiguity, we perceive that the sense of the passage conveys the heights of inspiration no matter where he may be, for he is sustained by them.

This double intention is confirmed by the ensuing stanza, which describes how the poet has been sustained even in those parts of the world where death constantly threatens: in battle, on land, and on sea. The importance of these verses lies not in their autobiographical detail, if indeed death had ever actually approached him on the occasions mentioned, but in their extreme expression. Death on the battlefield, or at sea, or by a falling tree, is always a possibility which it is foolish to ignore. But, because he is *amicum fontibus et choris*, he has been spared.

As has been indicated, the historicity of the details is not relevant. The details are illustrative of the power of the Muses, of art, to sustain life. By using himself as an example, the poet has been at great pains to illustrate the protection the Muses afford. From boyhood through young manhood he has been their friend. He goes on to declare that he will ever be so. The ideas of past and future are alternated in the stanzas beginning at v. 21 and continuing to v. 36. The Muses will always be with him whether he goes to the Bosphorus, Syria, Britain, Spain, or Scythia. The references move from water to desert to people to water. The first reference, *insanientem Bosphorum*, indicates the connection with the previous stanza and, when combined with the phrase *Scythicum amnem*, suggests water surrounding the earth. Earth encircled by water is a well-known metonomy for the men on the earth with whom he will be *inuiolatus*. Whether or not Horace might have planned to go to such interesting outposts is not the point. What he is demonstrating is that, amidst the most menacing people and places, the Muses' protection extends over him.

At v. 37 the poem ceases to refer to Horace, the "I" of the poem, and begins to speak of Caesar, Octavian the Emperor. Horace has cited himself as far as he cared to in order to indicate the power of the Muses toward their servant. He now proceeds to another man. The transition to Caesar is important, for Caesar is in some way like Horace himself. The point of vv. 37–40 lies in the salutary effect the Muses have had on Octavian. He has hidden (*abdidit*) his exhausted cohorts in towns in an attempt to end his labors. In other words the Civil Wars are over; Caesar has disbanded his armies and sought recompense for them. Now the Muses strengthen the weary Caesar. The first curious word in the stanza is *abdidit*. Why should the cohorts be regarded as hidden? The most reasonable answer is that the vast army has been hidden from sight; it has been taken away from common view. But, bearing in mind that something hidden can at some later time be exposed to view, uncovered, we grasp that such may happen to this army. Although Horace may develop this idea later in the poem, at the moment he does nothing with this implication. The army has been concealed by means of towns, for the *oppidis* of v. 38 is an ablative of means. We know from other sources that Octavian, after confiscating or expropriating land, settled his veteran troops often in new towns. But, even if we did not know that fact, the ode would convey a suggestion of it, for towns obviously have locality and thus are part of the land. We have already been shown in this poem that lands or places and peoples possess the power to menace. The use of *oppidis* after the preceding passage might well suggest something ominous. The word is, again, part of Horace's transition to the following passages. For the moment it is significant to note the connection with the previous portions.

The Muses seek to restore *Caesarem altum*. The *altum* obviously refers here to his august position in the state, but it too forms part of the transition to later passages. The interesting words are *Pierio recreatis antro* (40). The indicative mood indicates that the Muses, as a matter of fact, do re-create life. They do as a fact restore man and society to good health. We have earlier seen how Muses protected the poet. Here the Pierian cave becomes a symbol for the Muses' ability to help Augustus, to restore him to health. The next verses make it clear that the Muses give gentle counsel and rejoice as fostering spirits when their advice and aid have been accepted. The power of the Muses has been shown with regard to one man, the poet. The notion is now expanded to embrace another, the statesman, and from the fact of Octavian's position, we can infer that their power extends to the whole of the Roman state.

At v. 42 the topic changes to a discussion of the Titans' vain war with Jupiter. The passage begins with *scimus*. The plural instead of the singular is required by the verse, yet even so the plural form heightens the effect of the previous verses. The "we" may be a poetic form of "I," or it may be Horace and Caesar, or it may be all men, "we of Rome." All three notions function at once. *Scire* itself in the indicative implies factual knowledge. In this passage the source of the knowledge is the Muse. But what sort of knowledge comes from the Muses? The answer is clearly that which derives from art, not from history or politics. By the end of the poem we know what that knowledge is, how it comes to us, and what its importance is.

The explanation begins with the next verses. The struggle of the Titans was an impious one involving a vast throng which was ultimately crushed by the *fulmine caduco*. The story is a familiar one. The outline is given briefly. The poet moves on to a more interesting matter in the next stanza, which defines Jupiter, the subject of *sustulerit*. That deity alone rules the earth, the sea, cities, kingdoms, the living and the dead, and he rules *imperio aequo*. Jupiter is the divine analogue to Caesar. We see clearly why in v. 37 Octavian had been called *altum*: Octavian and Jupiter are parallel. But even more we can see a parallel existing between the areas ruled by Jupiter and those mentioned in vv. 29ff. Jupiter rendered his realms safe and so has Octavian. Both are responsible for maintaining the peace of the regions. Here the parallel ceases, for Jupiter can do it in his own right, or almost so; Octavian cannot. Though he has a powerful weapon in the hidden armies, a weapon comparable to Zeus' thunderbolt, he nonetheless needs the aid of the Muses and of the servants of the Muses. For Caesar as well as for Horace the Muses become the source of safety.

The significance of the Muses as the source of knowledge becomes clearer, for it is from them we learn about the war with the Titans and the power of Jupiter, information both Caesar and the Roman people can profit from. Let us explore the notion a little further.

In examining the tale of the Titans the poet concentrates on the convulsion caused by the giants against the *imperio aequo* of Jupiter. The description continues from v. 49 through v. 64 and involves a series of gods who aided Jupiter in the battle. The tale has obvious parallels to Octavian's suppression of civil war and affords an admonition against future civil discord. The story is a timeless one in that such disturbances always threaten and need constant vigilance to be held in check. This point is implicit in the way the story is told. Mythological tales are timeless, for they have no actual relationship to historical time. In a sense they exist forever and are forever true. The fact that Jupiter destroyed the force of the Titans is as true today as when Horace wrote it or even when the tale was first told. Such time as does exist in the story is relative to the events of the story itself. An examination of the verbs employed from v. 44 to v. 64 suggests that Horace took advantage of the timeless quality of myth. *Sustulerit* (44) is perfect subjunctive in primary sequence after *scimus*. Its time is in reality relevant to the tale, not to the main verb. Jupiter defeated the insurgent gods after something happened and before something else happened. *Temperat* (45) is present indicative implying the eternal quality of his rule. The pluperfect indicative *intulerat* and the infinitive *imposuisse* are past actions with regard to the story. The *possent* of v. 58 is in the subjunctive of a conditional relative clause which is contrary to fact and with the apodosis implied; the imperfect subjunctive implies that the statement that the giants could avail nothing is forever true. *Stetit* of v. 58 is a perfect indicative indicating action begun in the past and continuing into the present, and thus the verb implies that Vulcan and Juno forever stand. Furthermore *possent* and *stetit* are emphasized and opposed by the chiastic arrangement of the verse which reinforces the import of the tenses as well as the ideas of the verbs. (The ideas of *ruentes* and *auidus* gain support too by the chiasmus.) The notion of the eternality of this action is reinforced by the future active participle, *positurus*, of v. 60 and the present indicatives in vv. 61–62. The tale, as the verbs imply, carries the overwhelming weight of a timeless truth.

Another implication also exists which is equally true. The monsters are not destroyed; they, too, like Athena, Vulcan, Juno, and Jupiter, forever exist. Their power is forever crushed yet forever rising, or more exactly, in danger of rising.

If we turn to the Titans and the gods named by Horace, we see that the former are all symbols of brute force attempting to destroy the world by fire, earthquake, natural convulsions, anarchic impulses. The gods, on the other hand, are all constraining influences on the earth, symbolic of the civilizing rule implicit in the *imperio aequo*. It might also be well to note that the most important of the Olympian deities, so far as this poem is concerned, is Apollo whose connections with poetry and music are stressed in an entire stanza. He is given as much attention as was Jupiter.

What is implicit in the triumph of the gods over the Titans Horace makes explicit in vv. 65–68. Mindless force falls by its own weight, whereas force intelligently used even the gods' aid. The poet does not say that force should be expunged from the world. He admits its necessity and indicates how it can be strengthened. The illustrative tale of the war in heaven demonstrates the point not only for the giants and the gods but, as it goes on to show, for men as well. The use of *idem* and the chiasmus of *uiris* to *mouentis* underline the point. But how is force to be *temperatam*? We see in this stanza that *consilium* is necessary (*uis consili expers . . . 65*). That *consilium* comes, as has already been said, from the Muses. It is force taught or tempered by art, by poetry. This point is the heart of the poem. We have here as clear a statement as one can find about the power of art. To this point we shall return after a brief discussion of the final stanzas.

In those stanzas Horace draws once more upon mythology. Again the verbs are all in the present tense or in the present perfect in order to demonstrate that the statement is forever true. In the first reference *Gyas* harks back to the war of the giants as does the reference to *Terra*, mother earth, who bore the monsters and who, of course, is the means whereby they are punished. She grieves that she who gave them birth must also be the prison of her offspring. But others too are imprisoned: Orion, Titys, and Perithous, who are all guilty, as the poem indicates, of sexual excess. The juxtaposition of the giants who warred against the dominion of Jupiter and those who attempted rape suggests that the crimes are of a similar nature, and the similarity of punishment reflects the same notion. They are both explosions of anarchy, the one of an individual against the vital force of another individual; the other, of one community against another. The use of force without *consilium* is common to both, hence both are doomed to be suppressed. Horace perceived the connection, and concludes his poem by demonstrating the intermingling of the two as he illustrates the similarity of the individual and society.

In the light of the whole poem and its organization some general remarks can be made. The heart of the poem is, as has been shown, that strength, *uis*, in order to be effective in the world must be counseled by art. By beginning with the imperative *Descende caelo* and the address to the Muse, Horace has already begun to indicate the intimate connection he wants to make between art and the affairs of men. It is not in some other world that art has influence and power, but here and now in the world of Caesar and Horace, in the world of the individual and the state. The poem was written not to demonstrate primarily the danger of revolt against Caesar's rule, but to show the source of that rule and its inherent harmony. Stanza two prepares for the ensuing portions of the poem by underlining the fact of the author's conscious control and use of mythic elements. The myths of the war of the giants and the monstrous creatures are part of the bequest of the Muses. From them, from art, men learn the right moral and political conduct of life. By stressing those timeless actions Horace illustrates as clearly as possible the practicality of art. Furthermore the discussion of Horace's validity as an interpreter of the Muses is explored at length from vv. 9 to 20 and the consequent results for himself and for Caesar in vv. 21–40. The "I" of the poem functions in a complex way: as every man, as a poet, and as an interpreter of the Muses to Caesar, and even as Caesar himself. The notions are most interwoven perhaps in vv. 25–36 where we find intertwined the themes of safety under the protection of the Muses and, by implication, of safety under the rule of Caesar in whom strength is joined to *consilium*. We can see why Horace, as interpreter of the Muses, employed the legendary tales, for that is the kind of knowledge we receive from art. His own service to the Muses is not simply the rhapsodizing of a poetic sensibility, but the concrete practical matter of a man involved in the world and offering it salutary counsel.

The poem thus has a clear connection with the assertion made at the beginning of the "Roman Odes." Horace is a *Musarum sacerdos* who does indeed sing *carmina* not heard before. Self-consciously and confidently he asserts the power of art in opposition to the *profanum uulgus*. In *Ode* III.4 he demonstrates as clearly as one could wish the great power of art to order life, the power ignored too often from his day to ours.

❧

Quintus Horatius Flaccus (65–8 B.C.)

Ode III.5

Caelo tonantem credidimus Iouem
regnare: praesens diuus habebitur
    Augustus adiectis Britannis
        imperio grauibusque Persis.

5 milesne Crassi coniuge barbara
turpis maritus uixit et hostium—
    pro curia inuersique mores!—
        consenuit socerorum in armis

sub rege Medo Marsus et Apulus,
10 anciliorum et nominis et togae
    oblitus aeternaeque Vestae,
        incolumi Ioue et urbe Roma?

hoc cauerat mens prouida Reguli
dissentientis condicionibus
15   foedis et exemplo trahentis
        perniciem ueniens in aeuum

si non periret immiserabilis
captiua pubes. "signa ego Punicis
    adfixa delubris et arma
20   militibus sine caede" dixit

"derepta uidi; uidi ego ciuium
retorta tergo bracchia libero

portasque non clausas et arua
　　Marte coli populata nostro.

25　auro repensus scilicet acrior
　　miles redibit. flagitio additis
　　　　damnum: neque amissos colores
　　　　　　lana refert medicata fuco,

　　nec uera uirtus, cum semel excidit,
30　curat reponi deterioribus.
　　　　si pugnat extricata densis
　　　　　　cerua plagis, erit ille fortis

　　qui perfidis se credidit hostibus,
　　et Marte Poenos proteret altero,
35　　　qui lora restrictis lacertis
　　　　　　sensit iners timuitque mortem.

　　hic, unde uitam sumeret inscius,
　　pacem duello miscuit. o pudor!
　　　　o magna Carthago, probrosis
40　　　　altior Italiae ruinis!"

　　fertur pudicae coniugis osculum
　　paruosque natos ut capitis minor
　　　　ab se remouisse et uirilem
　　　　　　toruus humi posuisse uultum,

45　donec labantis consilio patres
　　firmaret auctor numquam alias dato,
　　　　interque maerentis amicos
　　　　　　egregius properaret exsul.

　　atqui sciebat quae sibi barbarus
50　tortor pararet; non aliter tamen
　　　　dimouit obstantis propinquos
　　　　　　et populum reditus morantem

　　quam si clientum longa negotia
　　diiudicata lite relinqueret,

55   tendens Venafranos in agros
            aut Lacedaemonium Tarentum.

NOTES

Meter: Alcaic Stanza.

3. *adiectis*—Horace regards them as already subjugated. In actual fact the project was not carried out by Augustus.

5. Reference is to defeat of Crassus by the Parthians at Carrhae in 53 B.C.

coniuge—ablative of association or accompaniment without *cum.*

6. *maritus*—predicate to *miles.*

9. *Medo*—used for *Partho*; metonomy.

Marsus, Apulus—i.e., the flower of Roman soldiers.

10. *anciliorum*—sacred shields kept by the Salii. One shield supposedly fell from heaven in the reign of Numa. Eleven others were made similar to it in order to serve as a protective device for it.

13. *Reguli*—hero of first Punic War, captured in 255 B.C. and sent to Rome in 251 B.C.

15. *exemplo*—dative with *trahentis*; legal phrase for assignment to a category; object is *si non . . . (17).*

17. *periret*—ultima is long. Subjunctive represents future indicative of Regulus' speech.

immiserabilis—predicate.

19. *delubris*—dative with *affixa.*

23. *non clausas*—litotes.

24. *Marte*—metonomy.

populata—used passively.

25. *acrior*—predicate.

37. *sumeret*—deliberative subjunctive in a dependent clause.

38. *duello*—archaic for *bello.*

40. *ruinis*—ablative of means.

42. *capitis minor*—*caput* is used in the sense of one's political rights or status.

44. *humi*—locative, but indicating direction towards.

48. *egregius exsul*—oxymoron.

53. *clientum*—poetic form for *clientium*.

55. *Venafranos*—Venafrum in Samnium near borders of Latium.

56. *Tarentum*—a Spartan colony originally.

QUESTIONS

1. Show in what ways this poem is connected with the preceding poems in the series of "Roman Odes."

2. How does Regulus' story differ from the tale of the revolt of the giants in *Ode* III.4? What are the similarities and distinctions between Regulus' speech and that of Juno in *Ode* III.3? What is achieved by these distinctions, and how does it affect our understanding of these three poems?

3. What importance does the Regulus story have in this poem? How is it told? What is the tone of the passage? Does it remain constant?

4. Carefully analyze vv. 27–30 and vv. 31–35. What connection do they show with the rest of the poem? Are they illuminating for the understanding of the theme of the poem, or are they merely decorative, that is added simply as illustration? Is there any connection between the two passages?

5. Explain vv. 50–56 and how they function with the rest of the poem.

6. *Ode* III.2 spoke of *uirtus*. This *Ode*, III.5, gives an illustration of a man who is virtuous. Are there any connections between the language, the metaphors, and the ideas of the two poems?

7. Explain the syntax of *Caelo* (1). What is Horace's intention in beginning his poem this way?

8. What is the significance of *prouida* in v. 13?

◆§◆

Quintus Horatius Flaccus (65–8 B.C.)
Ode III.6
Delicta maiorum immeritus lues,
Romane, donec templa refeceris
   aedesque labentis deorum et
      foeda nigro simulacra fumo.

5   dis te minorem quod geris, imperas:
hinc omne principium, huc refer exitum:
    di multa neglecti dederunt
        Hesperiae mala luctuosae.

iam bis Monaeses et Pacori manus
10 non auspicatos contudit impetus
    nostros et adiecisse praedam
        torquibus exiguis renidet.

paene occupatam seditionibus
deleuit urbem Dacus et Aethiops,
15   hic classe formidatus, ille
        missilibus melior sagittis.

fecunda culpae saecula nuptias
primum inquinauere et genus et domos;
    hoc fonte deriuata clades
20   in patriam populumque fluxit.

motus doceri gaudet Ionicos
matura uirgo et fingitur artibus
    iam nunc et incestos amores
        de tenero meditatur ungui;

25 mox iuniores quaerit adulteros
inter mariti uina, neque eligit
    cui donet impermissa raptim
        gaudia luminibus remotis,

sed iussa coram non sine conscio
30 surgit marito, seu uocat institor
    seu mauis Hispanae magister,
        dedecorum pretiosus emptor.

non his iuuentus orta parentibus
infecit aequor sanguine Punico,
35   Pyrrhumque et ingentem cecidit
        Antiochum Hannibalemque dirum,

sed rusticorum mascula militum
proles, Sabellis docta ligonibus
uersare glebas et seuerae
40   matris ad arbitrium recisos

portare fustis, sol ubi montium
mutaret umbras et iuga demeret
bobus fatigatis, amicum
      tempus agens abeunte curru.

45 damnosa quid non imminuit dies?
aetas parentum peior auis tulit
nos nequiores, mox daturos
      progeniem uitiosiorem.

NOTES

Meter: Alcaic Stanza.

  6. *principium*—trisyllabic.

  8. *Hesperiae*—poetic for *Italiae*.

12. *torquibus exiguis*—Parthians wore golden necklaces.

13. *Aethiops*—used for *Aegyptii*, subjects of Cleopatra.

17. *culpae*—genitive with *fecundus*.

22. *fingitur artibus*—*fingitur* is middle in force; *artibus* is ablative.

27. *cui donet*—indirect question and deliberative subjunctive.

38. *Sabellis*—for *Sabinis*; proverbial for sternness and simplicity.

42. *mutaret*—subjunctive of repeated action.

44. *agens abeunte*—oxymoron.

47. *nequiores*—*quam parentes* is to be understood.

QUESTIONS

  1. Carefully examine vv. 1–4, and show how they affect the rest of the poem.

  2. Examine the tone of the poem and indicate the ways in which Horace indicates how the reader is to respond.

ADDITIONAL QUESTIONS ON THE "ROMAN ODES"

After reading and analyzing the first six odes of Book III of Horace's *Carmina*, one should be in a fairly good position to judge their interrelationship and their success. Examine the repeated metaphors based on religion and law. What does such an examination reveal about those two institutions as conceived by Horace in this series of six poems? How does such an awareness help us to understand the works individually and as a whole? How do they affect our judgments about the success of the series as well as the success of the individual poems?

It has often been argued that great poetry needs vivid colorful pictures. Within these six poems very little color imagery exists. Does such an omission on Horace's part detract from an appreciation of the poems? What sort of imagery is used? Do the poems differ from others read in this book? Do your speculations on these poems lead you to any generalizations about poetry? Can you justify your arguments?

❧§❧

Quintus Horatius Flaccus (65–8 B.C.)
Ode IV.2

Pindarum quisquis studet aemulari,
Iule, ceratis ope Daedalea
nititur pennis uitreo daturus
    nomina ponto.

5 monte decurrens uelut amnis, imbres
quem super notas aluere ripas,
feruet immensusque ruit profundo
    Pindarus ore,

laurea donandus Apollinari,
10 seu per audaces noua dithyrambos
uerba devolvit numerisque fertur
    lege solutis,

seu deos regesque canit, deorum
sanguinem, per quos cecidere iusta
15 morte Centauri, cecidit tremendae
    flamma Chimaerae,

siue quos Elea domum reducit
palma caelestis pugilemue equumue
dicit et centum potiore signis
20   munere donat,

flebili sponsae iuuenemue raptum
plorat et uiris animumque moresque
aureos educit in astra nigroque
      inuidet Orco.

25 multa Dircaeum leuat aura cycnum,
tendit, Antoni, quotiens in altos
nubium tractus: ego apis Matinae
      more modoque

grata carpentis thyma per laborem
30 plurimum circa nemus uuidique
Tiburis ripas operosa paruus
      carmina fingo.

concines maiore poeta plectro
Caesarem, quandoque trahet feroces
35 per sacrum cliuum merita decorus
      fronde Sygambros,

quo nihil maius meliusue terris
fata donauere bonique diui
nec dabunt, quamuis redeant in aurum
40   tempora priscum.

concines laetosque dies et Vrbis
publicum ludum super impetrato
fortis Augusti reditu forumque
      litibus orbum.

45 tum meae, si quid loquar audiendum,
uocis accedet bona pars, et, "o Sol
pulcher! o laudande!" canam, recepto
      Caesare felix.

terque, dum procedis, io Triumphe,
50   non semel dicemus, io Triumphe,
     ciuitas omnis, dabimusque diuis
        tura benignis.

     te decem tauri totidemque uaccae,
     me tener soluet uitulus, relicta
55   matre qui largis iuuenescit herbis
        in mea uota,

     fronte curuatos imitatus ignis
     tertium lunae referentis ortum,
     qua notam duxit, niueus uideri,
60   cetera fuluus.

NOTES

Meter: Sapphic Stanza.

1. *Pindarum*—the greatest Greek lyric poet (c.527–438 B.C.). Only his triumphal odes are extant.

aemulari—"rival," "emulate"; takes in this sense the accusative; with the dative it means "be envious."

2. *Iule*—dissyllabic; name of a mythical ancestor of the Julian family and used as a *praenomen*.

5. *uelut*—postpositive.

9. *laurea*—adjective used as a substantive.

Apollinari—i.e., sacred to Apollo.

10. *dithyrambos*—an impassioned hymn to Dionysus.

12. *lege solutis*—probably not in strophic or stanzaic form; or, as some say, the difficult meters of Pindar suggest this notion.

13. *reges*—the legendary kings such as Theseus, Peleus, Perithous, in Pindar's poems or hymns.

15. *Centauri*—one had tried to carry off Hippodamia, the bride of Perithous.

16. *chimaera*—fabulous monster with the body of a goat, the head of a lion, and the tail of a serpent.

17. *Elea*—i.e., Olympic victors; Olympia is in Elis.

18. *caelestis*—predicate to *quos*.

pugilem, equum—most important events of games and used here as typical of other events.

20. *munere*—i.e., ode composed in honor of the victor.

21. *flebili*—active.

sponsae—dative of separation.

iuuenem . . . plorat—an allusion to Pindar's lost dirges.

22. Accumulated conjunctions comprise another figure of speech, called polysyndeton. Verse is hypermetric as is the following one.

23. *aureos*—i.e., hence worthy of admiration.

25. *Dircaeum cycnum*—i.e., Pindar. So called because of fountain of Dirce near Thebes, Pindar's birthplace. Swans were a common symbol for poets.

27. *apis Matinae*—Mount Matinus, spur of Mount Garganus on eastern coast of Apulia where Horace was born.

33. *poeta*—in apposition to the subject of *concines*, i.e., Antonius.

plectro—ablative of quality.

35. *per sacrum cliuum*—*Sacer Cliuus* was part of the *Sacra Via* from *Summa Velia* down towards the Forum.

decorus—i.e., *decoratus*.

36. *Sygambros*—though they had defeated Lollius, they made peace with Augustus.

44. *orbum*—"bereft." On festal occasions all public business was suspended.

57. *imitatus*—perfect participle but denotes contemporary action.

curuatos ignis—i.e., crescent of moon entering its third day. It is the first occasion when the new moon is visible.

59. *qua duxit*—clause limits *niueus*.

uideri—epexegetic infinitive.

60. *cetera*—accusative of specification; a grecism.

EXERCISE

Write a detailed analysis of this poem in which you discuss the metrics, the figurative language, the tone, and the theme, and in which you also give an evaluation of the poem.

GLOSSARY

The TERMS listed here are ones which in some way are technical, either referring to prosody or rhetoric. All have been defined in the text when they first appeared. This list is solely for the sake of the reader's convenience.

allegory: see *imagery.*

alliteration: repetition of same sound, usually the consonant, at the beginning of two or more words.

anaphora: simply the repetition of a word (with the same or a different inflection) but the repetition usually occurs at the beginning of successive phrases, clauses, or stanzas. Anaphora is frequently used to indicate antithesis between two pairs of ideas, for it is actually the arranging of the members of the two pairs in the same order:

> *rerum copia uerborum copiam gignit.*

Its opposite is *chiasmus.*

anastrophe: the inversion of the normal order of words, as when the preposition follows the noun, e.g., *haec inter.*

assonance: a repetition in more than one word of the same vowel sounds, although the consonants of the words are unlike.

asyndeton: the omission of conjunctions between two or more co-ordinate words, phrases, or sentences, e.g., *omnes di homines.* Its opposite is *polysyndeton.*

brachyology: omission of a word or words essential to either construction or thought. Usually the omitted element, frequently in a modified form, is to be supplied from a nearby clause.

caesura: the ending of a word before the end of the metrical foot with the result that there is an overlapping of metrical feet and words. When the word ends after the first long syllable in a dactyl, it is called masculine, after the first short, a feminine caesura. *Caesura-pause* occurs when the sense ends but not the metrical foot. It avoids the sharp break of a *diaeresis-pause.*

chiasmus (chiastic): the reversal of the order of words in corresponding pairs of phrases. The arrangement is crosslike. Chiasmus can occur with parts of speech, or case-endings, and, of course, with ideas. It is a variety of parallelism, and its opposite is *anaphora.*

diaeresis: the coincidence of a word's ending with the end of a metrical foot. When the sense also halts at the same time a definite break occurs, the result is called *diaeresis-pause.*

elision: a variety of liaison in which the final vowel or diphthong or vowel plus *m* of one word is slurred into the initial vowel or diphthong, alone or preceded by *h*, of the succeeding word. E.g., *utqu(e)inpulit.*

ellipsis: suppression of a word or words of minor importance to the logical expression but necessary to the construction. A kind of brachyology, e.g., "virtues I admire" for "virtues which I admire."

end-stopped: the pause in sense at the end of a line. Contrasted with *run-on line.*

enjambment: see *run-on line.*

foot: in metrical matters a foot is a unit of measure in a meter, e.g., in the hexameter, one dactyl $-\cup\cup$ or one spondee $--$ is a foot. When two feet are combined as in the iambic meters, the combination is called a *dipody* $\cup-\cup-$.

gnomic perfect: the perfect tense used of a general truth, especially with negatives. Although it refers to past time, its use implies that something which happened once, always does happen, and always will happen under similar circumstances. It is the Latin equivalent of the Greek gnomic aorist.

grecism: a Greek idiom which has come into Latin. Although not commonly regarded as a rhetorical figure, its effect in Latin poetry frequently seems to achieve such status.

hiatus: the failure to elide although all the conditions necessary for elision are present.

> *Deferri. Mane, inquii puellae.* (Cat. X.27)

The *e* of *Mane* would normally elide with the *i* of *inquii.*

Intermediate between hiatus and elision is *semi-hiatus.* That occurs when a final long vowel or diphthong retains its identity but becomes short before the initial vowel or diphthong of the following word.

> *ualē, ualĕ inquit Iola.* (Verg. *Ecl.* 2.65)

hypallage: a change in the relation of words, by which a word is made to agree in case with another word it does not logically qualify. Commonly called *transferred epithet.*

hyperbole: use of exaggerated term or terms, e.g., the use of "infinite" for "great," or "the best of men" when simply an average person is meant.

hypermetric: liaison (usually elision) between the last word of one line and the first word of the next line. Not only the sense but the sound as well flows over to the next line.

ictus: one of the syllables in each *metrical foot* is stressed to mark the rhythm of the meter. The syllable bearing the stress then bears the *ictus* or beat of the foot. E.g.,

$$\bar{\underline{}}\,\smile\smile\,|\,\bar{\underline{}}\,\smile\smile\,|\,\bar{\underline{}}\,\smile\smile\,|\,\bar{\underline{}}\,\smile\smile\,|\,\bar{\underline{}}\,\smile\smile\,|\,\bar{\underline{}}\,\smile$$

in the hexameter.

imagery: representation of any sense experience. Poetry continually appeals to the senses, which is to say that poetry is concrete, for the poet makes his statements and conveys his ideas through figurative language. The most common varieties of figurative language are *simile* and *metaphor.* Simile is a stated comparison; metaphor an implied comparison. Both are methods of comparison for the purpose of giving insight. Closely allied to metaphor is *symbol* which is a metaphor with the first term of the comparison omitted. The term symbol is used when an object or an action is thought of as standing for something else. Frequently symbols are conventional, that is agreed upon by everyone, such as the flag standing for a country or the cross for Christianity. In poetry, however, a poet often has to create his own symbols within the context of his poem, e.g., Mount Soracte is a symbol of old age in Horace's *Ode* I.9. *Allegory* is an extended metaphor in which the object and persons are equated with meanings lying outside the narrative, e.g., as in *The Pilgrim's Progress*. Allegory is frequently bad when the equivalents seem mechanical, arbitrary, or confused.

interlocked word order: see *synchesis*.

irony: the use of words which convey a sense contrary to what is meant. Irony can also involve statements, events, or situations in which there is a contrast between expectation and fulfillment. All may appear in a poem, but irony of statement, tone, and attitude is perhaps more important. The management of irony in poetry is one of the greatest problems confronting a poet, for he is denied the use of tone of voice, or bodily gestures or expression which can help to convey an ironical intention in actual speech. Some of the devices at his disposal are *paradox* (q.v.), *understatement* (q.v.), or *hyperbole* (q.v.), *oxymoron* (q.v.), etc., all of which involve indirection of statement which is the essence of irony.

liaison: the coalescing of a final syllable of one word to the initial syllable of the next. Commonly used in continuous speech in Latin; for its use in poetry especially, see entries of *elision*, *prodelision*, *hypermetric*, and *hiatus*.

litotes: the affirmation of a thing by a denial of its contrary, e.g., "not a few," meaning a great number. This is the precise usage. But the term is indifferently used for *meiosis* (q.v.), i.e., for any kind of understatement, e.g., "a rather deep hole" when referring to the Grand Canyon.

meiosis: any understatement, not necessarily a double negative, e.g., "a somewhat pleasant view" when the scene is one of extreme beauty. *Litotes* (q.v.) is used more frequently to describe this kind of phenomenon, although *meiosis* is the more accurate term. It is the opposite of *hyperbole* (q.v.).

metaphor: see *imagery*.

meter: the arrangement of metrical feet in lines for rhythmical purposes.

oxymoron: the combination of two terms that are ordinarily contradictory, e.g., "make haste slowly." The juxtaposition is therefore arresting.

paradox: a statement which seems contradictory but which in actuality has an element of truth.

parallelism: the parallel arrangement of the terms of two or more clauses. See also *anaphora* and *chiasmus*.

parataxis: the arrangement of ideas into co-ordinate clauses without subordination.

pause: a break in the sense within a line of verse or at the end of a line of poetry. When a pause occurs in a line, it involves either *diaeresis* (q.v.) or *caesura* (q.v.). When a line has a pause at the end, it is called *end-stopped* (q.v.); when none, a *run-on* line (q.v.).

personification: the representation of an idea or a thing as a person, e.g., the treating of Youth as a human being. (Horace, *Ode* I.30)

polysyndeton: the use of an unnecessary number of conjunctions between co-ordinate words, phrases, and clauses.

prodelision: a variety of liaison. It occurs when a word which ends in a vowel or diphthong or a vowel plus *m* precedes *es* or *est*. The *e* of *es* or *est* is dropped. E.g., *miserum (e)st; audienda (e)st*.

prolepsis (proleptic): the use of a word in the clause preceding the one in which it would naturally appear. It is often used of an epithet which is anticipatory, i.e., the applying of the epithet as if already true to a thing when in reality it only becomes true by or after the action now being stated. For example, "The two brothers and their murder'd man rode past," i.e., and the man who was to become their victim. In Latin: *inaequales procellae*

(Horace, *Ode* II.9.3); the adjective denotes the effect of the blasts.

quantitative verse: verse arranged on basis of long and short syllables which require longer or shorter amounts of time to utter. In general it was felt the long syllable takes twice the length of time to utter as the short one.

rhyme: repetition of same sound at the end of two or more words.

run-on line: one in which no pause occurs at the end of the verse; the sense overflows to the next line. Also called enjambment.

simile: see *imagery*.

stress accent: the syllable bearing the accent of the word is uttered with greater stress, i.e., more loudly. In Latin it was the dominant accent, and fell on the ultima in monosyllables, the penult of dissyllables, and on either the penult (if long) or the antepenult (if the penult was short) of words of three or more syllables.

syllepsis and *zeugma:* both involve a single word in relations which seem to be but are not the same with a pair of others. Syllepsis, however, is grammatically correct, that is the single word can grammatically function with each of the other two; all that is required is a slight shift in the meaning of the single word. E.g., "He left in the rain and a Rolls-Royce." In zeugma the single term is grammatically correct with only one of the other terms. E.g., "The men fired their guns and arrows at the enemy." In zeugma the context easily supplies the appropriate sense; e.g., fire the gun, but shoot the arrow. Although zeugma is quite commonly used for syllepsis, it is perhaps as well to observe the distinction between the two.

symbol: see *imagery*.

synchesis: interlocked word order in which the elements of one pair alternate with those of another, e.g., *et superiecto pauidae natarunt aequore dammae* (Horace, *Ode* I.2. 11–12).

synecdoche: the use of the part for the whole, or the whole for the part.

tmesis: the separation of a compound word into its original parts,

with the insertion of one or more words between them, e.g.,
quae me cumque.

understatement: a statement expressing a thought less strongly
than the truth allows, e.g., "she is a pretty girl" when she is a
great beauty. See also *meiosis, litotes, irony.*

zeugma: see *syllepsis.*

INDEX OF AUTHORS
AND POEMS

GENERAL INDEX

Accent (stress): 25, 32, 37, 51, 264
Actuality: 5, 50, 51
Adonic: *see* verse form
Aeneid: 32, 69, 82; II, 10; IX.435, 84;
   X.519, 61
Alcaeus: 23, 70
Alcaic: *see* verse form
Allegory: 64, 71, 190, 260
Allen and Greenough: 73
Alliteration: 33f., 39f., 43, 74, 171, 260
Allusion: 23, 165, 177, 179
   mythological: 140, 169, 175, 246ff.
Ambiguity: 14f., 17, 54, 68, 84, 96, 111,
   113, 120, 122, 129, 146, 150, 160f., 218,
   220, 242f.
Anacrusis: 41
Anapest: 37
Anaphora: 95, 102f., 106, 194, 260
Anastrophe: 145, 166, 206, 235, 260
Antithesis: 76, 96, 174
Archaism: 9, 26, 46, 58, 88, 95, 182, 252
Archilochian: *see* verse form
Aristophanic: *see* verse form
Asclepiadean: *see* verse form
Assonance: 33f., 40, 43, 161, 260
Asyndeton: 14, 106f., 166, 194, 260
Attitude (of poet, poem): 4, 23, 43, 51,
   70, 88, 91, 102, 150ff., 156, 174, 184,
   206, 215f., 219, 221f., 227

Brachyology: 166, 260
Bucolic: *see* poetry, pastoral

Caesar: 4
Caesura: 31ff., 36, 38, 43, 55, 261; femi-
nine, 32, 42ff.; masculine, 32, 42f.; *see
also* pause
Catalectic: 39, 41
Cato: 3
Chiasmus: 103ff., 107, 127, 183, 213ff.,
   221, 242, 247f., 261
Choliambic: *see* verse form
Cicero: 3f., 24, 129f.
Colloquialism: 20, 28, 72, 95, 112, 124,
   128, 145, 179, 180
Communication: poetry as, 3f.; of feel-
ing, 151f.
Comparison: 60, 63f., 157
Conceit: *see* metaphor
Contrast (as poetic device): 60, 71, 76,
   220

Dactyl: 24, 30f., 36f., 39ff., 42f.
Dactylic trimeter catalectic: *see* verse
form
Description: 5, 14, 49, 51, 54ff., 59, 63,
   70f., 80, 102, 160
Diaeresis: 22, 31ff., 37ff., 42ff., 163, 261;
   see also pause
Diminutive: 19f., 54, 110
Dipody: 37ff.
Drama (of a poem): 6, 10, 12ff., 15,
   17f., 20f., 23, 40, 49, 55, 62f., 65ff.,
   80f., 90, 102, 146, 150, 171, 180, 189,
   227
Dramatic event: 6, 22, 50, 96, 155
Dramatic scene: 14, 20, 49, 50, 58, 96,
   206
Duckworth, G.: 196

Elegiac couplet: *see* verse form

The text for *Reading Latin Poetry* has been set in 11-point Linotype Janson, a recutting of a charming book type first issued by Anton Janson of Leipzig. Modern methods of letter-drafting and punch-cutting have retained its sharpness and sparkle as well as "the beautiful clarity and comeliness of its drawing."

The paper on which the book is printed bears the watermark of the University of Oklahoma Press and has an effective life of at least three hundred years.